Negative H

Also available from Continuum:

The Politics of Aesthetics, Jacques Rancière (translated by Gabriel Rockhill)

Time for Revolution, Antonio Negri (translated by Matteo Mandarini)

The Way of Love, Luce Irigaray (translated by Heidi Bostic and Stephen Pluháček)

Infinite Thought, Alain Badiou (translated by Oliver Feltham and Justin Clemens)

Art and Fear, Paul Virilio (translated by Julie Rose)

Francis Bacon: The Logic of Sensation, Gilles Deleuze (translated by Daniel W. Smith)

Killing Freud, Todd Dufresne

life.after.theory, edited by Michael Payne and John Schad

Negative Horizon

An Essay in Dromoscopy

PAUL VIRILIO

Translated by Michael Degener

continuum
LONDON • NEW YORK

Continuum

The Tower Building
11 York Road
London SE1 7NX

15 East 26th Street
New York
NY 10010

www.continuumbooks.com

© Editions Galilée, 1984, *L'Horizon Negatif*
This English translation © Continuum, 2005
Introduction © Continuum, 2005

British Library Cataloguing-in-Publication Data
A catalogue record for this book is available from the British Library.

ISBN: 0–8264–7842–5

Library of Congress Cataloging-in-Publication Data
A catalog record for this book is available from the Library of Congress.

Typeset by Fakenham Photosetting Limited, Fakenham, Norfolk
Printed and bound in Great Britain by MPG Books Ltd, Bodmin, Cornwall

Contents

To the robot Hilare

Acknowledgements

It is a bit ironic that this work, preoccupied as it is with *acceleration*, should have given rise to a kind of inversely proportional effect. It seemed the closer I came to the negative horizon, the slower my progress! And the measure of this can certainly be taken from the fact that this project has spanned the passing of generations, first from Athlone to Continuum, and then, on the level of my personal contacts in Great Britain, first from Tristan Palmer and on to Sarah Douglas. And given my already established gratitude to Tristan, not only for all of his very constructive editorial assistance and encouragement for my previous project with him (*Desert Screen, War at the Speed of Light*, 2002), but also for his patience, I can only somewhat sheepishly begin to express my heartfelt thanks for the very human patience that Sarah ungrudgingly extended to me, hers only beginning where Tristan's left off. And so it falls to me to thank Galilée for their copyright extension on behalf of us all, and here I extend my thanks to those others at Continuum whom I have not worked with directly, but who in their various capacities have accommodated the delays.

Perhaps I might try to put some of the blame for this on the wee shoulders of my daughter (she can hardly object) – Belén – who chose the horizon of this time to make her very, very *positive* appearance in this world! Especially since such an 'excuse' also provides me with the opportunity to thank my wife, Henriëtte, for her ambidextrous juggling of the many demands that this project added to a wonderfully hectic time.

I am still very grateful to James Der Derian for his contribution to our awareness of Virilio in the English-speaking world, and more personally, for his long-suffering patience and stout efforts in collaborating with such a frenetic and distracted doctoral candidate, and in drawing me forth – at least a little – from that enforced reclusion, to begin to open out onto the broadened horizons of what has now become an unexpectedly sustained encounter with Virilio's work. And, of course, we are *all* indebted to Professor Virilio's gutsy work. While at times it has proved vexing for me as a translator, there is something very heartening in encountering the work of a thinker who never balks, who is always driving hard up against the threshold, whatever the risks.

I am very grateful to Susan Cope for her careful attention and patience in proof reading and line editing.

Others have helped with the translation. In Lausanne, my long-standing admiration for Ghislaine Vautier was deepened all the more as we wrestled back and forth in the no-man's land between languages which she calls home. Thanks also go to Lauren Osepchuk, to Max Statkiewicz in Wisconsin, especially for helping tackle some tough problems at the eleventh hour, and also to Edwin Gentzler, Mark Koontz, Pauline Leven, Tom Parker, Myriam Fontaine, William Sokoloff, Mikael Petraccia and Greg Spano. I would like to thank Michael Prince and Jackie Walsh for their ongoing professional support. Finally, a very special thanks to my consummate American editor, Martha Loomis.

Michael Degener

Translator's introduction:
Seven minutes

We are unknown to ourselves ... and with good reason. We have never sought ourselves – how could it happen that we should ever *find* ourselves? ... Whatever else there is in life, so-called 'experiences' – which of us has sufficient earnestness for them? Or sufficient time? Present experience has, I am afraid, always found us 'absent-minded': we cannot give our hearts to it – not even our ears! Rather, as one divinely preoccupied and immersed in himself into whose ear the bell has just boomed with all its strength the twelve beats of noon suddenly starts up and asks himself: 'what really was that which just struck?' so we sometimes rub our ears *afterward* and ask, utterly surprised and disconcerted, 'what really was that which we have just experienced?' and moreover: 'who *are* we really?'

On the Genealogy of Morals, Preface, Nietzsche

Seven minutes. For seven interminable minutes the Sovereign sat amongst the children.

T MINUS

Of course we would learn that he was already there *in place, sitting, (having been seated) – Da ... duh*sein, *dumbstruck like the rest of us – one tower burning and the clock already running, out, when the booming whoosh and screeling intake rang the second bell, the draw of the jet, weapon of negative, or nihil propulsion, post modern technology beyond a threshold of thrust, drawing now from the other side of that critical horizon that* 'creates before or above the vehicle a vacuum into which it would rush forth ... *creates the vacuum from the atmospheric void', of which Virilio, in 1984, prefines: 'The aspiration for drive ends in a suction, and* *the wish to attain to the horizon as quickly as possible corresponds with a profound inspiration'.*

And as the towers burn time stops, a vertiginous timeless 'high noon'. I cannot help imagining the thin, windswept strains of the theme from The Good, the Bad, and ... *whistling faintly in the ears of the distracted Sovereign, from on high, from* beyond. *A fateful and utterly impropitious* intake of time *as only about now the ash and leaves of paper float, in hushed silence, to the surface below. A screeling accelerating intake 'post-9-11' time; ponderous, lurching ascent – gain – an instantaneously 'post' time, fixed as a* past telos *for* bellum ad continuum, *future 'war' in* perpetuum, *war beyond and revelation state of emergency.*

For seven minutes the Sovereign sat amongst the children, in plain view, *before being withdrawn into the undisclosed location that is the constitutive* atopos – non-place – *of sovereignty as such.*

MINUTE 1

What does one experience when the bell tolls? What is the experience of shock and awe? Certainly the absent-minded haze evaporates, but what replaces it? Is one thrown back into, or upon, oneself? Does one take possession of himself in this moment? Or, in all fairness, should we not better ask: can one *really take possession of oneself, of one's self; can* one *take possession of* one self? *Or does not the Sovereign rather feel himself somehow apart, both from himself and from the others? No longer really among them as before, he sees an other worldly aura about the children. Or is it rather the aura of the* inner worldly? *A certain aura, or halo, about each of the children in the field of his experience as he continues to sit there –* da *– among them.*

But is there any there there, any *Da da*? It would seem Virilio, pace Heidegger, says no. In a work, not unlike his others, which is nowhere more than a couple of degrees removed from concrete realia, from the slipping concatenations of empirical series, his unexpectedly evident statement of purpose might go overlooked:

> Looking at this more closely, what have we [i.e., the West] produced that is more original, more specific, than this idea of nothingness, of

absence? It is in the final analysis our most obvious cultural contribution. It is precisely this *absence* that I wish to interrogate, where
is this void?[1]

For this statement points less to a thesis than the orientation of a
phenomenology. This orientation, however, does not locate a centre,
as with *Dasein*, but rather takes its bearing from a certain periphery
– *a negative 'Archimedean' horizon* – to advance a post-Heideggerian
phenomenology of speed, or, as Virilio dubs it, a *dromoscopy*.

Virilio's question arises from a practice in painting in which he
explores what he terms 'antiforms': an ever-shifting field of complex
visual formations, arising in the interstices between reified objects
through a sustained shift of attention from figure to ground in which
he describes 'sliding over to a secondary aspect [*sur l'à-côté*], just to the
side [*tout à-côté*]'.[2] He presents an abbreviated genealogy of the modern
'imperialism of apprehension' taking us back to the cave paintings of
Lascaux where mankind first marked out figures from ground and stabi-
lized a perception of what was 'good'. In time, with the consolidation
of the subject, these figures become fixed, except for those who perceive
transparence, perceive, that is, 'that everything is always moving, that
SENSE circulates among things like blood in the veins, in the forms of
the frozen object'.[3] Yet this perception itself arises from the movement,
or *déplacement*, of the subject just as 'a passenger on a train sees trees
and houses darting past, sees hills bending away'[4] and for those who
see with this sort of double vision 'the interval glimmers, distorting
ceaselessly thanks to the displacements of the subject'.[5] Thus, following
upon the post-Kantian moment in which Foucault would strive to
reformulate the transcendental subject as a *historical a priori*, we witness
a post-Heideggerian moment in which the displacement, or dislodging,
of *Dasein* – Virilio's term, *déplacement*, runs the full course of the text,
effacing boundaries between the subject and technologies – undoes the
integrity of the field of experience and releases an interplay between
destabilized objects and the interstitial antiforms. The result:

> on the one hand, an internal dynamic that assured the material
> reality of the object (stone, class, furniture) ... and, on the other

hand, an external dynamic that induced the void, the transparence, that gave form and value to absence.[6]

MINUTE 2

And just as he sees, self-consciously, the children each individually now for the first time, no longer an anonymous group, but rather each standing out individually one to another in the field of his experience, so also he senses himself standing out – standing out of himself (even though he is still sitting) and in this capacity set apart....

We may gain a deeper appreciation of the force of Virilio's *déplacement* of ontology by entering into Adorno's response to phenomenological ontology, or 'neo-ontology', at the point where he identifies two elements in which it remains tied to idealism. I will limit myself to the first:

> The first is the definition of the encompassing whole *vis-à-vis* the particularities included in it; it is no longer held to be a systematic whole, but rather a structural whole, a structural unity or totality. In conceiving the possibility of encompassing all reality unambiguously, even if only in a structure, a claim is implicit that he who combines everything existing under this structure has the *right and power* [*das Recht und die Kraft* – emphasis added] to know adequately the existing in itself and to absorb it into the form.[7]

Adorno is preparing a refiguration of the nature/history dialectic within the framework of Benjamin's aesthetics of allegorical constellations, but I am interested for the moment in how Virilio's interstitial antiforms challenge Heidegger's *Entwurf* (along with its implications of 'design' or 'sketch') in such a way that Adorno's characterization of Benjamin's project appertains: 'What is at issue is of an essentially different logical [although here I would interject 'phenomenological' or 'dromological'] form from that of the scheme of thought based on a project (*Entwurf*) whose foundation is constituted by a general conceptual structure'.[8]

Adorno's criticism is particularly applicable to Heidegger's engagement with the Pre-Socratics, especially in his imposition – his 'im-positioning' of *Dasein* in his reading of Anaximander. Based on my own reinterpretation of Anaximander[9] that stems from the abyssal cosmology inherited from Homer, and more immediately from Hesiod's *Works and Days*, I challenge Heidegger's ontological reading of the fragments in which beings (*ta onta*) are presenced forth into a *totalized*, or *bounded*, field of beings, that is, into a 'structural whole'. Here is how Heidegger states it:

> ... translated literally, *ta onta* means 'beings.' The neuter plural appears as *ta polla*, 'the many,' in the sense of the manifold of beings[10] [*Mannigfaltigkeit des Seienden*]. But *ta onta* does *not* [emphasis added] mean an arbitrary or boundless multiplicity; rather, it means *ta panta*, the totality of beings. Thus *ta onta* means manifold beings in totality.[11]

In interpreting Anaximander's *to apeiron* as *Sein*, i.e., the *Sein des Seiendes*, and in describing it as the 'boundless' that presences forth all that is to be gathered together within the bounded 'manifold of beings', Heidegger erroneously introduces the general (metaphysical) concept of *to on*. For any such totalizing concept of *to on* is, in fact, *neither articulated nor conceived*, implicitly or otherwise, prior to Parmenides' *originary ontological reaction* to what I counter is Anaximander's *tragic* vision of an *unbounded* 'field' – it is neither a field, nor a domain – of ephemeral *onta*, which are not to be confused with 'beings' understood as defined with respect to Being conceived as a general concept (potential or otherwise). We may translate Anaximander's ὄντα (*onta*) as '*Seienden*', but only so long as we do not make them the namesake of '*Sein*'. Anaximander's *apeiron* is not a name for 'Being', it is not the *archê*, or governing concept, of a bounded field of 'beings' according to that *version* of the fragment that bears the impress of its Peripatetic recension: *archê tôn ontôn to apeiron*; instead it names the *fault*, or *aitia*, of the unbounded (*apeiron*) 'field', the 'field' that is *not* a field precisely for not being bounded, the abyssal *atopos*, non-place, locus of earth in which *onta* arise only to perish *according to the taxis of time*, such as it appears has been preserved in another version of the fragment: aitia *tôn ontôn to apeiron*. The *apeiron* is the *aitia*, or *tragic* flaw, that precludes the bounding of a field precisely because earth, as the *atopos*, non-place, locus of *genesis* (and this *atopos* locus of *tragic* experience can now be definitively divorced from Heidegger's inner worldly), is subject to the *taxis of time* – here we glimpse the link to Virilio's dromology. What is more, the *atopos* locus of earth is opposed to *another proper sphere*, that of the eternal *bounded* sphere of the divine. Heidegger remains within the limit of the Peripatetic tradition in that he fails to recognize that Anaximander's description of the *genesis* and *phthorê* (perishing) of *onta* on earth is a description of only one half of the archaic cosmo-ontological structuring. We will see later that this bifold cosmology is reflected in the two terms in Greek for which we have only one, i.e., 'life': on the one hand, the term for the biological basis of the life of *genesis* and perishing, *zôê*; on the other, that which names the spiritual life of the citizen in the polis, *bios*.

MINUTE 3

… apart, *and it hits him. Where are the handlers? What is going on back there? Behind the scene? What do I do? Should I stay or should I go? What is taking them so long? They are whispering into their sleeves.*

While mankind is born on earth, born as a *zôon*, he lives his political life (or at least the citizen of the polis lives his life), or *bios*, within the light of the bounded sphere of the divine. However, he must pass away, according to the taxis of time, into the abyss of the unbounded, of Hades. I note here a certain confusion in the use of the term *bio-logy* that has been embedded in history. For more strictly speaking we should speak of a '*zoo*-logy' of the *natural* life of *physis*, that abyssal life that gives mankind what we erroneously call the 'biological' life (what in a couple of minutes we will see Giorgio Agamben aptly calls 'bare life') necessary to accede to his spiritual life – which would be more accurately called *bio*-logy – in the polis.

It is where *zôê*-life, or life-ontology, and *bios*-politics intersect that we discover the risk that Derrida points to. And we must not forget that the sovereign is still sitting there – well, if perhaps no longer quite 'there', at least sitting *by*.

Otherwise justice risks being reduced once again to juridical-moral rules, norms, or representations, within an inevitable totalizing horizon (movement of adequate restitution, expiation, or reappropriation). Heidegger runs this risk, despite so many necessary precautions, when he gives priority, as he always does, to gathering and to the same (*Versammlung*, *Fuge*, *legein*, and so forth) over the disjunction implied by my address to the other, over the interruption commanded by respect which commands it in turn, over a difference whose uniqueness, disseminated in the innumerable charred fragments of the absolute mixed in with the cinders, will never be assured in the One.[12]

Yet despite Derrida's criticism, Heidegger's Anaximander is still left too much intact as it is assumed into Benjamin's post-tragic historical messianism. For among the cinders Derrida also retains the most untenable of Heidegger's impositions, namely the imposition of the *Fuge*, translated as 'reck' – or, by Derrida, as 'jointure' – remaining inert among the *wreck*age of history. For Heidegger, the reck, or jointure, whereby beings are established to abide, *to be*, for a while, in being presenced forth over and against one another, unfolds the inward resonance of the *peripheral* boundary of the manifold of beings whereby the interstices that distinguish beings one from another are articulated. Yet my reckoning of Anaximander obviates at once, outwardly, Heidegger's peripheral bound – which is, again, nothing other than what Adorno detected as the vestige of subjective idealism – as well as, inwardly, the would-be stabilizing jointure of beings (that *will*, however, arise later in history, but only as the *aftershock* of the *representation* of the tragic as staged in tragedy proper). For the serial sequencing of the *genesis*, and *more importantly*, the *phthorê*, or *perishing*, of ephemeral *onta*, slips out along the *taxis*, or *axis*, *of time*. The *bios* life of the polis is ultimately exposed to the slippage of abyssal *zôê*-life, that is, to death.

It is the *thauma*, or wonder, of this tragic experience that underlies – or, in a certain *redoubled* way deep within history, still is – the *thauma* which Adorno mentions in reference to Lukács' second nature and the problem of natural history;[13] yet it would appear that this *thauma* also underlies what Virilio too described back in 'minute one' as that 'external dynamic' which induced the experience of 'slipping to the side' through which those fleeting interstitial antiforms emerge – those antiforms that he attributes to the *déplacement* of the subject, that is the displacement of movement, or, *time*. Dromology.

MINUTE 4

Cameras still rolling, the handlers signal to the Sovereign from the side, outside the frame: 'stand-by'.

Yet while the legacy of Anaximander's *apeiron* may account for the way in which reified objects come, so to speak, to be haunted in history by the interstitial antiforms – as some vestigial charge deriving from the *symbolic* fixed within the allegorical – it alone cannot account for the 'internal dynamic that assured the material reality of the object'. Nor can it account for the fact that the antiforms henceforth never stand alone, independently from presenced objects whose interactions determine their modifications. For even if Kant's subject has been ungrounded, is no longer quite seated there – as Foucault, looking back, relativizes the *a prioris* of time and space genealogically, and Einstein, looking forwards, relativistically – the subject is still in *force*, the Sovereign still at least appears to reign, even if in a kind of diminished 'stand-by' capacity.

Indeed, such stand-by sovereignty is everywhere implicit in this essay on dromoscopy, although the locus of the subject, of sovereignty, is destabilized or suspended by the centripetal manifestations of the peripheral negative horizon in the dynamic of *déplacement*. Thus while there are moments in which Virilio will draw in from the broader geopolitical register, the great interstices of military fronts, to consider the centripetal play of the negative horizon within the subject – for example, in his analysis of the effects of speed on the sensorium of automobilists, or, in the self-alienation of the video-mediated sports training of the modern manege – his dromoscopy never locates *persona*. The individual is either caught up as warrior in the broad movements of military forces: 'To sweep down upon [*fondre*], to strike precipitously, is also at the same time: to be swept up into [*fondre*], to dissolve into ...';[14] or is subject(ed) to the centripetal disarticulation of the negative horizon that works into the body itself:

> Each departure is a distancing [*écartement*] that deprives us of contact, of direct experience; each instance of vehicular mediation is nothing other than a drawing and quartering [*écartèlement*], a torture of the locomotive body, a sensory privation of the passenger.[15]

These tactics can, in part, be accounted for as resulting from the dromo*scopic* method laid out in his preface: Virilio intentionally shifts his focus, wilfully sustaining the double vision as a means of unleashing the secrets of speed – and for this reason his work lends itself to a kind of *speed reading*. If not as random as a stream of consciousness or automatic writing, nonetheless it careens across broad historical expanses at speed and provides few rest stations or fixed footings for discursive analysis. But there is also a political agenda at work in this method such that if the work is read *too* superficially, it might be mistaken for little else than a Foucauldian genealogy of the relationships between technologies and power. Which is not to say that Virilio does not share in some measure the tactics Foucault articulates in *The Archaeology of Knowledge* to subvert the juridico-discursive stratum of power:

> One remains attached to a certain image of power-law, of power-sovereignty, which was traced out by the theoreticians of right and the monarchic institution. It is this image that we must break free of, that is, of the theoretical privilege of law and sovereignty, if we wish to analyse power within the concrete and historical framework of its operation.[16]

Already, in his methodological discussion of *déplacement*, that is, in Virilio's focus on the play of the void in the interstices, and then as deployed throughout the work in his somewhat haphazard presentation of empirical series through history, it is obvious that his attention is directed against the tyrannizing hold of narratives of historical continuity, again in line with Foucault:

If the history of thought could remain the locus of uninterrupted continuities, if it could endlessly forge connections that no analysis could undo without abstraction, if it could weave, around everything that men say and do, obscure syntheses that anticipate for him, prepare him, and lead him endlessly towards his future, it would provide a privileged shelter for the sovereignty of consciousness.[17]

However, there is a critical and paradoxical distinction to be drawn between the two thinkers' orientations to the problem of history. For, on the one hand, the empirical content of Virilio's work remains more 'undigested' than what is found in Foucault – more haphazard, more exposed to *le hazard*, to chance and accident – despite the commitment to interruption Foucault inherits from Nietzschean genealogy: 'History becomes "effective" [translating '*wirkliche Historie*' – ED.] to the degree that it introduces discontinuity into our very being as it divides our emotions, dramatizes our instincts, multiplies our body and sets it against itself';[18] while, on the other hand, the critical distinction whereby Virilio's history is – if not *teleological* – nonetheless *organized* in its relationship to the *futurial* negative horizon departs from what follows in Foucault:

'Effective' history deprives the self of the reassuring stability of life and nature, and it will not permit itself to be transported by a voiceless obstinacy *toward a millennial ending* [emphasis added]. It will uproot its traditional foundations and relentlessly disrupt its pretended continuity.[19]

Virilio's negative organization of history is not teleological, it does not represent a progressive development of positive evolution or 'additive' advance; instead, the futurial draw or suction of the negative horizon of history – perhaps Virilio would not object to a metaphoric sense of the 'millennial', raising the question of the relationship of his negative horizon to Benjamin's 'messianic' history – unfolds a logic of *privation* or *subtraction*: obstacles are *removed*, spaces cleared, edges smoothed, resistance reduced by the wind of speed that whirls out of the future and draws (us) forwards in a careening advance at once broadly fateful – *pace* Foucault – *and* locally haphazard.

MINUTE 5

And again: 'stand-by'. But now he has been left out there too long. *And so in this moment he commits the error of hubris – somehow it does not quite seem to rise to the sin of pride, as pride entails a greater measure of reflection – for now he believes that he has 'found himself' in this experience of self that stands apart, stands alone. Does he feel that it is* this *self that stands before – is called before – his god? Is this the moment in which he senses, with an unexpected but misguided certainty, a renewed inspiration, this 'I' that was somehow previously absent, but which will henceforth be the 'I' that will have said, will have arrogated to it*self *the authority to say, repeatedly, 'I have decided …' and henceforth be the 'I' who will have self-righteously claimed* the right and the power *to distinguish between those who* are *good, and those who* are *evil – ontologically – those who are* with us, *and those who are* against us? *Is this the face of a man who is communing with the 'Lord'?*

Yet it is *because* it is *us* along with everything else, that is, it is because there is some relative *fixity* of the human subject, and of the state construction of sovereignty systemically, that is drawn forth that there is a *history*, and not just *life*, or *nature*, disclosed to us in the accidental character of events, its elusive meaning ever structured futurially beyond itself, on vanishing lines of sight. This futurial meaning, however, can only be read, so to speak, over the shoulder, allegorically, as Benjamin has shown, from the debris that is left behind and reclaimed by 'life' as second nature. Both Nietzsche and, following him, Foucault fail in this capacity, perceiving historical content as merely epiphenomenal to an essentially vegetative substructure of force relations, and it was this failure that occasioned Benjamin's superimposition of the *Ursprung* from the death's-head of *Trauerspiel*[20] upon Nietzsche's 'Dionysian' fascination with the *Geburt* – the birth from life – of *Tragedy*.[21] A more direct critique of Nietzsche's theory of tragedy would address his failure to distinguish correctly between the spheres of *zôê* and *bios*, or, rather, to see that abyssal *zôê* is distinguished from the bounded sphere of *bios* (the sphere of the eternal abiding gods of myth that Nietzsche reduces to the mere illusion of the Apolline) precisely in *not* being a sphere, as instead representing merely the unbounded *atopos*, non-place, of birth and death. In Nietzsche's enthusiastic bid to displace the modern subject he ultimately succeeds only in imputing its organic integrity – a gesture repeated in its own way, as Adorno points out, in Heidegger's 'whole' – to what for the Greeks was the truly abyssal unbounded *atopos* of the Dionysian. In Nietzsche, the 'Dionysian' becomes the organic mediating field of biological life, 'biological' in the historically misconstrued sense – itself just begging for a Nietzschean genealogy – discussed above.

Nietzsche's and Foucault's genealogies dissolve the 'eternal truths' and *a prioris* in the 'life' of a history that has neither any clearly demarcated origins nor any definitive future orientation; they may uproot the old trees of the 'eternal truths' of the past *but what do they do to prevent them from reseeding in the fertile field of life?* They present a view of history whose forward (nineteenth-century) progress suggests no more organization than that of vegetative evolution, one positive life/force impulse merely following upon and superceding another. Much of this is captured in Foucault's words:

It seems to me that power must be understood in the first instance as the multiplicity of force relations *immanent in the sphere* [this emphasis, as well as all that follow, added] in which they operate and which constitute their own organization; as the process which, through ceaseless struggles and confrontations, transforms, strengthens, or reverses them; as the support which these force relations find in one another, *thus forming a chain or a system*, or on the contrary, the disjunctions and contradictions which isolate them from one another; and lastly, as the strategies in which they take effect, whose general design or institutional crystallization is embodied in the state apparatus, in the formulation of the law, in the various social hegemonies. Power's condition of possibility, or in any case the viewpoint which permits one to understand its exercise, even in its more 'peripheral' effects, and which also makes it possible to use its mechanisms as a grid of intelligibility of the social order, *must not be sought in the primary existence of a central point*, in a unique source of sovereignty from which secondary and descendent forms would emanate; it is the moving *substrate of force relations* which, by virtue of their inequality, constantly *engender* states of power, but the latter are always local and unstable.[22]

But thus *history*, as dialectically opposed to nature, itself has no rootedness, all 'Apolline' structuring 'crystallizations' merely kicked up ahead as the luminous froth of the wave into which it all inevitably falls back again and dissolves. No Archimedean point.

In the place of the mediating field of Nietzschean/Foucauldian *zôê*-life, it seems Virilio offers not just the negativity of death, but arising from it an ether of speed, a temporal ether threatening to dissolve us in a *futurial* continuum, a continuum 'rooted' in the negative 'Archimedean' horizon of the future. And it might be ventured that it is this 'soil' that gives second nature its *bios*-'life', which accounts for the curiously organic, although alien, metamorphic qualities of the ergonomic and aerodynamic post-modern plastic forms that bleb forth like 'speed larvae': 'the embryos of a constantly *deferred* becoming [emphasis added to mark the distinction with Nietzsche's first-nature becoming], provisional figures of a defection the final outcome of which is perceptible only with the emergence of another machine, one of even greater speed'.[23]

Hold up! Let's stop a moment. Things are racing forwards, slipping past. Here is where I raise my critical question of Virilio: How can we resist simply slipping past, or askance of, our own presence/present into the even more baleful future continuum of speed, resist so as not to forego the *redemptive* potential of this dromoscopy's *de-finitive uprooting of first nature*? In other words: How can a *person* take a stand? *Take a stand* – however provisional or *tactical* (harkening back to Anaximander) – as opposed to just *standing-by* as events race past?

MINUTE 6

Almost trembling, he realizes he will have to speak. Take questions, extemporaneously, no handlers. *But as he stands apart from himself (still sitting) he can already somehow begin to hear how it will sound: 'I have decided' 'I had to make a de-cision'. The murmur of the children receding into the background, he believes he can hear, he listens to, 'him' – i.e., to the one who will pronounce the (unholy, hubristic – let us not forget that the Pope had no little badge to offer him in exchange) 'gospel' – even as if*

he – i.e., the one listening to the one who (mis)pronounces – were himself also among the children, of god.
Alas, for shame! Would that it were all just so much prattle!

In his work on *homo sacer*,[24] published one decade after the death of Michel Foucault and the appearance of *L'horizon négatif*, and one decade before this translation, Giorgio Agamben returns to the problem left unresolved in the late Foucault's sustained attention to biopolitics, which he describes as a 'vanishing point that the different perspectival lines of Foucault's inquiry (and, more generally, of the entire Western reflection on power) converge towards without reaching', that is, he raises the problem of 'locating' the 'zone of indistinction ... at which techniques of individualization and totalization procedures converge'.[25] However, already in 1984, we find Virilio projected far out ahead on these same perspectival lines, in an asymptotic approach, not to this vanishing 'point', but rather to the vanishing horizon, extending Foucault's attention to 'the passage from the "territorial State" to the "State of population"'[26] from manifold perspectives – *all, however, unlike Foucault's, resolving in the negative horizon.* Moreover, Virilio *propels* the biopolitical optic forward precipitously by reinflecting it in the 'light of speed':

> Now each vector administers the time of the passenger in expelling him through the unleashing of the beyond, speed is the progress of violence at the same time as its advantage; beyond the territorial body, each speed constitutes a fleeting 'province of time' where the old role of places disappears in the geographic annihilation of distances.[27]

The (bio)body-politic on steroids, or rather, *on speed*.
Before racing forward, however, before throwing ourselves headlong into Virilio's dromoscopy, I would like to take a moment, first, to propose an apposition of Agamben's theory of sovereignty, and, second, thereby to set the stage for a contribution of my own in response to Virilio's programmatic question: Where is this void? For although Foucault's biopolitics is, in certain measure, superceded by Virilio's *chronopolitics* – and the measure to which this is the case would undoubtedly constitute one of the more important measures of his

contribution – Virilio's presentation of this chronopolitics does still retain Foucault's tactic of circumventing a direct engagement with the juridico-discursive stratum of sovereignty. If Foucault strips away the sovereign as an 'Apolline' epiphenomenon and drops back into Nietzsche's *zôê*-life register, Virilio tends to outpace the *zôê*-life register (although this is not entirely the case, and in as much as Virilio still retains a keen awareness of the *physical* substratum of virtual force configurations, he is to be favourably contrasted with Baudrillard) such that these dromoscopic perspectival lines tend to resolve within the *bios*-life, second nature, register beyond what Agamben identifies as the sovereign threshold.

So, for expediency's sake, I will attempt to sketch out schematically the juxtaposition with Agamben's 'recentred' presentation of the problem of sovereignty in terms of what was said earlier regarding Anaximander's *tragic* experience and what it *anticipates* in the *staging* of tragedy proper to follow historically. Let me bring the discussion of Anaximander back into play here by recalling the problem of what it is that 'assures the material reality of the object' and by suggesting, again, that we may refer not only to such objects as we perceive in the field of our experience, but also to *ourselves*, i.e., ourselves as (*tactical*) subjects, as 'beings', i.e., *Seienden*, so long as we resist thereby deriving from this *any* notion of 'Being', i.e., *Sein*. For Virilio's *déplacement* suspends, displaces, what is too static in Heidegger's *Dasein*, which is still, as Derrida notes, preoccupied with the centring gesture of the (self)-same. Thus we saw that the role of the *taxis of time* serves not only to dislodge Heidegger's 'archaeology' of *Dasein*, but also to suggest an *aetiology* – that is, a causal origin in the *aitia* as tragic flaw – of Virilio's anti-forms, those descendents of Anaximander's ephemeral *onta* that still haunt *material* objects to this day. But what then about the *materiality* of these objects, and of *us*, disposed as we are each as one *Seiende* among *Seienden*? Perhaps we find ourselves standing by, and perhaps (even more than just standing by) we find ourselves in such a posture (i.e., disposed) that we are prepared to take a stand, that is, to take a stand politically speaking. Our disposition is one of being *tactically* there – *da* – and taking our bearing *tactically* by dint of what we encounter tactically arrayed, or *presented* – as opposed to merely presenced – to us there in the sense of Benjamin's privileging of *Dar-stellung*. The 'materiality' of objects represents merely the *relative* perdurance of what it *is* useful to think of now as constituting Heidegger's inner-wordly experience.

Returning now to Heidegger may, however, cause some confusion since I stressed above that his notion of the inner-worldly must be divorced from Anaximander's *tragic* experience, that is, from that originary experience of *thauma* that prefigures, and in a certain redoubled way, resurfaces, albeit metamorphosed, in what Benjamin and Adorn disclose of the *Darstellung* of *Trauerspiel*. A delicate distinction is required: I assert that Heidegger imposes *Dasein anachronistically* upon Anaximander, and that we would have instead to wait for Parmenides to find the *totalizing* gesture – at what constitutes the genuine origin of Western metaphysics – of the 'whole' of Heidegger's ontology which Adorno, and I, challenge. And it is the necessarily *totalizing* gesture of ontology *as such* that marked *both* Parmenides' and Heidegger's ontology as ineluctably *metaphysical* because what remains immanently undisclosed in Heidegger's ontology is the *sovereign gesture* whereby he simultaneously stands outside *and* within the field, that sovereign gesture whereby Heidegger claims, as Adorno put it, *das Recht und die Kraft*, the Right and the Power, to *command* the field in his own consciousness. (It is important, moreover, here quickly to point out that we must not fail to question whether Heidegger's gesture should not be thought of as a metamorphosis within the sphere of *logos*, i.e., ontology, of what Nietzsche sought in his flawed pretension at once to embody the 'Dionysian' *and* to speak of it, in order erroneously to account it as that whence tragedy is 'born'. Tragedy is no more born from life, nor from Nietzsche's misconceived 'biological' notion of the 'Dionysian', than is *Trauerspiel*.)

The question raised by Heidegger's sovereign gesture rejoins the one posed by Virilio, namely the question of the *where*. And this is where we may call upon Agamben to complement our understanding of how the peripheral dynamic of Virilio's negative horizon reverberates into the centre of the field. For in contrast to Virilio's moving target, Agamben presents a direct static articulation of the logic of sovereignty as defined by the state of exception. The Sovereign is he who is at once within *and* beyond the law. We might say the Sovereign is he who *insists* on being seated, and remaining seated, fixed, *da*, right there, *albeit oblivious* –

duh*sein* – in the centre of the field: death's head null point *Dasein*. The inertial centre whose mass it seems has captured the orbiting fool of *Trauerspiel* within itself, as that self sitting in audience before, listening to, *it*self, but which simultaneously commands the field from beyond its bounds, from the negative interstitial horizon of State power, the ersatz '*auto-da-fé*' of an *autos* that insists upon being both out there, *da*, and within, 'over *here*', *da* – *where?* But the enforced, *unnatural, deathly* fixity of the Sovereign also *deconstitutes* the field such that no others can be properly seated, being instead always constitutively *displaced* – even if 'materialized' through being contingently constellated by the artificial fixity of the sovereign null point centring the field – and *haunted* by what has always been the abyssal *zôê*-life underpinnings of every *bios*-life experience, and therefore ever predestined through history to the re-emergence of the threat of exposure inherit in the bio-, or what really *must* now be correctly renamed, zoo-politics of what Agamben aptly terms 'bare life'.

Where? In the palace of Argos.

MINUTE 7

The Sovereign withdraws to the undisclosed location. Long live the sovereign.
But where is the undisclosed location?

In taking up where Foucault left off, Agamben argues that the emergence of the biopolitical that Foucault identified as the mark of political modernity actually represents only the latest manifestation of the constitutive structure of sovereignty, a structure he argues that is intrinsically linked with the problem of 'bare life' and which is historically figured in the status of the *homo sacer*: one who 'may be killed and yet not sacrificed ... an obscure figure of archaic Roman law, in which human life is included in the juridical order [*ordinamento*] solely in the form of its exclusion (that is, of its capacity to be killed)'.[28] Agamben argues for a logic of sovereignty that, in brief, explores how sovereignty, on the one hand, and bare life, on the other, defy a clear distinction between inclusion and exclusion with respect to law, or, the polis. What

I wish to show is that what is being articulated here is a logic that is ultimately derived from the Pre-Socratic relationship between *zôê*-life and *bios*-life expressed by Anaximander, a logic constituted, however, only in the wake of the *representation,* or *Darstellung,* of Anaximander's *tragic* cosmology in *tragedy* proper, specifically Aeschylean tragedy. In other words, Agamben's logic has *its* underpinnings further back still in the archaic Greek relationship between the bounded sphere of the divine (*bios* – figured in the quasi-Heideggerian *world* of the polis) over and against the unbounded abyss of earth (*zôê* – the life-giving *earth* outside the city walls). Thus we see how *zôê* – reflected in what Agamben calls in the following simply 'life' – is included into the *bios* sphere, but only as an exclusion, that is, only while retaining the abyssal underpinning of the vulnerability of *zôê*-life:

> Life, which is thus obliged, can in the last instance be implicated in the sphere of law only through the presupposition of its inclusive exclusion, only in an *exceptio.* There is a limit-figure of life, a threshold in which life is both inside and outside the juridical order, and this threshold is the place of sovereignty.[29]

Only two modifications need be made here to disclose the pre-Socratic origins – *not* a *Geburt* from 'biological' life – of this classical Roman structuring of sovereignty: first, that the 'outside' to which Agamben refers here derives from the outside of Anaximander's *apeiron,* that is, the unbounded abyss of earth that lies *outside* the bounded sphere of the polis; and, second, that the *secular* sovereignty to which Agamben refers here is only constituted as the *repercussion* of the *Darstellung* in tragedy proper of a very specific experience of the threshold – and we will see in a moment how this brings us back to Virilio's negative horizon. Moreover, *homo sacer,* as he who may be killed yet not sacrificed, that is, he who can be killed by anyone outside the sanction of the law and yet whose killing cannot be religiously sanctified in sacrifice, emerges as the obverse *in history* of what I have demonstrated elsewhere regarding the sacrifice of Iphigeneia in Aeschylus' *Agamemnon*: she whose sacrifice by Agamemnon was actually *not* sanctioned by Artemis, and which results in the caesura, or *suspension,* of the mythico-symbolic order that allows precisely for the *advent* of civic, or secular, law in the Areopagus.[30]

Let us return, however, to the problem of the *where*. Agamben's 'centred' orientation, his exploitation of a static logic of inclusion/exclusion, fetches a powerful figuration for the localization at work in the establishment of sovereign territory:

> *In the city, ... sacred life is more internal than every interiority and more external than every extraneousness ...* sacred life is the sovereign *nomos* that conditions every rule, the originary spatialization that governs and makes possible every localization and every territorialization.[31]

Both the Sovereign, and the individual 'citizen'/subject through bare life inclusive exclusion, straddle the threshold of within/without while *transcending the spheres constituted by it*. While the spheres articulated by the threshold themselves are *deconstituted* by the symmetrical pairing of the sovereign and bare life – and this as a metamorphosed vestige of the pre-Socratic opposition of sphere/non-sphere – nonetheless the *threshold* itself is in place and, with it, the possibility, however contingent or unstable, of localizing territory.

But Virilio's (hyper)extension of Foucault's biopolitics would seem to propel us somehow beyond whatever contingent measure of territorial definition remains for Agamben, as the *déplacement* of his chrono-politics serves foremost as the moving force of *de-territorialization*:

> The 'liberation of colonies' brought about by the passage from the era of moving people from place to place to that of outright migrations is in fact only the most evident sign of deterritorialization; it announces the future of an anational 'state of emergency' beyond the old state of siege on the city, where the capitalization of speed attains to such a degree that the old geopolitics tends to become a simple chronopolitics, a true war of time, beyond that of space and territories.[32]

Are we simply left with an *aporia* in the gap separating these two post-Foucauldian theoreticians of bio politics – arising, on the one hand, from the mobile-peripheral optic and, on the other, from the static-inclusion/exclusion logic? The resolution to this problem comes from a horizon yet to be located, the threshold in tragedy that marks the passage from myth to history. We must turn our back for a moment upon Virilio's futurial horizon, and go back further still in history than what Agamben locates in the name of *homo sacer* on *this* side of the myth/history divide. We must go back to Argos to find the *obverse* of what is more internal than every interiority, more external than every extraneousness, in the tragic no man's land *between* myth and history.

We are running out of time, the Sovereign is gone and the Sovereign's handlers are anxious to strike the set, so this must be brief. I turn to a couple of lines from Aeschylus' *Agamemnon* in which the prophets of the palace of Argos reveal the spectral dynamics of Helen's *opsis*, or image, unleashed by Menelaus' longing. The lines occur at the crux of a pair of strophic-antistrophic odes, lines 404–36, the structural intricacies of which I will only be able to hint at here.[33] The strophe opens with the chorus' recounting, at the close of the ten-year war, first, the effects of Helen's departure for Troy – the clamour of equipment in preparation for war throughout the city of Argos – and then, reversing the sequencing of events, the cause, describing her physical departure through the all-important threshold of the palace gates. At this juncture the chorus, themselves debarred from entering the palace, recount the words of the prophets of the house. They describe the erosive effect of Menelaus' longing for Helen, how his passion for her wanes in the blankness of the stone eyes of her statues, which once amplified her presence throughout the city in supporting outwardly his active Empedoclean gaze.[34] Now, however, his outwardly directed gaze finds no purchase in the blank stone eyes, revealing the concrete nihility of sheer materiality (the direct precursor of the 'sacredness' of Agamben's bare life), collapsing instead into the inward void of *pothos* [at 414], that is, the void of longing. And it is this *pothos* that is my answer to Virilio's question: Where is the void?

In the antistrophe the prophets describe the folly of grasping after the splendours of mere dream images, the spectral images of Helen's *phasma*, or phantom:[35]

> ... *parallaxasa dia*
> *cheirôn bebaken opsis, ou methusteron*
> *pterois opadous 'hypnou keleuthois*

[A. Ag. 424–6]

These lines have heretofore only ever been seen to describe Menelaus'
'inward' experience of Helen's *opsis*, as he pines for her, attempting in
vain to capture her image in the metaphorical hands of his mind:

> ... the image slips [*parallaxasa*] through [*dia*]
> the hands passing away, not a moment later, 'within'
> down the winging paths of trance.

However, according to a carefully prepared ambiguity, the lines also
describe the 'outward' active Empedoclean movement of the *opsis*:

> ... the image *goes 'out'* transposed [*parallaxasa*] through [*dia*]
> the physical hands (put to the oars), not a moment later
> on the winged ships in pursuit....

The *would be* distinction between a psychic interiority and concrete
exteriority is *collapsed* by the dynamic of Helen's disembodied *opsis*
that literally puts the physical hands of the warriors to the oars while,
not a moment later, slipping through the vainly grasping 'metaphorical'
hands of Menelaus' mind, it simultaneously *goes off in pursuit* of its
corporeal counterpart in Troy. While going 'out' and 'in', it also stands
'positioned' as a *static* baleful bottomless hypostasis above the mythic
debacle. It is the simultaneity, the *timeless* simultaneity – *a tragic
timelessness opposed to any mythic* or metaphysical *notion of the eternal*
– that at once collapses the strophic/antistrophic structuring of the odes
from within, in an exquisite moment of formal and thematic conson-
ance that I refer to as the *ingression of the threshold*. For these lines
describing the mobile/static dynamic of Helen's *opsis* respond to the line
in the preceding strophe that describes her *physical* departure through
the gates of the palace, this inward strophic collapse anchored in the
nodal cancellation of the exact responsive position of the one key term
that most incisively problematizes the threshold itself: *dia* [407≡424],
'she stepped lightly *through* [*dia*] the gates ...'.

The ingression of the threshold 'prefigures' – although we can only
say this inasmuch as it is being *presented* on stage before spectators
– the spatiality so precisely identified by Agamben of what is more
internal than every interiority, more external than every extraneousness,

for here, in the constitutive interstice of *myth and history* not only is the very distinction itself of interiority and exteriority effaced from within, disclosing the Sovereign's undisclosed *atopos* location, but so also correspondingly is the disposition of time in its relation to space effaced, such as was anticipated already in the abyssal pre-ontological disposition of Anaximander's *onta* arrayed according to the taxis of time, and such that the aneternal timelessness of the 'moment' of this past horizon is revealed as being the *same* screeling intake moment as Virilio's negative *futurial* horizon: these are 'both' the same *negative Archimedean horizon(s) that 'bracket(s)' history on both 'ends'*. It is the aura of Helen's *opsis* that is revealed by the *parallax*, that is, that which slips off to the side, *para-*, that Virilio glimpses just off to the side, *tout à côté*, in the interstitial *déplacement* of objects.

It is this *atopos* horizon that *organizes negatively* what is to be structured henceforth in the constellations of the wreckage of history, as the aneternal timelessness punctuates what vestiges remain of the continuum of myth and are restructured in history thus providing for the possibility of the event. While Foucault was still caught within the limits of Nietzsche's 'biological' 'Dionysianism' – Aeschylus' 'sacred' (in Agamben's sense) moment has *nothing* to do with the Dionysiac – he did at least make the useful contribution of translating Nietzsche's unconscious *zôê*-life-forces into the terms of the unconscious contents of historical discourses. Why is this useful? Because if we push Nietzsche's and Foucault's genealogies back far enough, we *do* find a *de-finitive* origin – not a *Geburt*, but rather that *Ursprung* that resurfaces, albeit metamorphosed, with all the 'sacred' *thauma* still appertaining thereto, as Benjamin's within the frame of history – for the negative horizon not only butts up against the future, but backs up against the limit of the tragic *crisis* that disarticulates the fixed discourse – *that lacks any unconscious content whatsoever* – that is the literal meaning of the term *mythos*.

T(ER)MINUS

The wind of speed blows out of the future overhead, swirling back down and catching up the angel of history, drawn careening forward, back turned to the future, gaze fixed, *however, resolving inwardly, as it takes its bearing from the vanishing horizon of the past, gazing in wonder upon the wreckage of history worn ever smoother by the erosion of time....*

So where are we now? What really was that which we have just experienced? What is this well-worn road that leads to Baghdad?

> ... a linear clearing offered to the 'divine celerity' of the war chariot, earth scorched by vehicles, the surface scoured, the Mesopotamian road is defined independently from the land they pass through, a geometric abstraction; uniformity, unidirectionality, *speed* [*la vitesse*] *provokes the void* [*le vide*] *and the void* [*le vide*], *speed* [*le vite*] ...[36]

I was struck by the strange contrast between the ballyhooed Rumsfeld-doctrine speed of the advance, with all its embedded drama, and the strange anticipation at terminus Baghdad, cameras in place, already there, waiting for the first tentative and anti-climactic arrivals of a few scattered Bradley units. It seemed to me captured best in Virilio's description of how, through the course of the history of speed, everything is first reduced to points of departure and arrival, and eventually *merely of arrival*:

> Such is already the case with audiovisual communications where the observer and the auditor are matched up before the screen, *the departure for the meeting has come to an end, it is replaced by the arrival of images* on the screen....[37]

And the images ... for shame.

So where has the road to Baghdad led us if not, indeed, to the camp. Ah, but it is not just Baghdad of course. We would really have to stop now and compare Agamben and Virilio once again with another striking juxtaposition. First, Agamben's territory, where the camp is the *exception* which establishes the rule that *defines* for him modern politics:

> The paradoxical status of the camp as a space of exception must be considered. The camp is a piece of land placed outside the normal juridical order, but it is nevertheless not simply an external space.

What is excluded in the camp is, according to the etymological sense of the term 'exception' (*ex-capere*), *taken outside*, included through its own exclusion.[38]

The *exception* that threatens to 'Gitmo-ize', what – the entire world? The *atopos* which has already been taken deep into the body politic – I picture a young mother walking with her child in a buggy, vaguely distracted, past the 'secret' detention centre in *Brooklyn* where the one unlisted detainee we have yet learned of was stripped, brutalized, and placed in solitary confinement for three months in a 6 by 9-foot cell lit 24 hours a day before being allowed to return to his home in the capital of Buddhist Nepal (for his only infraction was found to be overstaying his work visa), allowed to return only it seems thanks to the fluke of the *exceptional* conscience of one interrogator who said, 'I felt some – not responsibility, but I felt that there was no one else' – an accidental case of an exception to the exception that has become the rule.[39] In the end all that Mr Barjracharya asked was that he be allowed to wear his one modest suit, asked simply to retain just that much of his dignity, but this was denied as he was repatriated in shackles in the now nauseating orange jumpsuit.

The Gitmo *exception* that Tony Blair all too correctly, casually, and I must only assume, unwittingly, described as an '*anomaly* [emphasis added] that has at some point got to be brought to an end'.[40] Yes, at some point indeed, Mr Blair, but, not to put too fine a point on it, *when*? When does the 'war' end? When should we set about correcting what is *a-nomos*, that which is *outside the law*? Or would you have us accept the *a-nomos as* the law? Or, if not the law, then the Rule? We are wondering: Whatever became of *your* voice of decency?

Or was the world already Gitmo-ized from the moment we set out? Was the *road* itself already Gitmo-ized as Virilio argues:

The expressway is not a pathway of transmission, but the concentration camp of speed; segregation and incarceration stem far more from the violence of displacement than from various police controls. *A highway colony*, similar to the staircase of Mauthausen ... [41]

But it is America's destiny to export freedom to the rest of the world:

> ... the passenger is no longer of this world, and if the *freedom of movement* (*habeas corpus*) would seem to be one of the first freedoms, the liberation of speed, the *freedom of speed*, seems to be the fulfillment of all freedoms.[42]

It would seem that only Bush's note to Blair really outdoes Virilio's irony here: 'Let freedom *reign*' – the phrase just strikes me as oxymoronically appropriate – as the reins were supposedly being passed over....

So if I have, in this introduction, held Virilio back momentarily with the rei(g)n of the Sovereign, it is because ultimately I find it necessary to try to pause for a moment to consider what is at the other end of the leash....

> In this parody of the religious state ... lies the beyond, the hereafter [*l'au-delà*], of progressive perspectives, the end of hope for any 'paradise on earth,' for any economic and social success, the obscure advent of a *universal purgatory* for supernumerary populations deprived of civil rights, in deferment, in permanent suspension, subject to the decay of the quotidian and the many recent excesses that betray the scandal. *It is hard to imagine a society that would deny the body just as we had progressively denied the soul. This, however, is where we are headed.*[43]

The images tell it all. Detainees in restraints, and those we discover moving about in the periphery of the frame once Susan Sontag[44] pulled the camera back forcing us to ask the question, now in a different context: 'Who *are* we really?'

To the robot Hilare[44]

Foreword
The Enterprise of Appearances

*The nature that places the mask of the visible over the invisible,
is only an appearance corrected by a transparence.*
(Victor Hugo)

These days I have taken up painting, and in particular the still life. I have always been resistant to the formulas of mathematics but open to the figures of geometry and geography. When I was quite young, I would draw from memory on a blackboard, all sorts of maps, the relief, the network of rivers. I was, on the other hand, quite incapable of remembering a single date, and history and arithmetic were like foreign languages to me, each as foreign as the other.

Figures always spoke to me, the inanimate was clear to me, perimeters descriptive, I found shapes all around me expressive. I was always better able to perceive this language than the other, the sound of utterances disrupted the content of statements, the signs meant more, often, than their composition in formulas, language, or discourse. I must be a bit of a tracker, one who follows trails, an illiterate. I was always drawn to the inanimate, by this standstill movement. The inanimate is merely a derogatory term used by those who read only appearances; those who perceive transparence know well that nothing is immobile, that everything is always moving, that SENSE circulates among things like blood in the veins, in the forms of the frozen object.

I was therefore occupied or rather preoccupied with painting and depicting, that is to say, with attempting to interpret lines, values, and colours, but these seemed to me much less luminous than forms. My first life drawing was of a woman walking down the pavement on the rue Saint Jacques in Nantes, the second was one of a bridge on the Loire. A coincidence, these two most banal subjects would later prove to have a certain meaning: the bridge, or rather the arch, one of three architectural archetypes along with the crypt and the nave, and human movement, for my first subject was less the woman than her gait, a transcription of the gait like those first films that rendered the human gait in movement, a white phantom outlined against the black base of the chronophotographic image. At the time, I wished to do animated drawings and I could only see the future of painting as forms put to movement; imagine the drawings of Da Vinci, the cataracts, the vortices of water, or the grimaces of his caricatures, in movement.... This is how I came to understand the contribution of the technology of photo-cinematography to the old art of drawing. I was fascinated by Emile Cohl's metamorphoses, those personages that moved by successive distortions in as many figures seducing me without my any longer being able to guess at the reason for this attraction. Far Eastern painting also interested me, not for its exoticism, but for its will to represent the non-representable: the wind, the void, currents, withering, softness, all things essentially tactile that seem to us still beyond the possibilities of the art of drawing.

One could thus translate with a pencil, brush, or ink, what we experience by touch, by the skin, and no longer solely by vision. Forms no longer instruct us merely concerning their nature, concerning what constitutes them materially, they inform us also concerning what they undergo in the moment, in time. By their movements, from the more infinitesimal to the more abrupt, they reveal to us the nature of the void, the force of winds, the currents of rivers ... this was for me a discovery and a confirmation: forms, things, emit and receive, they emit their sensible reality and what they have undergone, they receive and return the totality of the sense of their milieu and their immediate surroundings, and this throughout the course of their existence. It thus made little difference to me to learn soon afterwards that with carbon 14 we could now date matter, or that with tree rings we could date back several centuries. For it was already clear to me that we could turn our inquiry to the silent appearance of objects, of things, of figures, and that this inquiry would necessarily become an art of painting the pictorial as questioning and not as representation, just as writing is questioning before being a discourse or a novel – before, well before.

To reflect – since, as Paul Klee contended, 'objects perceive me' – the phenomenology of figures, the origin of geometry, this was my territory. There is no abstraction, everything presents a figure; the formless is an innovation of the West, the void, the null, nothingness, barbarian words introduced by a civilization of predators, destroyers ... ours.

Looking at this more closely, what have we produced that is more original, more specific, than this idea of nothingness, of absence? It is in the final analysis our most obvious cultural contribution. It is precisely this *absence* that I wish to interrogate, where is this void? This is the quest I take up. We often speak of an *abstract* art, a riot of marks, streams of colours, surface effects, opposed to an abstraction called *geometrical*. And this we claimed was a new reality: once the figure had been captured by photography, by the lens, all that seemed to remain for the painter was the subjectivity of the effect; we would be able to discover all the sensible qualities in these specimens of an allegedly contemporary art, and the critics did not hesitate in offering their commentary. Unfortunately, none of this helped much at all in seeing, it was a matter of castes and systems of iconoclastic castes that traded or turned down the messages. The figure, the silhouette, remained there, among us; trees remained trees with their leaves which moved and their trunk which did not move, with the sky and the sun dappled among the branches and the cylinder of the trunk opaque and immobile. We had managed as always to divide reality in two: the figurative and the abstract, and we established them as being mutually exclusive. The figure was dated, passé, while art informel[1] dominated the salons and galleries. We reversed the terms. Yet while the problem did not change, we were trapped as always in the West by the ancient dichotomy, by the exclusion of the other, by the exclusion of that which is different. During this period, my consideration of objects for what they are was so heightened that I became absorbed in the most banal; my still lives were composed of valueless kitchen utensils, laid out on the ground, on the floor of my apartment. In fact, every array of objects seemed to me quite free from any need for a sensible arrangement: strictly speaking, there was nothing interesting in the positioning of the things and I made it a rule not to pay any attention to the positions of the articles in my compositions. It was a study of a real asceticism and those who came to see me then simply could not understand the interest of such an exercise, above all since it was not a question for me of a 'miserabilism' but exactly its contrary, the richness, the affluence of that which does not appear, the life of that which seems to be *absent*.

It was of course quite difficult to contemplate a plastic salt shaker, a little steel spoon, or an empty cheesebox for hours … it was at times unbearable. I have spoken since of the infraordinary, it is just this that was already at issue in my paintings, but was it really a question of paintings? Almost everyone doubted that the result of this would be of any artistic interest, that is, that what I was striving to expose, to bring to appearance, mattered much.

I have always been convinced that everything that will determine the novelty, the originality of tomorrow, is already present in the moment, concealed in the everyday vision of each person, which accounts for this constant will to practise a perspicacity worthy of my desires for change and renewal. The field of vision always seemed to me comparable to what the ground is for archaeological exploration. To see is to be lying in wait for what must spring up from the ground, nameless; for what presents no interest whatsoever, what is silent will speak, what is closed is going to open, it is always the trivial that is productive, and so this constant interest in the incidental, in the margins of whatever sort, that is, in the void and absence.

So it is that after several years of pictorial contemplation, my vision abruptly diverged. From my focus upon the valueless object, I slid over to a secondary aspect [*sur l'à-côté*], just to the side [*tout à-côté*]. The banal object did not turn into a privileged object, there was no 'transfiguration'. Something more important happened. Suddenly, before me, new objects appeared, bizarre serrated or notched figures; an entire collection of articulations had become subtly visible and these objects of observation were no longer banal, in any way, or insignificant. Quite the contrary, they were extremely diverse, they were everywhere, throughout space, the whole world was full of these new forms, they were nestled in the hollows of the slightest forms, it was like an unknown vegetation that proliferated around me, useless objects brought forth the appearance of momentary objects of great complexity, the position of things triggering new exotic forms, forms that escape us although plainly visible, habituated as we are to trivial geometries. While we perceive circles, spheres, cubes, or corners perfectly, our perception of intervals, of the interstices between things, between people, is far less acute. These configurations, cut out by bodies, stamped out by forms, escape us … in every case, these passing figures barely leave any sensible traces in our vision of the world, their fleeting character, tied to the instantaneity of a relation, never seems particularly important. These figures have a far too immediate obsolescence for our analytical consciousness, for our scrutinizing minds, we have always more or less despised this movement that displaces the lines. But I found myself suddenly at the heart of an enriched space, the feeling of being in the desert disappeared, now, each time I opened my eyes, I could by choice contemplate the banality of formal modern presentation or just as well view to the side [à côté], just to the side [juste à côté], the richness of the antiforms. I enjoyed moving to the left, to the right, in order to see them metamorphose into so many new forms. In contrast to manufactured objects where symmetry plays such a significant role that the movements of the observer barely modify his perception of things, with the exception of distancing which miniaturizes the object, the interval glimmers, distorting ceaselessly thanks to the displacements of the subject: what I see here is only valid for a brief instant, I will see something else soon, something else unexpected that I could never guess. Thus this interstitial geography offers me surprises and discoveries of a kind of scaled-down journey, a pool of space will in a moment take on the appearance of an isthmus, of a peninsula of emptiness. I am aware that it is the movements of my body that are producing and destroying this landscape of transparencies, a bit like a passenger on a train sees trees and houses darting past, sees hills bending away; by my own speed, however weak it may be, I form or deform these particles of emptiness, these holes, these hollows, it is a game of construction that I develop without accessories, simply through being here or there. These forms of transparence have another value, they allow me to see, beyond the succession of planes, other forms, there are hollows within hollows, intervals within intervals, these successions of planes, of thresholds, form a complexity transparent as a mirror, but a mirror that would not be a frame, a mirror that one could contemplate continuously from all angles, in front, to the sides, behind, a crystal ball where one would divine the future of the forms.

I decided, therefore, to set out on the hunt for figures of intervals, we speak of the *space between* [*l'entre-deux*[2]] (the space between two seas, for example), it is a common way of speaking, yet this figure is only the first in the encounter: between-three, between-four, between-forty, between-one hundred ... these are just as real even if they usually escape our notice. This escaping was precisely what I was setting out to hunt for, I sought to flush out the antiform, I was convinced that there are certain species of them, unknown, unperceived, families, races, and I was quite determined to discover them and make an inventory of them. I knew then that they hide everywhere, as in those line drawings where the silhouette of the beautiful young women is hidden in the old hag by observing the image from all its aspects. I decided to contemplate my environment in all its facets, reality had become abruptly kaleidoscopic, I was no longer in this urban desert of identical, repetitive, and fixed forms in a pseudo-eternity, I was in the arborescence of counterforms, I navigated through the hollows of intervals, in transparence, this transparence that I had discovered during the war, in the destruction of the urban landscape, I now perceived that, fragmented, exploded, it remained in the midst of the reconstruction and that I had only to will it [*vouloir*] to see [*voir*].

I had gained the liberty to orient myself in the formal universe, I had the choice no longer solely between the negative and the positive, arbitrary terms, but between form and its generation: antiform. I set out for the adventure and for the discovery of this legacy concealed within everyday vision, like Poe's hidden letter, hidden in the open.

Now there were for me two states of the evident: the evident of the explicit and the evident of the implicit, I was irresistibly attracted to the latter, but here I was intrigued by something: the vision of the between-world was extremely fragile, the image of transparence could only be maintained by an effort of perception, the antiform only persisted as long as this effort was kept up, afterwards form reclaimed its stake and concealed the field of the void, the ground [*fond*[3]] appeared only for an instant. Vision became a phenomena of voluntary focus, as with a camera, I had to choose the object to be focused upon and direct myself to it to be able to observe it in all the distinctness of its contours, as soon as I let go of this focus on the ground, on the antiform, on this transparence, the form again became distinct, quite naturally, as the void previously perceived receded.

This subtle equilibrium was quite an astonishing phenomenon,

I tested its duration, the provisional character of the exhumation of transparences in the heart of the opacity of materials and things.

The forms of transparence could not subsist by themselves, they receded into the ground as soon as the attention of the observer abated. I found this transient character most intriguing, I could not accept this game of hide-and-seek where the form constantly prevailed over the ground just at that point when forms had become for me impoverished, not only because the formal space of the city that surrounded me had become meaningless but also since the dynamic of the architectural outlines threatened to reduce further what remained of diversity in the city. The eclipse of the antiforms appeared to me here to be the consequence of a sort of imperialism of apprehension. Vision, my vision, was rejecting, in the same way as Western culture, the ground, the margins, difference. No matter how hard I tried, as soon as I relaxed my attention the object of my perceptive choice disappeared, giving way to what I had rejected. Of course, the awareness that I had of optical phenomena was there to reassure me that this was a matter of physiological and psychological causes and to counter any idea of cultural influence on what could only be an optical illusion. But I could never convince myself of this scientific neutrality, for me, two plus two now made five. In fact, between four, there was room for the fifth: the antiform, the anticipher. For me, number appeared in a space and time, it did not appear in the mathematical series but in the common span of time and extension of space [*la durée et l'étendue commune*], everything was bathed in this, people, things, concepts, notations, languages, there was no scientific heaven where one plus one made two, but the rapprochement in the continuum of two times one inevitably produced the third through the interciphers. Thus each time I directly observed two objects, I would perceive a third, formed by their conjunction, the void, the transparence would take shape between them, the interform had at least as much numerical value as each form taken separately. Why deny it? Why deny the generation of forms? Why deny induction? The dynamic of things seemed to me to double (indeed, I was seeing double ...), on the one hand, an internal dynamic that assured the material reality of the object (stone, class, furniture ...) or, in the case of a drawn figure, that assured on the paper the geometrical reality of the circle, of the roundness within the circumference, and, on the other hand, an external dynamic that induced the void, the transparence, that gave form and value to absence. The surface of the object, the line of the drawing, the outlines, served two purposes: one of internal individuation that established that it was a case of a circle or square, the other of external information that produced a field. When one brought a second figure alongside the first, the external fields would meet each other and the antiform would arise and show itself, a bit like when one throws a stone into a pool of water and then a second alongside, the concentric circles finish by joining and mixing together thus forming a new figure.

Meanwhile, in making my drawings, I was able to distinguish the moment of reversal between (internal) individuation and (external) information, the line of the pencil running over the paper, deciding between two zones still open, then, in closing up my form with the outline of a cup and an ashtray, all at once, there would be a first form and a second form, there was the image in two dimensions of the antiform revealed by the presence of the two figures.

In reproducing two quite real objects on the surface of the paper, I could not avoid causing the transparent object to arise from their reciprocal information.

I found this fascinating. Here was the tropism of the point where the form and the antiform still oscillated. If by running the lead of my pencil further, I passed this specific point, the form would get the upper hand. If I stayed just to this side of it, the antiform became the only apparent object, the object both of the drawing [*dessin*] and of my intention [*dessein*]. In measuring the traced line, I was able to mark out the boundary where primary form and secondary form switched over.

Thus I became a specialist of the tropism since I had taken on the goal of making visible the invisible, and I no longer drew within the narrow limits of these points of reversal that marked the limit between the trivial forms of objects and the non-trivial forms of their effects. At first glance, the decoupling might have seemed insignificant; the antiforms that I exhumed here or there were nothing other than a series of edges [*échancrure*] ... who ever paid any attention to such figures? Of course we speak of a pretty bay, but this is always in the context of the seaside or the sky, the water and the rocks playing together.... As far as the neckline [*échancrure*] of a corsage, we imagine simply a way of catching a glimpse of what is usually hidden ... no, in fact, this type of form was always taken to be quite common. In technical languages, however, all this is present, named. What is full and what empty gather together and are arranged in the construction of movements, forms have their location and this is not considered secondary. The mechanics of *perpetual motion* consisted precisely in harmonizing the passage from one form to another, from one movement to another, by a series of repetitions that required managing the effects of the inductions: what is full will empty itself and vice versa, only the cycle, the chain, is taken into consideration, since in normal observation we only perceive the world as a solution of continuity, of objects, of separate things. In the construction, we assemble this and that in an ensemble that we name structure, flux, machine, etc.

I find this supreme hierarchy of the forms of normal vision a veritable enigma. Has this hierarchy always existed? Or rather, has it been gradually constructed through experience, through the use of groups, of past societies? Was it still possible to live perceiving the word in reverse: on the first level the void, the transparence and its figures, on the second level, material, objects as ground [*fond*] and no longer as form? My ongoing efforts to live in this way proved to me that it would be extremely difficult and that this would require at the very least quite an extraordinary measure of will.

This phenomenon that defined the hierarchy of a perception of the world at the expense of transparence, was it legitimated by the demands of an orientation to the contrary, was it a question of a kind of alienation, a hallucination? An alienation inherited from a distant past, from these peoples lost in the infinite, or rather the indefinite, of the primordial landscape, this jungle where the vegetal dominated, abundant with rich formal complexity, where everything was chaotic and without name.... This first society lost in the flux of vital impressions, the flux of the landscape and of its seasonal renewal, would have gradually developed a logic, a rule of perception, somewhat as we have invented the yardstick and the clock, it would have invented form and ground so as to find itself, or at least to prevent losing itself.

Perhaps this was the goal of the rupestrian art that we are inclined to take as representations similar to our own; perhaps, for those who drew them, it was still solely a question of an apprenticeship in marking out the forms from the ground. The origins of the beautiful, of the good, entailed the attainment of a means of orienting oneself within the surrounding landscape, in the midst of what is good to see and good to consume. Why wouldn't we expect this to be associated with the invention of alimentary customs, the selection of edible plants, of those traced on the walls of the caves? Perhaps we see here an exercise in selection, in the edible character of forms, of substances, of what could be exchanged as signs, as reference marks in a jumble of inextricable outlines. There is not only one perspective, that which comes to us from the Renaissance; the aborigine or the Eskimo find themselves in the places where we could not survive. Perspective is only a hierarchy of perception and there probably are as many perspectives as there are visions of the world, of cultures, and of ways of life.

This original process of definition must have been preliminary to the fully constituted language, a language that must have taken over in facilitating the marking out of the initial continuum with its beginnings of what would become toponymy. Why persist in the belief that the dichotomy of form/ground had always existed? I was trying, albeit in a rather clumsy way, to apprehend this non-distinction but I was only able to do so by an attempt at an exhumation of transparences, I had to invert the significance of what is full and void. Were we, in our encounter with the antiform, facing the residual content of a perspective that was once itself dominant? Did the value of the void actually precede that of plenitude? My drawings, my paintings were above all exercises for interrogating the interstices of vision, a mode of *vision* that I could no longer take for granted. In fact, I could no longer believe my eyes and I had already decided to remain in this rather particular *atheism*. I categorically refused the privileges of perception, I was on the edge, on the shore, and this extreme point seemed to me the only one worthy of interest. I found these multiple shorelines to be my true homeland, and I was like that humorist who said: 'I must meditate on the limit of something, it matters not much what, the important thing is that it be on the limit...'. All this would meanwhile lead me quite logically to the boundary of the sea and to architecture.

These sites, where simultaneously something ends and something begins, literally fascinated me: at the edge of my window, the silhouettes of buildings outlined against the sharp edge of the blue sky drew me, the greater or lesser sharpness was intriguing. It is this that finally determined the greater or lesser presence of the antiform, the blurred contours shade off one into the other, the form and the counterform disappear as in Turner's impressionism. I preferred Cézanne whose pictorial approach abandons nothing of the formal problematic. This way of visually testing the perimetric limits of things was quite comparable to a kind of Braille, there was one part of voluntary blindness in my way of seeing, I was all at once persuaded that vision was presenting less to be seen, that it was above all a process of concealment, a very old process where the old customs of marking out fashioned the everyday image. Something chose for me the figure I would contemplate: 'One only really sees what one already has in mind ...', this maxim confirmed for me the clandestine voluntarism at work in the most ordinary vision, and it made me indignant, as vision consisted precisely of constantly revealing, of unmasking.... To cease to reveal would be to be blind, dazzled by the overexposure as opposed to a physical disability of underexposure. I found then several points in common between this and the other blindness: in the case of the disability we were directly deprived of images, in the case of the one who sees, we were deprived of the freedom to discover truly new images, the usual images that presented themselves everywhere were only the screens destined to mask the appearance of new forms, to conceal life, the flux of renewal, the changing of forms. Once certain institutionalized figures had taken hold, as had been the case for a long time, they occupied the foreground of the scene of visual apprehension and they defended their position ferociously.

Old phantoms battled before my eyes, this rediscovered slicing up of reality was from a world forgotten, a world in which forms proliferate and crowd in on us, where the distinction form/ground was the only means to orient oneself. But to find oneself there has since become a narcissistic vice, that which modern man needed was no longer markers, or reference points, he had become quite saturated with them in the meanwhile; the entire world was no longer anything but a system of commands, for a long time everything had been labelled, listed, recorded. But meanwhile *chance* had practically disappeared, and with it the profusion of animal and vegetal life. The vegetative proliferation of natural forms had been progressively replaced by the organization and normalization of the social field, space had been measured, mapped, time had since become clock time, the diversity of relief, of topography, gave way to topology, there were immense museums filled with every form of creation from dinosaur skeletons to the tiniest fly, everything was consigned to the display windows of the natural history museum, and comprehension started on its way to miscomprehension, there was always someone who knew the name of things, generations of specialists busied themselves with the global inventory of living things, this was the last jungle, this underbrush of labels, figures, dates, maps, which, superimposed, formed the new landscape, one of a geodesic procreation. The world had become a great worksite, all that was to be seen were the excavations of those who dug up the origins, the scaffolding of structuralists, signposts for every little roadway, the slightest trajectory, to the left, or right, up, down, it was all this that finally led modern man astray; designation, by dint of abundance, abandoned its own justification. Today we are prone to succumbing to the labyrinth of signs as we were once prone to succumbing in the absence of signs. The situation of contemporary man is the inverse of the primate's, he must make his way in the heart of the proliferation of landmarks, or rules and orders, this is why the processes of the organization of perception seem to me so poorly suited to the epoch. An updating of perception must be at work in the composition of the immediate image: to see cannot constantly be to see again. Today we are no longer truly *seers* [*voyants*[4]] of our world, but already merely *reviewers* [*revoyants*], the tautological repetition of the same, at work in our mode of production (i.e., industrial production), is equally at work in our mode of perception. We pass our time and our lives in contemplating what we have already contemplated, and by this we are most insidiously imprisoned. This redundancy constructs our habitat, we construct on analogy and by resemblance, it is our architecture. Those who perceive, or build differently, or elsewhere, are our hereditary enemies.

If we are really so worried today about our resources, about the exhaustion of natural energies, it is also necessary that we consider the *sensorial privation* to which we are now subjected. The phenomena that obscure our perception of the world deprive us of sources of energy, our relative blindness masks from us inestimable sources of information. In order to survive, we must change our view [*vue*], just as we must change our lives [*vie*] to subsist. It no longer suffices to speak negatively of 'zero growth', it is necessary to endeavour positively to reinvent our vision of the world. As long as we maintain this brutal dichotomy in our sight, this abusive hierarchy of form over ground, our temperament will lead us to ruin, to the degradation of our milieu, to the rejection of the other and of what is different.

Our vision is a battlefield in which the movement of our culture towards nothingness and disappearance is concealed in the obvious. 'Less is more', declared Mies van der Rohe. We have perverted the terms, reversed the poles, and we are at work on a culture of desertification.

Like the old lords, we respect the phantoms of the past. The object of our attention, the landscapes of our regard, are no longer museographic forms, it is not necessary to go to the National Gallery or the Louvre to see scenes from the eighteenth-century in order to contemplate the figures of the past, it is enough to get up any morning and stroll along in a museum of fashions and styles of outdated observation. Unconsciously we repeat the typologies of apprehension: from the initial separation of the figure from the ground – the detachment between the line of the earth and the sky, between the shoreline and the primordial ocean – to the elaboration of scientific perspective.

He who dreaded that the sky would fall, he who feared the liquid mass and movements of ocean, tore apart a logical structure of vital importance, an essential continuity between the solid and the liquid, between the gaseous and mineral, between presence and absence: he destroyed the relativity of the instant of vision.

First Part

The Metempsychosis of the Passenger[1]

> If you have no woman, go into the bush,
> follow a mare and make her your woman.
> (Dogon adage)

Man is the passenger of woman, not only at the time of his birth, but also during their sexual relations, hence the taboo against incest as a vicious circle, or rather, voyage.[2] Paraphrasing Samuel Butler, we could say that the female is the means that the male found to reproduce himself, that is to say, to *come* to the world. In this sense, woman is the first means of transportation for the species, its very first vehicle, the second would be the horse [*monture*] with the enigma of the coupling of dissimilar bodies fitted out for the migration, the common voyage. Pack animals, saddled horses, or draught horses – the metabolic vehicles present themselves as the exemplary products of a scorned zoophilia, forgotten with the rejection of bestiality. At the origin of domestication, woman preceded the raised and bred animal, the first form of economy, even before slavery and husbandry. She begins this movement that will lead to the pastoral societies, patriarchal societies organized for war, beyond the primordial hunt. In fact, it is at the close of these first acts of carnage that what is to come is first sketched out: war. From the *animal hunt* for the purpose of immediate subsistence, we pass on to the hunt for woman in passing on to the hunt for man. But this hunt is already more than a slaughter, an execution; it is a capture, the capture of female livestock. The waste of energy ceases, as far as the female sex, once the males are again executed and consumed. This is the case practically up to the agricultural stage that will see the institutionalization of slavery, thanks to the taking of men as prisoners.

It is useful to consider this transfer of violence for just as war arose from conflicts between members of the same species and not from a confrontation with animal kind, so also did its sophistication further develop in connection with internecine struggles as opposed to conflicts against outsiders.

Patriarchy arose with the capture of women and then established and perfected itself through the husbandry of livestock. In this economy of violence that signalled the pastoral stage, beauty preceded the beast, it is the coexistence of this twofold livestock that favoured the establishment of the dominant sex; but looking again at these metamorphoses of the hunter, domestication is the fulfilment and perfecting of predation. Outright bloodshed and direct slaughter are contrary to the unlimited use of violence, that is to say, its economy. From the confrontation ending in the carnage of the first ages, we witness an evolution that leads hunters to the point of gaining simple control of the movements of certain selected species, then with the help of the dog, the first 'domesticated' animal, we pass on to the shepherding of semi-wild herds and finally to breeding. The domestication of the female stock has its place in this process. Some time before the pack animal, woman served as a beast of burden; like the herd, she worked in the fields, controlled and supervised by men. During migrations, in the course of conflicts, she carried the baggage. Well before the use of the domesticated donkey, she was the sole 'means of transport'. In attending to transport, woman allowed the burdened hunter to specialize in the homosexual duel, that is, to become a *hunter of men*, a warrior.

The first freedom is the freedom of movement, the 'woman of burden' [*femme-de-charge*[3]] provided the man of the hunt with this, but this freedom is not one of 'leisure', it is a potential for movement that is identified with a potential for war, beyond the primitive hunt. The *first logistical support*, the domesticated female establishes war in taking over the hunter's maintenance for him; just as the territory will be laid out by the invader for the best movement of his forces, so also the woman captured and taken as a mate will immediately be changed into a means of transport. Her back will be the model for later means of portage, all auto-mobility will stem from this infrastructure, from this pleasing conquered croup; all the desires of conquest and penetration are found here in this domestic vehicle. This woman-of-burden who will continue this portage from gestation and early infancy gives the warrior time, sometimes a *good time*, but above all *free time*.

On this level, the heterosexual group will be more formidable in the homicidal fight than the homosexual, and the purely logistical dimension of the weaker sex will be essential to the emergence of the patriarchal order. On this side of reproduction and sexual customs, bisexuality asserts itself as a veritable 'mode of subsistence'. For the nomad, survival was identified with the pursuit of prey; with pasturage, the pursuit of the enemy. The group finds its subsistence in its faculties of adaptation to movement, its 'fortification' is only 'time gained' over prey, over the adversary, it is not yet the 'obstacle' of the sedentary agrarian, but the course and its means: 'pack-woman',[4] the mare, anticipating later conveyances. In offering him free time, along with her back, woman became the 'future of man',[5] his destiny and destination. Thanks to this first stock, the hunter-breeder comes to possess what in military terms we call 'a good payload capacity' thus allowing him to prolong conflicts and therefore to succeed, since he was no longer obliged to procure food on site.

Conflicts, limited up till then by the limited mobility of groups, could henceforth be extended because woman brought to the warrior his projectile weapons and served as supply. With the breeding of the horse, war will last even longer and extend over a greater area, simply because the horse's capacity and speed is superior to the human metabolic vehicle.

Let's take the example of the Maya: in the Yucatan, the wars that preceded the arrival of the Spanish were always of short duration, for on that continent the women were still the only transport vectors.... On the other hand, with the conquest by a trifling company of mounted invaders, we witness a debacle without precedent that is no better explained by metallic weapons than by the spiritual disposition of the native people. It is the differential in time, the speed of the conquerors that enabled the extermination of a civilization by a few dozen horsemen. The introduction of the horse on the American continent is the probable cause of the extinction of a people and a culture that faced their conquerors together in the same place, but in a different unity of time, the Spanish possessed this 'dromocratic' superiority that always compensates for any inferiority in numbers.

In sum, with the origin of the first expansion of combat, woman was the first 'transportation revolution'. She allowed the hunter to specialize in the obscenity of the narcissistic and homosexual duel, far more formidable than the contest with wild animals because it requires constant changes in tactics, as well as strategies. By her domestication, the weaker sex allowed the invention of an enemy beyond prey; later, this extension of the assault was pursued with pack animals, *the invention of the mount*, the cavalry, the use of chariots and the sorts of infrastructural constraints specific to Mesopotamia, *the invention of roads*, in anticipation of the railway ... but this is another history, that of the specifically technological revolution in transportation as opposed to the metabolic vectors. We saw in the nineteenth century how man came down from his horse to mount the train, and this in the same era when he discovers himself curiously descended from an ape-like anthropoid ... I would here like to make an inverse move and attempt a guess at how man mounted his horse [*monté sur la monture*] in descending from the arms, from the back of woman.

To leave is also to leave behind; to leave the dock, the port, to prepare to launch out, but also to lose one's sense of calm, *to be swept up in the violence of speed*, this unsuspected violence produced by the vehicle, this celerity that tears us away so abruptly from the places travelled through and in which we abandon ourselves in shared transport.

Each departure is a distancing [*écartement*] that deprives us of contact, of direct experience; each instance of vehicular mediation is nothing other than a drawing and quartering [*écartèlement*], a torture of the locomotive body, a sensory privation of the passenger. Borne along, walled in by the violence of movement, we merely attain acceleration, that is to say, the loss of the immediate. Speed, by its violence, becomes a *destiny* at the same time as being a *destination*. We go nowhere, we have contented ourselves solely with leaving and abandoning the vivacious and vivid [*vif*] to the advantage of the void [*vide*] of speed.

The term 'mount' [*monter*] shows [*montre*] this clearly: we mount horses, we 'mount'[6] automobiles, we climb up [*élevons*] to be carried off [*être enlevés*], stolen away by the prosthesis that extends our mobility; *this abduction is at the heart of accelerated travel*, travellers taken up by the violence of speed are 'displaced persons', [«*personnes déplacées*[7]»] literally deportees.... However, this modern transmigration seems to have been overlooked; the acceleration of movement [*déplacement*[8]] has been assimilated to a progression, to progress, as a curious blind alley in the history of movement.... The mount would seem, therefore, indispensable to the assumption of the passenger, this rider levitated above the ground, hostage to the celerity of his course, deprived of his own motility. Eliminating the fatigue of its passenger's locomotive limbs, the horse, the mount, in its saddle, resembles a seat that moves, a piece of furniture, a hippomobile that is not satisfied merely in assisting the body in the requirements of parking, of rest, like a chair, but also in moving from one place to another.

The invention of the mount would be in some measure a military tactic of the locomotive body: just as we exercise our limbs standing in place in order to alleviate extended sedentary immobility, so also, in the mobility of the saddled animal, we spare ourselves from the discomfort of pedestrian travel by manipulating the speed of movement. Sliding bit by bit, drifting stage by stage, from the slightest shifts to the most far-reaching, we play this game of hide and seek with our body which we call: assistance, comfort, support, well-being ... *in order to feel our animal body less we are constantly on the move* (motility), *so as to forget the expanse of the territorial body, we travel rapidly, violently.*

This constant search for an ideal weightlessness is at the heart of the problems of domination. The epiphany of the horse, celebrated in the Middle Ages, illustrates this particularly well: in equestrian heroism, the horse is the bearer of death at the same time as being the protector of life, but 'wasn't it only the protector because it was the bearer?' as Fernand Benoit asks.[9] This theme recurs again in the bearer of Christ, St Christopher, patron saint of motorists. The celerity of the warhorse protects the rider from his pursuers but also from his own weakness, *the mount protects its passenger from the weakness of his own constitution*, but only by disqualifying it, explaining why the horse and the bird[10] would be portents of death at the same time as being portents of power and domination: it is necessary first for the passenger to join corporally with the divine celerity of the warhorse, to lose his soul in an immediate metempsychosis in order to accede to domination. He who is 'mounted' dominates those on the ground, he dominates them by the height of his mount, but also by the mobile force of his horse with its tack on. His adversaries will no longer escape him, they are driven before him in the hunt and widely dispersed, *the martial role of the horse is to disperse the fleeing enemy in order to exterminate it*, the charge of the cavalry breaks through the mass of infantry like an explosive charge tears open the mass of walls and ramparts.

The differential in speed and violence between the infantry, those who fight on foot, and the cavalry, those who fight on horseback, leads to the disqualification of the former (just as the pack animal had disqualified the 'pack-woman'), only to be followed in turn by the even greater differential between technological means of transport and all types of metabolic vectors.

The violence of speed is only an extermination; mounted, raised up by his speed, the passenger is nothing but a dead man who rides[11] both elevated [*élevé*] and carried off [*enlevé*], the mounted rider no longer really belongs, instead, he belongs quite entirely to the violence of the warhorse and, just as the expression 'to take [*enlever*] a position' means in military terms to take it by crossing over it, the phrase 'spur on [*enlever*[12]] to the gallop' signifies that the rider is leaving the earth, losing his footing in an accelerated errantry.

Speed resembles senescence, and death, this death that brushes up against the evil that carries him off and bears him away from his people; to mount the horse or ride in the automobile is to prepare to die to the moment of the departure, and thus, to be reborn in the moment of arrival (to die a bit ...). Speed is identified with a premature aging, the more the movement [*mouvement*[13]] accelerates, the more quickly time passes and the more the surroundings are stripped of their significance; 'displacement' [*déplacement*[14]] becomes a kind of cruel joke: it is said 'The shortest trips[15] are the best!' Like one who has passed away, the passenger is no longer of this world, and if the *freedom of movement* (*habeas corpus*) would seem to be one of the first freedoms, the liberation of speed, the *freedom of speed*, seems to be the fulfilment of all freedoms.[16] In fact, the course arises in history as the sublimation of the hunt, speed perpetuates the hunt and mobilization of forces, extermination. The dromocratic hierarchy of speed [*vitesse*] renews nobility: *vitesse oblige*! The society of the course, society of the hunt, the dromocracy is merely a clandestine organization of a social and political hunt where speed extends the advantage of violence, a society where the affluent class conceals the class of speed. The last 'economy of violence', where the transmigration of species goes beyond portage, in the 'transportation revolution' where riding, a metempsychosis of origins, is illustrated by the myth of the centaur[17] but also by the myth of the motorist.

The progress of speed is nothing other than the unleashing of violence; we saw that breeding and training were economic forms of violence, or, if you like, the means to sustain violence, indeed render it unlimited. The conservation of metabolic energy was not therefore an end but an orientation of violence: *the means to prolonging it in time*; the technological motor resulted in the long-standing pursuit of the *perpetuum mobile*, and with it the release of this violence. Two questions present themselves:

How did we ever guess at the vehicle within the animal? The motor in their limbs?

How did the primate come to have this desire to couple with the mount? What sort of seduction is at work here?

This desire for a *foreign body* following as it does the desire for the *different body* of heterosexuality seems to me a major event on a number of points, comparable to the invention of fire, but an innovation that has been lost in the obscurity that surrounds animality.

From the *zoophobia* that signals the earliest hunts and that ended in the slaughter for immediate alimentary needs, we come to this *zoophilia* of the training of the animal for transport....

How is it that we get beyond the necessities of mere subsistence? How did we guess at the motor beyond the reserve of meat on the hoof? The means of locomotion on this side of alimentation?

What sort of economy, what sort of subsistence is at issue in the costly upkeep of a large animal for the course?

Domestication seems to be a quasi functional end of predation: bloodshed was a waste of violence, the enclosing of semi-wild animals, and above all the breeding which followed, brought forth an initial type of economy. Domestication is a form of *conservation of energy* necessary for subsistence. With the training of the mount, this underwent a transformation: the economy of violence is no longer that of the hunter in the breeder but that of the hunted animal. With the mount, kinetic energy was preserved, the speed of the horse as opposed to that of proteins. From a direct subsistence economy to an indirect one, we proceed on to an *economy of survival*, the animal of locomotion was now useful almost only for combat, his passenger will be only a *parasite*, the body of the race animal was nothing other than a first *speed factory*, a motor, the standard for the modern measure of horsepower.

Whereas the *hunter* aimed at stopping the movement of the wild animal by a systematic slaughter, with domestication, the breeder is satisfied with conserving it, finally, thanks to training; the *rider* is linked up with the movement, in orienting it and in prompting its acceleration. From the desire for death to the desire for incorporation, it seems we witness a phenomenon of the *metempsychosis of the living*, the couple at odds from their origins henceforth form only one body, as in a marriage. It is the erotic desire for this prosthesis that sets it off in the beginning.

But in this instant, the race becomes a higher form than the hunt, *the eruption of the beyond*, of a beyond of physical bodies, territorial and animal, an image of delirium and possession that will, in medieval belief, become the 'diabolical hunt' where the horse takes on an apocalyptic dimension, where the four riders symbolize the end of time and the extermination of history.

After having signalled the suppression of distances by the speed of the course, the eruption of the beyond signals the annihilation of time. The speed of the warhorse symbolizes the terror of the end, but it must also be carefully noted that fear and speed are in fact linked: in the animal world, speed is the fruit of terror, the consequence of danger. In fact, the reduction of distances by the acceleration of movement is the effect of the instinct for self preservation. *Speed being simply the production of fear*, it is flight and not the attack that prompts the violent distancing, the sudden burst of speed. The constant acquisition of greater and greater speed is only therefore the curb to increasing anxiety; in this sense 'the transportation revolution', in producing in the nineteenth century the factory of speed, industrializes terror: *the motor manufactures fear*. The speed of movement[18] is only the sophistication of flight and not the attack, as the fascist philosophy of the thirties claimed ('All grandeur is in the attack' in other words, in the eruption of the beyond of bodies and in particular the territorial body). Unfortunately for the 'futurists' this war manoeuvre is never anything but a *flight forward,* a prevention of the end and not a projection forward!

If distance is place, it is also the body. To sweep down upon [*fondre*], to strike precipitously, is at once: to be swept up into [*fondre*], to dissolve into ... we find here the vehicular function of the warhorse to disperse (*skedasis*[19]), to drive the enemy astray [*écarter*], but also, to be carried astray oneself [*s'écarter*], taken beyond the familiar horizon.

'Fear is cruel', says a Nordic maxim, 'it never kills, but it impairs life.' The sublimation of the hunt in the course also makes it impossible merely to abide....

Let us return to the invention of the vector. Very early, the hunter must have been struck by the swiftness of animal movement and fascinated by the instant reflexes of game. Conversely, pursued by wild animals or enemies, the hunter must have perceived a real change in the acceleration of his performance. In the terror, the power, and in his forces multiplied by fear, he must have perceived a formidable 'weapon'. The aptitude for accelerated movement appeared to him as the aptitude for survival, before the invention of tools designed for killing, movement was for the fighting body what range would later be for the power of projectile weapons: a question of critical distance, a problem of retreat and not solely of penetration.

It is meanwhile significant to note that the extended range of sidearms resulted from the development of the cavalry. If tools *extend* the body of man and extend it to a great distance, thanks to the projectile; it is the invention of the mount and the vehicle which will attain its greatest extension, the mount will be the warrior's first 'projector', his first weapons system. 'At the beginning of the second millennium before our era, the copper poniard in use in the Aegean region, will give birth to the dagger, the longer weapon that spread through all of central Europe. The dagger was very valuable for the soldier on foot, but for the cavalry an even more imposing weapon was needed. It is therefore with the cavalry of the last period of the bronze age that the dagger gave rise to the sword', states General Fuller, and continues: 'The increase in the numbers of cavalry armed with lances and swords will bring about the suppression of the sledge and battleaxe of those who lived in the steppes.' In fact, for this last category it was a question of tools more than weapons. It was extension that will make of the hunting knife a specialized weapon, and of the sword, a 'lance' ... from a series of polyvalent prostheses we progress on to the 'weapon' that, according to Sun Tsé, is only an 'ill-omened tool', an obscene prosthesis, literally! ... and this in order to offset the speed and the elevation of the mount.... We saw previously that before the domestication and breeding of the war horse, woman had contributed to the protraction of combat beyond the duel; with the horse this protraction extends not only to war and its duration, but also to the entirety of its means: weapons, logistics, infrastructure, etc.

Extension and protraction come to be identified with protection and defence, the 'protracted wars' of agrarian societies, which have survived right into contemporary times, are sketched out in this transfer from woman to the horse, then to the chariot and the road; as the military space develops, the cavalry, as a parasite of the mount, gives way to wheeled vehicles, while harnessing replaces the mounted coupling and requires the construction of roads, that is to say the void, the clearing out and straightening of the path. First 'military glacis', the road is only a linear clearing offered to the 'divine celerity' of the war chariot, earth scorched by vehicles, the surface scoured, the Mesopotamian road is defined independently from the land it passes through, a geometric abstraction; uniformity, unidirectionality, *speed* [*la vitesse*] *provokes the void* [*le vide*] *and the void* [*le vide*], *speed* [*le vite*]....

After the pack animal, the draught animal, comes this line that stretches out and extends beyond the bends of the road, this straight route that predetermines the displacement by inducing the violence of movement, this infrastructure, the 'static vehicle' that is nothing other than a memorial to the celerity of fear. The steel that stretches out in front in the sword, in the lance, in the knife as in the rail, is like the road, that disappears over the horizon in a movement of shock and distancing, signalling one violence, one terror.

In Mesopotamia, possession of the earth is always linked to the techniques of the 'war of the course'; the monarch distributed the territory to an elite of movement, *those who move quickly possess the earth*. On the other hand, the charioteers had important administrative roles, their teams allowing for a global surveillance in support of the central power. In Rome, we find again the *stallion-standard*[20] [*cheval-étalon*] in the aristocracy of breeders and then, with the Roman equestrian order and the octroi by the State of the 'public horse', we note that this elite of speed is in fact economico-militaristic. Among the knights of the *equite romani*, we find prefects, tribunes, but also 'military tradesmen'. As Nicolet notes: 'This second very influential aristocracy, who play a very important financial and political role in the *publica* and the tribunals, never lose the character that their military origins confer upon them.'[21] The 'knight-banker' administers the movable and transportable assets. His affluence results from transfers and from their celerity. The profit of war results from the portable character of assets, without the transfer of spoils war would be futile; economically if there was nothing to be won, it would no longer be profitable.

To sum up, from the 'hunter-breeders' up to the 'ocean-pirates' passing through the horsemen and charioteers, the elite of movement represents a misunderstood and underestimated order without which accumulation would not have been possible. The accumulation of energy and of speed in the vectors of transport (horse-drawn or seagoing) is indispensable for the capitalization of goods and riches, the occult character of this dromocratic 'society of the course' reveals the strategic dimension of the vectorial politics carried down through the ages.

Desire for a metallic body – the passenger enclosed in the cabin of the automobile repeats the primary coupling. As if the materialist West, with the revolution of transports, installed its metempsychosis in the present moment of bodies; without awaiting the transmigrations of birth or death, the industry of movement accelerates, transfers, from here to there, from one to the other, we 'cast off' [«*appareillons*»[22]], enclosed in the differential of speeds, walled in by the energy of the travelling, we are less human than we are station.[23]

Site of ejection and no longer election,[24] territory becomes the margin [*lisière*] of an incessant cabotage: disembarkation, embarkation, *break of load*, technical rhythms build us up and break us down relentlessly. The excess of speed is a driving school, it trains our reflexes, our responses, as the fascist Marinetti once wrote:

Our heart is not in the least weary!
For it feeds on fire, hate, and speed.

The Great Vehicle

> If we all manage, to the very limit of our
> networks, to respect the hour down to the second,
> we will have endowed humanity with the most effective
> instrument for the construction of a new world.
> (Audibert, railway engineer)

With the invention of the vehicle as animal, man arrives at one of the
very first forms of relativity, his territory will no longer be what it was,
he is increasingly detached from it through the celerity of the warhorse.
Places will become points of departure and arrival, shores which are left
behind and arrived at, the earth's surface will henceforth be nothing
more than the promontory of an equestrian cabotage. In the saddle,
or on foot, the cavalry changes the territorial body into nothing more
than points of embarkation and debarkation, thresholds for a 'break of
load'[25] such as was already hinted at with the transportation revolution
of woman.

   In providing for an elevated traversing of the greatest expanses, the
animal's body becomes a *body-bridge*, a mobile bridge, whereas the
body of woman was only a precarious *body-footbridge*, the horse's body
becomes the symbol of the hipparch and beyond him of the monarchy,
the leader who harnesses and directs these animal energies. Well before
the invention of the arch among sedentary cultures, the body of the
mount sketches out the construction of the bridge that spans the
distance of the moat, the gap of the river; the symbolic function of the
horse that disperses (*skedasis*[26]) the enemy doubles with the function
of exchange, the mount becomes an 'elevated crossroads', literally, an
interchange [*échangeur*], as the cabalistic tradition would call it later
on…. To finish, these points [*points*], these bridges [*ponts*], produce
the *port* [*port*], this site where the animal lays down its load will mineralize into the architectonic of the *portal* [*porte*], veritable 'port of
earth' of caravan transience, a gearbox [*boîte de vitesses*] where the value
of movement is exchanged for the octroi of a taxation on invasion

trades; a value that repeats, in the economy this time, the power of the transshipment of the cavalry, this 'charge of rupture'[27] that will trigger the progressive development of the urban ramparts erected against the assault of waves of animals like the quay against the ocean. In fact, the slanted postern that allows the connecting route to pass through is similar to the entrance to the fortified port, *between the defence towers of the urban enclosure and those of the port citadel, a similar 'liquidation' is at work*: in the example of the 'portal', it is a question of the turbulence of the dry flux of passengers that must be controlled by the design of the surroundings; in the case of the 'port', it is a question of the flow that 'ports' the vessels. The defence is thus double since it is necessary to protect oneself not only from the water and tidal movements by the erection of the quay, but also from naval manoeuvres. In the continental city, the entrance is merely a 'dry port' where the defences control access based in the immediate outlying area where the topography has been levelled off, worn down, to facilitate control of various movements. The port with its customs control, allowing for the engagement and disengagement of internal and external movements, is the most important thing for the art of Western fortification and will be taken up later by the railway stations and airports.

The *rail poliorcetic* [28] results in this theory[29] of networks that the systems of roads will only regain later in the instrumentation of the motorway; the projection of the sword of the rail will contribute to the perfecting of the vectorial politics of the assault.

The point of transshipment [*rupture de charge*] of the rampart, as with all durable structures elsewhere, masked the charge of rupture [*charge de rupture*][30] that gave rise to it. Comparable in each point to the dialectic between the weapon and armour, that of transport and port is never really recognized. Despite the problem of customs, the question of borders is taken solely as a 'question of property' as opposed to being identified as a front of movement and speed.

In sum, the passenger's desire for coupling [*appareillage*] with his mount is comparable to the rite of passage of marriage, for in this the interconnection and the departure[31] are linked, as is still suggested in the dance terms *cavalier* and *cavalière*[32].... Nevertheless, if yesterday, with the equestrian heroes, the horse would suggest the presence of the absent cavalier, today the dancing couple suggests the absence of the mount. We should be concerned about this forgetting of the animal vector in the choreographic rhythms, sexual coupling has too much obscured the act of tact, the preliminary organic touching of the joining of bodies, from the handshake, arms on the shoulders or around the waist, to the various conjoinings of collective work and play, to the 'galop' and 'quadrille',[33] these zoo-choreographic couplings from the nineteenth century. Each of these couplings frames a 'matching up' [*appareillage*], the *mise-en-scène* of a break of load [*rupture de charge*] at once effective and affective where corporeal proximity is performed, and is constantly drawn into question. In this sense, *the invention of an animal partner directly interconnected with the human body seems to me to be an event comparable to, indeed inseparable from, exogamy.*

The coupling of the passenger and the mount pertains to an economy of mutation, it is a graft propitious to the performance of the driving couple where the rider acts as a rein on the pace. In anticipation of what will follow, the driver of the movement becomes also its accelerator thanks to the western innovation of the spur, the key symbol of medieval chivalry.

The apparatus composed of the linked combination [fondu-enchaîné] of man mounted on his mount completes the exogenous unity of the heterosexual couple.

The exogamic coupling of the equestrian body and the pedestrian body pertains to the same external regulation: woman comes from elsewhere, she is carried off and the animal vector is in certain cases the means of this transfer. In ancient China, for example, the transport of the betrothed in the ritual cart constituted, from the legal point of view, the essential act of marriage as if to signify the degree to which *the passage and the wedding are associated,* as if the exogamous marriage was merely the symbol of the shared passage from one group to the other.

There are three obvious couplings, of which the last is rarely mentioned:

- the homosexual couple of the dual;
- the heterosexual couple of the marriage;
- the transsexual couple of the passage.

The institutionalization of the nuptial abduction [*rapt*] pertains to the logic by which being carried away [*enlèvement*] conceals the accelerated movement of the race, as a substitute for the hunt. The detachment of the geographic and terrestrial body, thanks to the domestication of the animal body as a vector of transport, is also the inauguration of a desocialization. If yesterday, in the unity of the neighbourhood, the other was both known and recognized through the daily repetition of encounters, with the transportation revolution, this neighbour will become a 'spectre' that one will only see again accidentally, the foreigner will remain hidden among us. . . . The opening to outside influences will not only favour a better communication between groups, the perfecting of exchanges, it will also bring about this *fleeting presence* of the other: the very notion of a neighbour will at some point disappear for ever, this kinetic addiction to the sudden disappearance of the congener will have the tragic character of a social divorce. The corporeal presence of the other will seem to lose its reality; in passing, as a passenger, fleeting, the other will be identified with its cinematic image millennia before the invention of cinema, the fugacity of the horseman pertains to an identical phenomenon of retinal persistence where the irreality of the course will now hunt the physical reality of bodies advancing the formidable persistence of signs.

We live today in a dramatic addiction to the urban metastability and no one seems at all disturbed by associating with phantoms at every turn: we will probably never encounter this woman we see in the street again, and the same applies to virtually all those around us, a meeting with an acquaintance from the neighbourhood being no longer anything more than a brief encounter. . . .

On the other hand, are we to imagine a universe of stability where foreignness was the exception and the relation of bodies the rule? It is, however, this reversal that the revolution of animal transport brings about, the innovation of the mount at once the 'factory of speed' and disappearing machine . . . leading to the steam engine that will one day enter the station of La Ciotat, and to the camera that Fromiaut, the inventor of camera dollying, will perch on top of a train, and on the escalator of the Eiffel Tower.

The device for recording images will, in its turn, benefit from the violence of the first camera dollies, those fast-moving vehicles which allow the layout and relief of territories travelled through to be seen 'filing past' [*défiler*[34]] as in a parade. Unfortunately, this optical illusion prompted by speed produces a double phenomenon: if, on the one hand, in the exhilaration of the accelerated movement, the passenger casts his gaze upon things that appear to be moving although they are actually at rest while it is he who passes by; on the other hand, in contemporary urban life, those around us give the impression of being stationary, of being our neighbours, even though they will soon disappear forever.

We note therefore that the *liquidation* of the world goes on, the liquefaction of the port (of the railway station, the airport) is mirrored in the extermination of the passenger in the transport. The other, the alter ego, is henceforth identified solely by greater or lesser fixity of his brand image; the working citizen is no longer so much a full 'member of society' [«*sociétaire*»] as a 'temporary' one [«*temporaire*»], whose fugitive political and cultural presence is constantly declining.

Meanwhile, with regard to this transition, it should be noted that the rail revolution came to us from a *maritime power* that perfected the 'sport of the transport' to such a point that it became an entire politics. It is from Britannic insularity that this demand came to us, new for the Continent, of *comfort in travelling*. This Anglo-Saxon ideology of 'well- being' is encountered in both the bourgeois furnishings [*mobilier*] of the eighteenth century and in what was first maritime mobility[35] and then rail mobility, *the comforted body of the traveller comes to complement the assisted body, the sedentary*. It was the Scot MacAdam who, in 1815, invented the smooth road surface for high-speed transportation. And these furnishings that simulate in apartments the cabins of sea-going vessels come from the same horizon. The marine element and its restful swaying motion became a norm of Anglo-Saxon comfort. The adage of oriental metempsychosis '*every body deserves misericord*' is taken up by the gentry before the rest of the West. Moreover, the manufacture of speed technologies contributed to the disqualification of metabolic means of speed: *the locomotive body of the privileged man deserves the misericord of assistance*, he whose prestige was in the past determined by his animal mount, its musculature, will henceforth be protected from the assault of the velocity of vectors. It will be necessary to make the road smooth and cushion the cabin of the vehicle and the seats. An entire *politics of comfort* develops in this epoch. With the violent acceleration [*emballement*] of the motorized machine, it will be necessary to promote the value of the corporeal 'packaging' [*l'emballage*] of the passenger, of this traveller squeezed into his upholstered mantle, in the arms of his armchair, an image of a *body mummified that moves* and that the British practice of 'sports' will attempt to revive, yes, to resuscitate once it has arrived safe and sound.... Whether it is a question of furniture [*meuble*] or shelter [*immeuble*], comfort fools us, it leads us into error in our experience of our own bodies. Comfort is nothing more than a subtle trap into which we fall with all our weight, the addiction to the comfort of artificial assistance is comparable to that of a narcotic, it deprives us of the physical realities of an actual body like those of the places traversed. With the high speeds that are only one of the outcomes of comfort, we are fooled by the duration of the trip. Doped by the cushion, by the depth of the seats, duped by the celerity of the course, the addiction to comfort leads us to lose our sense of touch, the muscular contact with materials and volumes giving way instead to a series of caresses, light strokes, and fleeting slidings.

The effect of the surface of things, the touch of surfaces, is definitively evaded by the improvement of 'well being' thanks to the interposition of mediating elements destined to cause us to lose complete contact with primary materials.

Enveloped, hidden beneath a cover that conceals solid reality, a bit like the way accelerated automobility veils the image of landscapes traversed, the padding of seats or the lining of clothes destroys all sense of localization, every possibility of getting one's bearings.

In sum, comfort is nothing other than a collection of ruses that aim to erase these infinitesimal inconveniences which are, however, themselves the proof of the existence of weight, scale, and a natural motility.

Meanwhile in order to outsmart the adversary – but also to circumvent our own fatigue – we have ceaselessly sought to perfect this vehicle that bears us along while we rest our lower limbs. If the seat relieves our legs from bearing our mass, the car or horse does even more to relieve the fatigue of the road, but this *economy of exhaustion* masks the economy of violence; the subterfuges of assistance cleverly conceal the fact that the comfort of the assisted body is nothing other than a *sophisticated domestication*, the progressive immobilization of physical bodies set flush in their furniture [*encastrement du meuble*], in the framing of their domicile [*encadrement de l'immeuble*], illustrating the 'democratic' illusion of the social and spatial integration, the illusion of a concentration-camp system that is finally nothing more than the vehicular system of the transhumance of an effectively dromocratic society.

Imperceptibly, the route [*la voie*] reproduces the convoy [*le convoi*], the alignment of troops; in marching order, the unwinding band channels us together in a column for the sequencing [*défilé*] of accelerated travel [*voyage*]. This aligned disposition of bodies in movement repeats that of the body of the trained animal: man entrained [*dressé*] is a man trained [*redressé*], in rows by two, by three; the multi-lane motorway inscribes the procession of convoys in the crossing of conquered landscapes. Victory of the sequencing [*victoire de défilement*] or victory parade [*défilé de victoire*], the high-speed route institutes the invasion as the colonial division of lands institutes the occupation ... the route installs its first line, its front in the conquest of time; here as elsewhere, to vanquish is to advance, and the allotment of territory in the interminable band of the route of penetration is nothing but a dynamic form of colonization, the route straightened for acceleration is nothing other than a 'deportation' camp, the punishment of modern asylums arises from the linear and continuous character of the movement and not simply from incarceration. The route that gives rise to the column of vehicles also prompts the colonization of passengers; whether deportees of work or deportees of leisure makes no difference! The transit camp of a final war where the domestication and normalization of motorists is continuously perfected.

Site of ejection and no longer of election where the alternating transmigration renews the classical territorial transplantation, it does indeed seem as if transfer must be indispensable to the State. The State apparatus is in fact simply an apparatus of displacement [*déplacement*[36]], its stability appears to be assured by a series of temporary gyroscopic processes of delocalization and relocalization. Let's look again for a moment at the Peruvian world: despite its inferior mobility due to the absence of the horse, it relied upon the distances between outposts to maintain state power; however, these distances would prove fatal with the arrival of the European equestrian forces: 'In the Incan Empire borders and subjugated provinces were defended by garrisons, strategic points were guarded by fortresses, *pacification was effected by moving people from one point to another*: the conquered tribal colonies were installed in secured areas and colonies of the dominant race were established in the subjugated provinces'.[37] We note that 'pacification' is accomplished here, as elsewhere, through a complete distancing between the vanquishers and the vanquished, and a similar practice is at work among the Guarani Reducciones. *Transport is at the heart of the State apparatus just as it is at the heart of war*, while these logistical necessities are to be traced back to their beginnings assured by the woman of burden. Nevertheless, these displacements are still only displacements in space, transplantations from one place to another and not yet *transmigrations in the time of acceleration*; the weak and irregular performance of vectors is up to this point incapable of prompting a dromocratic revolution of the State, beyond the walled city, the limits of the town or region. The distancing occurs through territorial conquest, it does not yet occur through the conquest of time. If invasion contributes to the institution of public law, its speed is not yet the Law of the world, the State is as yet only *the state of siege* of citadels, and not yet the *state of emergency* of vectors. Delocalization is effected through colonies of populations until it comes to be realized in the perpetual movement of columns of vehicles, and this will last until the nineteenth century, when the rail will contribute less to consolidating the colonial conquest than to preparing this historical transformation that today takes the illusory title of 'decolonization'. The 'liberation of colonies' brought about by the passage from the era of moving people from place to place to that of outright migrations is in fact only the most evident sign of deterritorialization; it announces the future of an anational 'state of emergency' beyond the old state of siege on the city, where the capitalization of speed attains to such a degree that the old geopolitics tends to become a simple chronopolitics, a true war of time, beyond that of space and territories.

As Lamarche declared in 1846, 'He who speaks of *a great colony* speaks nonsense if by these words he does not understand *a great navy*'. At the same time, to speak today of decolonization we must understand that is a question of the liquidation of territory.

Deterritorialization inaugurates the sublimation of domestic pacification, the bringing about of great movements of colonists announces the age of massive and accelerated migrations: beyond *exocolonization*, an *endocolonization*, the acceleration of a distancing, the incessant quotidian bustle and the absence of settlements beyond the city limits, the gyrovague cycles of work and leisure and no longer the ostracism of deportation. 'This mass of individuals visible in the smallest military unit unites in a common voyage' that Clausewitz described long ago, *public transport* generalizes it today: transport became civilization. Both the long highway convoys of holidaymakers and the suburban trains of the proletarian itineration define a *political isobar*, a new frontier, literally a last front, that of movement and of its violence. Already the German geographer Ratzel defined war as the 'promenade' of one's frontier over the terrain of the adversary, the front being merely a wandering frontier, its line being merely a military isobar. From this point forth the front line will pass through the centre of towns, through the heart of the countryside, and the common voyage of the task force advances with the incessant movement of traffic. High-speed routes are the next to last figure of the fortification, but a fortification that is once again identified, as during the pastoral era, with time saved and no longer with permanent obstacles. If the capacity for sudden onset is indeed the essence of war, it is also that of the modern State. 'The weapon of the Army Service Corps', the totality of supply networks functions like a last place/non-place of political power putting the full scope of the state apparatus into play. 'An army is always strong enough when it can go and come, extend itself and draw itself back in, as it wishes and when it wishes.' This phrase of the ancient Chinese strategist Se Ma presents the pneumatic dimension of the transit camp, or rather, of the unspeakable social migration, vectorial image of a combat without battle but not without fear, that gives rise to an extermination that extends throughout the world and spreads its victims across the field of excess speed. At the beginning of the transportation revolution, Field Marshal von Moltke wrote: 'We prefer the construction of the railway to that of the fortification' – a phrase that could have been interpreted as pacifist if the invasion of France in 1870 had not introduced a cruel contradiction to the ideology of 'progress through the increased speed of transports'. Whatever one may say, to vanquish is always to advance, and to gain in speed [*prendre de la vitesse*] is always to take power [*prendre le pouvoir*], since there is always a dromocrat to declare, like Frederick II on the subject of the Austrians: 'Indolent in their movements, slow in executing their projects, *they regarded time as their own*'.

Let us not forget, we are all Austrians, the slow [*lent*] and the violent confront one another in this 'battle between classes of speed' that has gone on since the innovation of that first logistical support of space that was the woman of burden. Transports govern production, including the production of destruction; since the problem of the transport is parallel to that of munitions, the speed of action always depends upon the state of the logistical system. After von Moltke, it was Luddendorf who stated in 1918: 'The Allied victory is the victory of French trucks on the German railway'. It was no longer the victory of a people, a nation, or even of a general, but rather the victory of a vector. The place of war is no longer the frontier that bounds the territory, but that point where the machine of transport moves. And with the beginning of the Second World War, General Guderian, practitioner of the *Blitzkrieg*, concluded: 'where we find the tanks, there is the front'. Thus he fulfils Goebbel's designs, who already in 1929 claimed: 'He who can conquer the road, conquers also the State'. All is front from this point on, since everything is mobilized at all times and in all terrains. Where we find the travelling machine, there is the State, the country has disappeared in the non-place of the State of emergency, territorial space vanishes, only Time remains – but only the time that remains.

Now each vector administers the time of the passenger in expelling him through the unleashing of the beyond, speed is the progress of violence at the same time as its advantage; beyond the territorial body, each speed constitutes a fleeting 'province of time' where the old role of places disappears in the geographic annihilation of distances. The urban motorway is not a pathway of transmission, but the concentration camp of speed; segregation and incarceration stem far more from the violence of displacement than from various police controls – *a highway colony*, similar to the staircase of Mauthausen, that motorists extend by the increased performance of their vehicles, by the tolls or tickets that sanction excessive speeds far more than the excess of speed.

In reality, with the dromocratic revolution of transports, it is the administration of Time that starts to take shape. The interest in dominating time far more than territory already made its appearance in the cult of the train schedule. Frederick of Prussia's desire for conquest became that of every industrial state: *it is no longer invasion that forms the foundation of the law but its speed, pure speed.* The direct line [*droite ligne*] of the pathway of penetration indispensable to its celerity symbolizes the extermination of public rights [*droit public*]; the emergency literally caused the traditional political structures to implode. In contracting distances, it causes the forces of the marching order to intervene in every sector of public life. Under the virtuous pretexts of risks and dangers resulting from the acceleration of relations, the project of a rigorous management of Time, following that of space, tends to become that of a *prevention of the moment....*

In metamorphosing into an 'integral security', defence finally brings about the perfection of the principle of fortification that Vauban announced as follows: 'War must be immediately superimposable on all habitable places in the world'.

Since movement governs the event, it is appropriate to ponder the emergence of logistics as the essential actor in the development of technologies. In fact, and despite the Logistes[86] of a Roman army expert in the organization of marches and retrenchments, it was not until the eighteenth century that the term 'logistics' came into use. In France during this period, it designated the reasoning applied to the problems posed by the movements and provisioning of military forces in the field, movements that thus tend to take on an increasing importance in the conduct of offensive operations which henceforth take precedence over the actual acts of siege.

As Field Marshal Montgomery notes in his history of war: 'When the Generalization of offensive tactics encouraged the leaders to search out the enemy to destroy him, *there was a need for greater mobility and more space,* and this was associated with an enlargement of political economy and the necessities of control over massive armies. Since these armies could no longer live off the land where they were operating, it became essential to assure the security of their line of resupply and inversely to cut the enemy's. *From that point on questions of logistical capacity competed with the political imagination.*' This was the dawn of the war of movement, the preliminary stages of the transportation revolution, but also the premonitory resurgence of the *column*, the *line*, that would result in the abandonment of tight and closed order, a rampart of bodies that repeated the structure of fortified spaces and stone walls. The *square* will only resurface later as a defensive mole, in the defence of the rivers, but it is also assimilated to a *front line* and precedes somewhat the *line of the railway* as a line of operation at the time of the American Civil War. All this served as a prelude to a considerable poliocretic and political event: *the substitution of the breakthrough for the encirclement.*

After the disciplinary formation of troops in a square on the massive front that Vauban had previously reduced from a width of six to three rows by introducing the rifle and bayonet as a replacement for the pike and musket, *linear formations become the rule, the means of maximal exploitation of fire power.* Line of fire, mobile columns, flanked and reconnoitred by a cavalry, regarding which Guibert would say that the most important thing is 'less the depth of its resources than the quantity of speed of which it is capable'. *The stretching out of infantry divisions would continue to increase with the progressively more powerful individual weapons*, to the point of dangerously isolating the individual infantryman. If the Swede Gustave-Adolphe's brigade was, in the seventheeth century, 'a little mobile fortress with curtains and ravelins', in the eighteenth century Frederick II would state that 'a battalion is a moving battery'. As Guibert stated in 1772, it was becoming possible for a leader to divide his principal forces *into separate offensive columns, forming a network of convergent detachments.* An enterprising general, he suggested, could ignore the fortresses with which the century had been obsessed and *march straight to the enemy capital that would constitute the principal objective.*

This vision, which prefigures our modern transportation networks, and in particular the French rail network, is realized during the period thanks to the considerable improvement to the roads by the civil engineering corps, but this new conception of logistical movement still required a development of the administrative organization of the territory during times of peace. This passage without transition of a statistical and punctual character of masses of columns in perpetual and linear motion based on the course of water or the communication route inaugurates, secretly, what will become the revolution of transports, the breakthrough substituted for enclosure, prelude to the fragmentation of corps of troops of which the 'corps-franc' will later be the model. Meanwhile this 'movement' of the army from the seventeenth to nineteenth centuries may be traced clearly in history: first, with this strict geometry of the corps, the line of the file of soldiers only comes to be used with parades and as troops march in approach; next comes the difficulty of organizing a mass mobility in the absence of rapid vectors other than the horse; and, finally, the ambition of inventing a new mode of combat, a dynamic war, that relies upon the natural infrastructures but also on these new frontiers, these last *fronts of movement* that defined the networks of roads and rails after those of streams and rivers.

This *line of assault* would finally acquire, with considerable firepower, a speed of movement equally considerable, realizing the perfection of the binomial fire/movement and thus giving its full significance to the line of the road and of the linearity of the troop, now *an integral projectile*, so much so that in 1878 General Cluseret would describe the German army as 'a formidable projectile hurled forth by a precision weapon: the major state'.

The shortest route had suddenly become the most violent route; in the same way that the dagger had extended to the sword, and as the pike extended into the lance in order to respond to the needs of the cavalry, the lance in turn lost its value with the employment of firearms; the penal colony stretches out and it is finally the entire army projected into an accelerated assault that will later become the *Blitzkrieg*.

Against this moving and mechanized force, the armouring of some fortified posts will still prove to be useful as a break, as regional reinforcement, at the point where the terrain allows a massive penetration; such is the era of *fragmented forts* that repeat the fragmentation of the corps of troops in defined units, up to the zero degree of the commando. A precocious disintegration of a fighting corps organized for the persistence of resistance and that voluntarily dislocates itself in order not to be dislocated involuntarily by the enemy.

The disappearance in disintegration now becomes the last form of protection. In the past it was a question, as in a game of hide and seek, of momentarily concealing oneself in the fortress by locking oneself away behind the shelter of ramparts in order not to be encircled by the assailant; it is necessary today to dissolve in order not to be totally encircled, and definitively this time. The citadel, mausoleum of sedentary peoples, hides a moving nomadic reality in these stones, these ramparts mineralize the value of the celerity of the assault, the thickness of these walls signalling the violence of the shock, just as the route signals the violence of speed. The war of movement will *dissolve* this permanent fortification at the same time that it dissolves the body of the combatant masses. The history of the avant-garde is exemplary, it reveals this progressive dissolution: Scythian horsemen charged forwards pushing before them their herds of horses; and the Mongols opposed a front of prisoners to the first shock of battle. More recently, in the fifteenth century, the Swiss, premier warriors, will set up an obstacle to Charles le Téméraire in casting before their troops, in the battle of Morat, their hoodlums, lost boys of the outlying Helvetian lands, barely armed, without any military command, left to move freely, who would sow confusion in the ranks of the duc de Bourgogne by misleading them regarding the intentions of his enemy, before the mass of peasants armed with long pikes and the cavalry of merchants would intervene.

We know the specific influence of the Swiss infantry on the French army: the lesson had not been forgotten when, at the beginning of the seventeenth century, we find in each company a handful of 'lost children,' the first human projectiles, to whom were conferred the first grenades in order that they might undertake the most perilous solitary *coups de main*, earning them the name, 'grenadiers', which they would receive officially under Louis XIV. At first there was one company of them per regiment, but eventually entire regiments of grenadiers were formed. The same evolution is evident in the cavalry: during the first Italian wars, lightly mounted corps were assembled, destined to defeat the country and capture convoys, they were first called Stradiots, then Argoulet, and finally 'household cavalry'; the carabiniers also had an origin comparable to the grenadiers. In the hierarchy of the movement of war, the last became the first: the first to possess portable explosives, the first to mount the fastest warhorses, the first to fire with carbines rifled for long range.

After having brought about, in the past, the lengthening of side-arms, the solitary horseman is the first to *extend the range with the portable firearm.* Because he was free in his movements, the bad boy of the Helvetian outlands came to take precedence over the disciplined soldiers of the close order. After the corps of the troop is divided into 'groups,' 'detachments', the sole effective means of evasion becoming the density of the invisible projectile of the firearm, against which no shield, no armour, serves as worthwhile protection, it is the column that will be cut up into restricted units next, allowing for the embarkation of soldier-passengers in the first vehicles designed for land battles.

In the binomial fire/movement, firepower merely serves as a deterrent against the interruption of the movement in progress; weapons fire, the explosion of munitions, aims at deterring the enemy from stopping the advance. Fire is used less for the purpose of killing men than for convincing the enemy to allow the movement to continue. In fact, the objective already lacks value, all that matters is the advance, to advance straight on, *the course is no longer the sublimation of the hunt, it has suddenly become the sublimation of war.* As General Fuller wrote: 'Movement is to the organism of combat what range is to the power of the weapon'. What artillery had anticipated with the art of ballistics, war-speed would amplify as the mobile machine gave birth to the works of Huygens, as well as the invention of the military engineer Cugnot: the fardier.

When we signal the military importance of the binomial fire/ movement, we are forgetting nonetheless that since mechanization we now see nothing *but* fire. The automobility of the vehicle is only the consequence of the fire of the steam engine, or the successive explosions of the battery of cylinders of the gas motor. The logistical perpetuation of movement is only therefore the result of the perpetuation of ballistic movement, *mobilization is not war but the progress of its violence in the time of the acceleration of movement.*

When Maurice of Saxony writes, 'I am not for battles and I am persuaded that a clever General can make war all his life without really being committed to it.... *It is necessary to dissolve, in a manner of speaking, the enemy*', he pronounces the significance of movement as conflict in itself, without reference to fire. The activity of displacement is not yet *the speed-activity* of Napoleon, but it pronounces nonetheless the war of movement, well before the revolution of transports that will reproduce, with its rail 'convoys', the marching formations of regiments, of battalions, the long theories of soldiers proceeding on a common voyage, a prefiguration of train cars, this *train* that gets its name from the 'artillery train'. Military convoys anticipate the tapestry of trajectories (Valéry) that the industrial revolution will later cast all over the world.

With the Marshal of Saxony's strategic innovation, conflicts become a series of Brownian movements and of furtive shifts. Mobilization becomes the essence of war, but of a war that is no longer identified with combat. Regarding these detachments that comb the countryside, the Marshal predicted: 'They can traverse an entire kingdom without being observed'. Here it is already a question of an aesthetic of disappearance, of a disappearance in mobility and no longer under shelter, an aesthetic that modern war will perfect without end thanks to the acquisition of greater speeds. With Maurice of Saxony as with Frederick II, the technique of movement is opposed to the tactic of confrontation.

Let us remember: it is invasion that establishes the law that he who passes possesses. Henceforth, he who swoops down [*fond*] the fastest upon his prey most solidly founds [*fonde*] his power. Along with the monetary standard of wealth, we have the military standard of speed: the greater the speed, the greater the control.

In the war of movement, all must be successively trained, straightened, extended, pursued, and then dispelled, the *course-pursuit* as the sublimation of war beyond the hunt is only the perpetuation of the protective extension. First set out in the arms of hand-to-hand combat, the prostheses of the body, and the Mesopotamian or Roman pathways of communication, war extends now to the time of movement thanks to the invention of the motorized machine, to the point where the technological breakthrough will become, by the end of the twentieth century, the sole form of manoeuvre, a tactical 'manoeuvre' without any other field of action than the propaganda of the arms race. Take Napoleon for example: 'The force of an army, like the quantity of movement in mechanics, is estimated by the mass multiplied by the velocity'.

The art of war is already the art of the warring motor. It is a question of unleashing rapid movement and maintaining it in order that it remain constant as long as possible; speed thus becomes an actual dimension of movement. However, between the Napoleonic empire and Caesar's, the difference in speed had barely increased, the horse was always the principal vector, but the desire for acceleration continued to increase; we need only consider the evolution of horsemanship between the eighteenth and nineteenth centuries in order to be convinced. In 1776, for the pioneer of scientific horsemanship, Dupaty de Clam, it was already a question of 'extracting from custom and routine a *truly mathematical art*', it was necessary for man and his mount to become nothing but one harmonic body. In his treatise on the rapport between horsemanship and physics, geometry, mechanics, and anatomy, the master horseman had the research of the physiologist Jules Marey in mind. The animal body of the mount is already nothing more than a passive machine as its progressions come to be controlled mathematically, like an engine in a simulator. Indeed, a bit later, certain methods that allow one to *drive a horse like a boat* will be proposed. It is, meanwhile, in the British Isles that the criterion of speed as the essential criterion of equestrian sport develops with the 'thoroughbred', the Anglo-Arabian horse.

Equestrian studies, considered as an exact science of the movements of the horse, introduce us to the truly mechanical art of the motor. The analytical geometry of the gallop of horses, in Muybridge's studies, for example, renews the all-too-elementary geometrical attraction of the body fighting on foot. *Now the object counts less than its path, than its trajectory*; with these cinematic studies, it would be necessary to give chase and pursue these unknown movements that propagate themselves in the object in movement. Thanks to Marey's *chronophotographic gun*, the running of horses, the flight of birds, and the gait of man will be reconstructed in the sequential magic of the hidden gestures of movement. The last hunt will consist of a 'safari-photo', making it possible to see not so much the animal as the invisible succession of the instants of movement: the line of flight, the stroboscopic structure of the moving body.

In geostrategy, apart from differences in the environmental conditions, *offensive forces are always employed in the same sense* (Mackinder). Also we would need to investigate not simply 'the logic of sense',[39] but the logistics of the sense of movements of displacement that affect the economic and political life of states, in attempting to comprehend the correspondences and the correlations that exist between their transmission/transport vectorial politics and statistics.

Since, *for every man of war, memory is science itself* (Napoleon III), let us recall the circumstances that allowed Vauban in 1684 with his counting formulas to invent statistics, the basis of our political economy.

During the many expeditions that led him away from the court, that is, from the centre to the frontiers of the kingdom, expeditions to inspect the marching formations as well as the construction of the 'great immobile machines' that constituted the fortifications, Vauban observed, with an inventory of the regional resources, the evolution of morals and customs and he derived laws from them. It is thus from the *state of the places* passed through, both on going and returning, that later he would derive, along with the geographical descriptions of these regions, *inductive statistics*. And yet, let us not forget, these constantly repeated movements – movements that could be said to be industrially reproduced, and this in a manner quite exceptional for the period – are all situated on the lines of geostrategic force at the far west of Europe, *in the same way that the famous advanced deployment forces exert themselves*. Up until this period in history, apart from certain great religious routes, *long distance movements could not be reduced to the repetition of the same deployment, to the same logistical sense*.

The old courier transports still represented only tactics of exchange fluctuating along with concurrence or of conflicts, and, with the exception of the couriers of the 'chevaucheurs royaux',[40] whose fixed timetables were established in 1626, these old passages were still rather episodic, and strategic tendencies were rarely evident. Curiously, the periodic expeditions of a marshal would anticipate by two hundred years those of the railway routes; for the itinerant inspector of the frontiers of the kingdom, each fortified site functioned rather as a turntable, orienting his trip, and thus prefiguring the central railway stations, those other great immobile machines, with their roundhouses of locomotives arranged like so many redoubts on the railways, *in the same logistical sense, on the same axes as those deployment forces* followed in the seventeenth century by the strategic statistician. For each of these trips, Marshal Vauban, 'commissar general of fortifications', became a

sort of 'commissar of watches'[41]; the kingdom marching under his eyes
in a grand review of details where the territory is exposed to inspection.
It is no longer the marching of troops in the training camp entrenched
before the reviewing officer logistically responsible for the proper order
of the army, it is the general review of the country, *the recruiting board
of the geographic body.*

It is no longer the body of the army that passes back and forth
in tight ranks beneath the regard of the intendant,[42] now it is the
inspector general that files past in review of the provinces, aligned as in
a parade. Yet the repetition of these reviews that triggers *the unfolding
of the regional film is only an artifice, only a cinematic special effect* which
benefits the itinerant observer. Perceiving the sequence of geographic
locations in this isolated fashion, the general loses sight of the local
realities and immediately demands the reform of the *common law* in
order to advance the *administrative standard.*

With Vauban, the old process of disciplinary unification manoeuvres
of the corps of troops extends to the entire social body [*corps*], since it
is a question this time of rendering homogenous and uniform not only
weights and measures but also the time and space of a territory which is
in this way symbolically identified with the glorious body [*corps*] of the
king. An entirely military way to inaugurate the French Revolution: for
Vauban, this 'regulation of essences' is nothing other than good *logistical justice*, such as was needed to bring about tax reform, whence his
project of the 'royal tithe' (1707) and the conflict with Louis XIV, who
did not understand that a soldier would only conform symbolically,
since he the king is the state. Contrary to the polemarch, the absolute
monarch has no interest in seeing *war seize all the habitable areas of the
world for the sake of his legacy*, thus relinquishing control to a chief of
staff. Lazare Carnot was not yet born; and as for the Empire, that is for
later. . . .

With the Sun King, Versailles became the home of the monarchy;
the old mobility of sovereigns and of their *retinue* (*curia*) was abruptly
brought to a halt. Hence the immobilization in the station of Versailles
of the old train of the court of nobility. Henceforth, the king of France
will only move under the constraint of revolutions; first with the flight
of Louis XIV, then with Louis XVIII's departure for Gand, and finally,
with the departure of all the monarchs from Charles X to Louis-Philippe

without exception. The immobilization of the monarchy was a prelude to the mobilization of the masses with the 'raising of the masses' in 1793 which prefaced the future revolution of mass transportation. This universal regulation of space and time sought by Vauban was made possible only by the rise of the steam engine. Favouring the extreme regularity of routes, rail transport would popularize this cinematic repetition of movement where, in anticipating the Lumière brothers, one region after another would file past before the passengers' eyes. Episodic trips would thus become normative tendencies that the traffic graphs would reconstruct for travellers in the listings of departures and arrivals. In anticipation of the State of emergency, the Nation-State appeared in the nineteenth century as the State of destinations.

If, previously, the ballistic plans of the military engineer would tend to reduce operations of siege into a geometric procedure of calculating the trajectories of the 'plane of fire', henceforth the entire nation becomes a strategic machine where railway stations, that is, the junctions, assure the regulation of the routes [*trajets*]. With the effects of these logistics applied to the entirety of economic and social movements, the travelling machine [*machine de voyage*] ultimately inherits the whole world from the engine of war [*machine de guerre*]. And with this comes the end of the old integrity of containment, the rejection of natural viscosity to make way for the uniform flow of states of flux.

In the great design of increasing the conductibility of forces, the map of the territory is progressively replaced by that of railway innervations; the *line* and the *front* come to be pre-eminent over the punctuality of places, the geometric reign of design, but above all the forced drive of the movement of people and goods.

If the strategic course of a geometrical soldier contributed, in the seventeenth century, to the invention of the statistical discourse of the eighteenth, it is the tactical course of a theologian-mathematician to which we owe the origin of the theory of networks. The poliorcretic schema is, however, the same, since it is a question now of resolving the enigma of the seven bridges of the old city of Königsberg. *Presenting problems of encirclement and penetration,* these seven bridges could not be crossed one after the other, in the course of a single movement, without the pedestrian being required to cross the river that encircles the centre of the city again by one of the bridges already used to enter.

Leonhard Euler understood that a mathematical principle was in play and demonstrated that it is geometrically impossible not to retrace these steps since, in such a network, the access points converge in three points, or, that is, in an odd number.

With this route it is not the centre (the city centre) that is important, but rather the site of convergence, the point of reversal of the movement of displacement. It is the non-Euclidean origin of a geometry where orientation takes precedence over control, where the controlling axis accords more importance to the pole of reversal, to the nodes, to the shunt and the interchange.

Meanwhile we note, curiously, that at the same time military manoeuvres [*manoeuvres militaries*] prefigure railway switchings [*manoeuvres ferroviaires*]: it is a question here of a series of complex movements consisting in bending [*ployer*] and deploying parallel lines and columns in order to pass successively from one order to another: *the reversed front battle of Guibert, the oblique order of Frederick, these movements prefigure those of railway lines, since the rows of troops are already arrayed like trains in the shunts*

All the military literature of the seventeenth and eighteenth centuries is filled with the description of these translations of detachments that trace out the splitting up of the train. As Jomini explains: ' *The French Revolution brought about the system of divisions* that disrupt the great monotony of the old formation and *created parts capable of moving on their own account over all sorts of terrains*'.[43]

'March separately, fight united', an old maxim that the railway organization will take up, since *the control of the railway will be directly translated onto the control of the military.* The cult of exact timetables will amount to a strategy of the tension made necessary by the demands of managing the safe running of the trains; thus it will be decided to apply the optical telegraph to railway signals with *semaphore.* Later this will lead to the bloc-system: 'In this, the line was divided into sections each several kilometres long and the access to each section was controlled by a semaphore. *This device only allowed entry if the section was entirely free*; the electric telegraph was absolutely indispensable for this in allowing various sections to be in communication with one another'.[44] Such extreme precautions resulted from the risks of collisions and derailments of trains on the single track of that era: 'As soon as shunts and signals were put into service, the agents in charge of switching [*manoeuvres*] had to be careful not to allow them to go in the wrong direction; with a switch closed but the signal indicating "open track" – catastrophe!' This innovation of the rail catastrophe, contemporary with the advent of the railway, *demanded that the authorization to take certain routes is only possible on the condition that others be prohibited.* All this led to the need for a series of control mechanisms, guarantees of greater transportation safety; after the processes put into effect by the English Saxby and Farmer to assure the perfect synchronization of the speed of the traffic, it was in 1898, height of spatio-temporal control, that a Frenchman, Albert Moutier, succeeded in making it possible to direct an entire itinerary with one single switch. One man alone, one flick of the wrist, in one sole moment – this was the beginning of the ministry of Time.

In 1800, the Emperor Napoleon I created the 'artillery train' [*train d'artillerie*], in 1806 'the train of engineers' [*train du génie*], ... and in 1807, the 'resupply train' [*train des équipages*] that would later become the 'armed train' [*arme du train*] destined to act *with the full array of forces.* Initially charged with the transport of supplies, then with the transport of troops, this 'weapon' will finally be engaged in combat, in reinforcing the units on the line, prefiguring the mechanized brigades of the future. Beginning with the Empire, we observe for the first time in fortifications the phenomenon previously seen in infantry formations: the geometry of the fortified places tends to disintegrate to the rhythm of the improvement of munitions. As Lazard will say in his thesis, *every increase in the power of the artillery leads to a corresponding decline in fortification.* After the age of bastioned systems, these 'great immobile machines of various designs', comes the age of 'fragmented forts' spread all along the length of the imaginary border line. The goal of fortification *is no longer to stop armies but rather to control, indeed to facilitate, their movements* (Colonel Delair). It is exactly the role that will be assigned to the controlling railway stations during the First World War. Thus we understand better the apparently paradoxical choice of Von Moltke as he declares: 'I prefer the construction of railroads to fortifications'. The train and its locomotive are in the end the effect of a very long logistical tradition that goes back to the first strategic routes of the war chariot.

In the twentieth century, in order to respond to the administrative necessities of a good praxis of vectorial politics, the major states would assume an increased significance; their organization had, on the one hand, to take account of the increase in the space where they undertook their operations because of the numbers in play and the *strategic dispersal allowed by the railways*, but they also had to account for *the tactical dispersal made necessary for battle by the use of guns with rifled barrels and soon thereafter the machine gun*. From that point on, logistics was divided in two components: the first concerned with routes [*trajets*], the second with trajectories [*trajectoires*]. General logistics encompasses not only the circulation of means and of masses, but also the circulation of munitions and projectiles, as deputy Abel Ferry wrote: 'The transport problem is parallel to the munitions problem'. Greater logistics tends thus to compete directly with strategy in becoming a sort of greater ballistics, managing all movements. Paraphrasing the inventor-precursor of the steam engine, Salomon de Caus, we can affirm that *logistics came to be the Reason of moving forces*, realizing the dream of Vauban to render war immediately superimposable over all habitable areas of the world. Between 1820 and 1830 the first regular railway lines were inaugurated. In 1848, in his *Principles of Political Economy*, John Stuart Mill declares: 'To produce is to move', without yet having any idea that transports would soon come to command production to the point of inverting his assertion. In 1861, it was the US Civil War and the first strategic use of the 'iron horse' by the Union General McClellan. In 1865, England acquired the first 'corps of engineers and railways of a major state', in 1866, von Moltke created the first 'office of communications lines'. In 1875, in France this time, we have the beginnings of the administrative organization of the military railways. At the end of the century, the chief of staff of the army will take up the direction of the military service of railways under the control of the ministry of war.

As 'the art of moving armies', logistics would therefore seem, Werner Sombart noted in 1913, to arise with industrial concentration and specialization. It is the economy of destruction, along with mass production, that demands the calibration of firearms (cannon, musket) and the standardization of the bore of pipes. Then it demands the standardization of munitions and, therefore, indirectly, ballistic performance and range along with the cylinders of machine motors. However we look at it, the reference to war as the origin of the rise of technology is clear: in 1673 it is the gun, internal combustion engine of one cylinder, that will serve as the model for Christiaan Huyghens' gunpowder engine. The definition of what will later become the internal combustion engine is significant: 'In my engine', writes Huyghens, 'the violent effect of the powder is reduced to a movement that can be controlled'.

Thus, the control and safety of the motile machine is not overpowered by its movement, that is, by the direction of its movement. Less than a century later, in 1769, military engineer Cugnot's wagon will be nothing more than an artillery dolly designed for his backer, General Gribeauval, first inspector of the royal artillery. In fact, the more that mobility increases and is extended to greater and greater spaces, the more the requirements of control intensify: to the control of the ballistics of projectiles it is necessary to add that of vehicles – logistics – and thereby increase continuously the conductibility of territories. In conclusion, since it is *time that separates weight from force* (Napoleon), movement can be summarized in one single proposition: 'Force and the change of speed are vectors that have the same direction' (Einstein).

After the gun, it is the rifle that will inspire, a century later in 1773, the coppersmith Olivier Evans. 'He witnesses a village festival, where a game catches his interest: it consists of putting water in the barrel of a rifle, stopping it up with a plug and heating it up to the point where the plug pops out.'[45] From this came the use of high pressure which Watt feared because of the risk of explosion. Evans denounced this fear and introduced boilers where the steam pressure would rise to eight or ten atmospheres.

With the steam engine, therefore, we are in the presence of a weapon of movement that extends that of the engine of war. All through the evolution of technology, we find this archetype, the 'fire tube' *capable of managing both the power of the energy (powder, steam, petrol) and the movement of the vector (projectile, vehicle ...).*

In Stephenson's machine of 1814, the boiler is traversed by a *single fire tube*. In 1828 Seguin invented the tubular boiler containing up to 40 tubes permitting an exposure to the fire of an increased surface of water, and thus increased energy. In 1867, Belpaire increased the power again by introducing up to 100 tubes in the cylindrical body.

Curiously, this multitube system had already existed since the seventeeth century in the arsenal of weapons by virtue of the old military desire to continuously increase the rate of fire. In 1832 Samuel Colt patented the first revolver and put it into production in 1851 in London. We may note in passing that this weapon served as a model for Janssen's 'photographic revolver' (1874), and then for Marey's 'chronophotographic gun', forerunner of the Lumière brothers' camera. Also in 1851 a Belgian captain invented a 'battery of guns' comprising twenty five gun barrels combined in a turning cylinder, mounted on a two-wheeled mount. In 1861 the American Gatling, *inventor of a steam plough*, brought forth a machine gun capable of firing six to twelve hundred rounds a minute. In 1893, by electrifying his system, it attained a rate of fire of three thousand rounds. This saturation weapon would give rise to General Electric's gun driven by a 28-volt motor, *incorporating an electronically controlled firing cadence*. But let us turn back to the travelling weapons and, more precisely, to the Stephenson brothers, creators in 1829 of a locomotive with a predestined name, the Rocket.

In 1850 Robert Stephenson constructed the first metal bridge, the Britannia Tubular Bridge, *an enormous iron tube more than 400 metres long*. This cellular structure, *designed to resist weight and vibrations caused by the passing of trains*, behaves like an artillery tube on the mount of its pillars; steam locomotion demands in its turn the calibration of the bridge, the new light in this tunnel transformed the soul of the gun.

After penetration was substituted by encirclement, it seems that all of a sudden emptying out and piercing become a necessity of the speed of transport. The levelling off programmed by the railway was not enough, it was necessary to penetrate under the ground, *as if speed demanded not only the absence of obstacles but also the absence of matter*.

A prefiguration of the conquest of the atmosphere and space, where acceleration itself will become the path; the tunnelling [*percement*] of subterranean networks will be the unperceived logistical consequence of the progress of the violence of speed. This power of transpiercing (geologically and geographically) will prove to be analogous to that of the projectile that is just as much concerned with the increase in the rate of ejection as the capacities of perforation. *Absolute speed necessitates the absolute void*, the increase in the performance of the engine goes along with the expansion of the desert. *After having contributed to straightening, then to scraping bare the surface of the route (roads, railways), the locomotive vehicle still demanded an airtight course, the production of a perfect void.*

Around 1860 in Saint-Germain Eugene Flachat produced his project of a *pneumatic train* where 'the train was interdependent with a piston that moved in an *airtight tube*. When the machinery created the void in this tube, the piston advanced and propelled the train in motion'.[46]

This system, comparable to pneumatic message tubes, anticipates an electromagnetic system: in 1941, the Germans, experts in ballistics, attempted to produce an electromagnetic rapid-fire gun: 'The engine appeared in the form of a long tube of seventy metres, equipped with numerous electromagnetic coils. When current was passed through the first coil, it would automatically be transmitted to the following coil, and then the shell, that had acquired a certain acceleration by the initial attraction, would be attracted a second time, thus receiving a new impulse adding to the first. By this means, from electro-magnet to electro-magnet, *the speed of the projectile increases continuously attaining up to one thousand eight hundred metres per second* by the time it leaves the mouth of the barrel. The whorls of the electro-magnets, heavily overloaded, were crossed by thin aeration channels and equipped with cooling blades. When the shell proceeds through the tube, it expels in front of it the contents of air which check the propulsion; to overcome this drawback, certain orifices between the coils were designed through the path of the barrel.'[47]

This utopian logistics, worthy of Jules Verne, has just been revived by Robert Salter, an engineer with the Rand Corporation, in the Planetran project. In this *linear motor train*, it is no longer a question of casting projectiles down upon the enemy, but rather of passengers chained to their seats in a shell-like cabin, the station of departure strangely resembling the breech of a gun without recoil.

Capable of linking up the east and west coasts of the United States in 35 minutes, *this metro, attaining Mach 20 (22,500 km/h), must move in a tube ruled by a near perfect void*: 'Propelled by a magnetic field, the engine moves above a stator. The magnetic field engendered by the coils of the stator (a kind of a rail file running the full length of the tunnel) moves with great speed over the several thousand kilometres of the course. This field maintains both the levitation and propulsion of the vehicle: in effect, a very powerful electromagnet with a coil refrigerated with a cryogenic device maintains the lift; at the same time, the field produced by the alternating current sent through the stator triggers the advance of the vehicle' (A. Dorozynski).

When we consider the impact of the deregulation of tariffs on domestic flights in the United States, on mass land transit, and, in particular, the two thirds reduction of Amtrak in 1980, we understand better the relevance of this *first project of supersonic land transport, ten times more powerful than air transports,* since Concorde only travels at Mach 2 and the hypersonic project of the hydrogen plane, currently under study at Lockheed, would only barely attain Mach 5, some 6,400 km/h.

At the end of the nineteenth century, Cecil Rhodes declared: 'The train is an instrument of pacification that costs less than the gun and reaches further'. *In this supersonic conquest of the West, what remains to be pacified?*

If the deurbanization resulting from the invasion of the European region by the 'barbarians' of the first centuries corresponded to a first dissemination, *the dispersal in the extension of the geopolitical field,* the deurbanization that is currently resulting from the invasion of time amounts to *a dissipation in the restriction of the chronopolitical field* due to the speed of various means of displacement. In this sense, it can be affirmed that if political importance was once identified *indirectly* with the populating of space (regional, national), it is henceforth recognizable by a depopulating (territorial, spatial) that results to a very high degree from the mobility of people, messages, and goods, that is to say, *indirectly* from the paradoxical populating of the time of displacements. In fact, the *deportation density* has supplanted politically the *population density* from the era of geographic populating; the disintegration of alternating migrations renewed the social integration of migrants in metropolitan areas, but this deportation in the non-place of the speed of displacements is not comparable to that of the past. Total mobilization (travel, leisure) does not so much aim *at transporting* populations

from here to there, as was the case during the epoch of local mobiliza-
tions, in the levy en masse of the eighteenth century or in the attraction
of people to the city from the country of the nineteenth century, but
at the shifting them out of *phase* [*déphaser*] to an accelerated rhythm.
This social deregulation and carefully maintained desynchronization
between the space and time of human activities came to be key
to a vectorial power that is nothing more than the perfecting of the
dictatorship of movement.

   This observation clarifies for us the contemporary urban crisis: this
is not foreign to the political crisis, the Polis is no longer the political
site *par excellence*; the delocalization of the means of communication
initiates a poorly understood phenomenon of deurbanization, since it
does not yet strike visibly at the site of the metropolitan concentration.
The social and political problem of populations is translated from the
place to the non-place of exchanges and of quasi-instantaneous migrations; *the state of emergency becomes the new city of a sort of populating of*
time, in that 'place' where the state of siege once determined the populating
of space.

   The management of time thus necessarily succeeds that of territory,
but it is a question of the time of a total mobilization, that is, that of
an absolute social deregulation.

   A pseudo-territory, the late city functions like a residue or, rather,
like the essential fallout of the transportation revolution (that is, the
revolution of the war machine in its capacity of speed machine); as a
communication infrastructure, the habitat henceforth persists merely
to form the 'outskirts' [*banlieue*] of an accelerated errantry; now a
mere reminiscence, or semblance, geographic place is no longer the
foundation of human experience but rather a pole to be reached in
the round-trip exercise. For some time now, these poles of attraction
and repulsion have constituted the quartiers of a late cadastre, but it
is necessary to thoroughly understand that this limited relativity of the
late city is itself menaced by the vehicular incontinence.

   This extreme congruence puts us to the test, it is not solely, as we
might claim, a temporary event [*événement*], but a cultural and political
advent [*avènement*] that poses to us, outside the ecological question
of limits, the no less important dromological question of residual
proximities.

The past and the future of the economy of the management of time replaces what is proximally in front and behind in the management of space; with the advent of this instantaneity, power moves toward a hypothetical centre of time, an axis of convergence of an absolute mobilization where the intensive succeeds the extensive and where the *maximum State, the providence State,* gives way suddenly to the *minimum State, the destiny State,* the upcoming destination of a political class where opposition and majority will come to be confused, enslaved to a *stereopolitical effect* of vectorial power, in a 'temporal compromise' that succeeds history.

Second Part

The Aesthetics of Disappearance

> The greatest glory of a State
> is to make of its frontiers a vast desert.
> Julius Caesar

To hide, to disguise the entirety of the fighting corps in order to obtain the secrecy necessary for surprise, 'to disguise' [*maquiller*] and 'go underground' [*prendre le maquis*] as with the French Resistance,[1] these words have one meaning. In altering nature or reverting to the shelter of the underbrush, the objective is to evade the obscenity of the enemy's gaze, of disappearing in a single movement of withdrawal [*retrait*] and retreat [*retraite*]. For those who pursue, it is necessary to overcome the interval, fill in the gap; for those who are fleeing, their weapon is less a means of destruction than a means of distancing, they occupy only what separates them and depend solely upon the maintenance of the distance that underlines again the isolation of their march.

The protection of the 'disguised' member of the Resistance [*maquisard*] depends upon topographic continuity, upon uninterrupted nature. It is necessary to evade anything that signals habitation – roads, buildings – in order to tuck oneself into the folds of the terrain. He 'occupies' the underbrush and trees, atmospheric disturbances, night. Just as he outmanoeuvres space through the care he takes in avoiding all contact, so also does he outmanoeuvre time through the speed of his movements. With his war paint, he even outmanoeuvres form, concealing his body in a series of occultations of the object [*objet*], subject [*sujet*], and trajectory [*trajet*].

Logistical necessities, tactical constraints, strategic preoccupations, it is combat that first sketches out and develops the game, while the enterprise of destruction begins with the production of disappearance.

Secrecy and speed are at the heart of the 'instrument of great funerals' (Charles Peguy). It is the objective of strategy to make life here on earth the invisible domain of the spirit; all that escapes the perception of the opponent passes into the reserve, what goes unrecognized becomes the arsenal of the warrior. The art of war pertains to an aesthetic of disappearance that is probably the whole issue. Since 'for the warrior, memory is science itself' (Napoleon III), the most far-reaching memory is needed, from the history of battle to the history of reason, the military apparatus mobilizes secrecy before nationalizing it. Let us not forget, the engine of war is first and foremost an 'engine of surveillance' and then an engine of assault. The armed authority is before all else the militarization of the hidden, the conscription of the unknown, the unknown whose tomb would become a national idol of France.

The invisible is commandeered in the service of the State, all that evades the enemy's intelligence, or simply what no longer appears, constitutes a weapon, in the maritime sense of preparations for war. In the dialectic of the weapon and armour, he who reveals himself demobilizes himself, the visible is already lost since it evades the foresight that is the rule of the game of war, this *Kriegspiel* that we meet in society games, from chess to playing cards where the figures originally symbolized military values: soldiers, horsemen, jacks, lieutenants ... later, the soldiers disappeared, replaced by point cards and the ace replaced the lieutenant of companies, as for the kings, the French Revolution overturned them to the advantage of the engineers of war, of peace.... The game is only a civilized duel for the cabaret, a battle of the salon that prepares for the *guerre en dentelles*. Combat is a game before being a spectacle for the court that follows in the train of the monarch; the field of stratagems of bastioned systems is a curiosity, and there is a new dedication to castrametration. The churchmen value these pastimes highly, and the dangerous liaisons of the Cholderlos de Laclos are incomprehensible without this reference to the attraction of strategic subterfuges. Fatal man is the model of woman, the guise [*maquillage*] of the preliminary rites to the kill precedes that of lovers. The seduction of the warrior in disguise [*travesti*] is, as for every animal species, the characteristic of the male. The homosexuality of the duel is at the origin of the beautiful, this conception of the beautiful that is merely the first degree of a torture inflicted upon the body, by features, scarifications, marks that anticipate mutilations and death. The beautiful is perhaps the first *uniform*....

The question of the equipment of the fighting body intrigues me, and here, the link between two museums suggests itself: the *Imperial War Museum in London* and the *musée de l'Armée* at les Invalides.

In the first are to be found for the most part vehicles and representations of different theatres of operation from the last century up to the Hiroshima explosion; in the second, work clothes, uniforms and flags, weapons and armour.

In London: the place or rather the non-place of the war, in particular of the Second World War, with extensive halls treating the Allies' air offensive against Germany; in Paris: a catalogue of weapons and cycles dating from the Middle Ages to the Forties with armourer's masterpieces sparkling in their displays.... In the British capital we get the impression of being in a garage; in Paris, of being in a wardrobe, the cloakroom of troops with gala costumes from the Empire and the metallic phantoms of armour, down to the drabbest and dirtiest clothing from the last world wars. In the middle of the trophies and banners – a bit like a store for theatre accessories with its panniers and rigging lofts – the museum at les Invalides presents the faded old tatters of past and bygone combatants. The army presents itself to us in the French capital like a department store with its summer fashions, its winter collections, and its springtime sales, while in Great Britain we picture instead a travel agency. From the phantoms of bygone combatants that haunt the lofty galleries of les Invalides we pass on to the maps, snapshots, and figures of a past empire as presented in the Bethlehem Hospital that shelters the London museum. This phantasmic character goes beyond mere nostalgia, or some mere reminiscence of a lost grandeur or even bygone aggression, instead it refers to a constant in war that is not solely associated with the art of destruction, but rather involves a practice of disappearance.... But let us turn back to the metamorphoses of warrior's equipment, metamorphoses Kafkaesque in more than a couple of ways. During the classical era, the nobility was scandalized by a certain *uniform*, an ornate costume that distinguished the officer from his troops. With feathers and a fancy hat, military stripes and ribbons, the goal was to demonstrate the wealth of the one who possessed a regiment. The adoption of standard uniforms is at once a means of integrating the corps, an incorporation like a valet's livery, and, as well, the mise en scène for the great tableau of battle. ... Rebellious peasants do likewise as they don their distinctive shirts, the camisards,[2] or their party costumes like the Protestants that gained their nickname of '*parpaillots*'[3] because they were as multi-coloured as butterflies [*papillons*]. The showy colours, reds, golds, also serve to conceal from sight the appearance of blood like the bullfighter's outfit, the fighting body, just like the square of the corps of troops, stands out as a target for the enemy. The relative lack of mobility of the infantry goes along with the geometric rigour of the military game. No one shies away, each maintains the alignment, each remains standing, they revert to the ancient legion – however, without the shield – signifying the great historical movement that leads first from the screen of the shields, from the helmet to the shield and the overall protection of the body by armour, then, with the appearance of the use of muskets, the gradual abandonment of protection in order finally to take up again certain individual forms such as the breastplate of the cuirassier, the helmet, and today, the bullet-proof vest....

This evolution of the soldier's equipment is clearly linked with that of the means of destruction, with the emergence of armaments and with the style of manoeuvres, but also with a certain politics of the fighting body. The term *army corps* has a far more precise sense than is commonly recognized. From the eighteenth to the twentieth century, in the English army, one retained one's place sometimes from birth, and connections were solicited in order to gain access to this or that regiment. The warrior elite is not constituted solely of troops more or less effective in combat, it also stemmed from the greater or lesser notoriety of families, from royal privileges and from the powers accorded to this or that service, from the lavishness and beauty of the uniforms of regiments.... We find all this again today in recruitment propaganda – uniforms pleasing to women, apprenticeship in certain technologies, piloting of various weapons of war ... all this already existed under the ancien régime in the recruitment propaganda of the time. The uniform is, therefore, from the moment of its appearance, at once the 'livery' of the master, a sign of membership of a group or caste, the social mise en scène of a pomp held over in the most cruel

conflict to come out of the salon; the '*guerre en dentelles*' designates a
period where the distinction between peace and war is not significant,
it is a question still of the elite.

However, the uniformity of the pomp had immediately been lost
in an attempt at the domestication of the nobility (in particular in
the provinces), and the nobility, despite the brilliant ornamentation
of their costumes, guessed that behind their uniform was hidden, for
them, some new losses, some disappearances important in other ways.
What the establishing of specific military units seemed to justify in this
era comes later to legitimize the end of the aristocratic privileges first
in the army, and then on the international scene. All this will continue
with the various movements up until the great industrial war that will
overturn, thanks to the dialectic of weapon and armour, the equipping
and arming of the fighting corps.

After the massacres of the first months of the war of 1914–18, where
the French were beaten both by the new firing capacities of the German
machine gun and by the *madder-red colour* of their own uniforms, 'the
military authorities came to agree on the obvious interest in renouncing
the showy colours of their uniforms and in adopting clothing of a
neutral shade to decrease the visibility of troops in the field. Numerous
experiments were attempted, but even if the red trousers and kepi were
to be condemned, opinions regarding the appropriate colour differed:
the Russians, grey; the Italians, their green grigio, and the Germans,
Feldgrau.

'*It was difficult to find an invisible colour distinct enough from the others*
so that there would be no confusion. However, on the eve of the Great
War they were just on the point of agreement. An ingenious manufac-
turer had found the means of reconciling the opposed opinions,
imagining a 'tri-coloured woolen cloth' woven of blue, white, and red.
The white threads and the red threads were in a minimal proportion
such that the overall shade gave the impression of a clear blue scattered
with points of red, such was the origin of the sky blue cloth that
differed from the tri-coloured cloth only by the decrease in the number
of red threads as a means to simplify and increase production.' This
extract from the 1916 Hachette almanac is extraordinarily useful in the
analysis of recent metamorphoses of the soldier: *from uniformity, we
pass to invisibility*; the ravages caused by the new weapons necessitate

the disappearance from view of the fighting corps, its concealment in the environment. To merge [*se confondre*] before being dissolved [*se fondre*], such is now the objective, and from this come various neutral, dull colours, the palette of more or less ochre greys. This is true even of the officers who end up having lost their distinctive markings, their stripes, left only with a number, that of their regiment. Those who were suicidal enough to risk wearing plumes and white gloves were in contravention of the rules even if they rarely risked being punished…

One question remained: *it was difficult to find an invisible colour that was nonetheless distinct enough to distinguish one force from another.* It was necessary to conceal one's troops from incoming strikes, from the impact of projectiles, but also to retain a minimum of 'national identification' so that on the field of battle, one could distinguish between allies and enemies. The battle clothing consists essentially of the warrior's overalls. It allowed him to crawl through the mud of the trenches, the great 'public works' undertaken then in the northeast of France.

Just as the worker is undifferentiated in his 'blue-collar suit', in his blue overalls, so also is the soldier in his 'sky blue', while his leave uniform is a bit like 'Sunday best' of the soldier on furlough…. This difference between national colours, between the French and their partners, will not survive the First World War. The process of stand-ardization will demand an even more total disappearance. After the classic uniform destined to magnify the combatant, and render the hero as visible as possible on the stage of the theatre of operation, we witness the uniformity of the total concealment of the corps where each nation will define its type of disappearance, its *invisible colour.* Some in a return to the earth, from yellow ochre to verdigris, others in the blue tint of distant views, *the blue line of Vosges,* as if the country of Bleriot and Vedrine wished to identify itself by an aerial colour. The troop is no longer the 'theatre troupe' of the great century, there are no longer leading roles, even if certain officers still wear their *formal uniform* at the time of the assault which will see them effectively and definitively exit off stage … now there are only extras, masses of extras assembled to make up the numbers! After the all too brilliant madder-red, one might have rather chosen the somewhat faded rose of skin tone, the rose of women's lingerie, *the rose of canon fodder.* As for those who chose khaki, the colour that is much more than a colour, their preoccupation was less that of identification than disintegration, since the word comes from the Hindustani *khaki*, the colour of dust. *The fighting body is no longer truly integral, truly one*, it is instead a number in the roll that one lifts from a cadaver. In these battles in the open field, not only intelligence and shrewdness become useless before the saturation of the mitraille, a storm of steel from the cannonade, but the body of a man no longer amounts to anything. Many fighters admit to never having seen those they fight at a distance, fear arising most often from the invisible presence of the enemy.

There are some very important episodes in the stories of this buried war. At the Battle of Somme, for example, the impossibility of making sandbags led to corpses being piled up to form ramparts, or also, in certain trenches, in soil dug and redug where there were numerous cadavers, one would hang up an accordion or mess kit on some member that had re-emerged....

The modern warrior is not only desocialized through the atrocity of the assault, he is also deanimalized; he, who once identified himself with the lion, or the eagle, or with the wryneck of the heraldic bestiary, is totally lost, he has become a *phantom*. The combatant deprived of recognition by his body is already nothing more than a shroud before the ossuary (the ossuary of Douaumont that was fated to take up the form of fusiform projectile responsible for their disappearance).

The phenomena will continue through the end of the Great War, we will see again the *trompe l'oeil*, the false appearances, camouflage, on the flanks of the first assault tanks, the 'terrestrial battleships' [*«cuirassés de terre»*] as they were called then.

Through the course of the Second World War, twenty years later, the camouflaged uniform, dappled with neutral tones, would first be developed among the parachutists. We will also see Finnish and Russian winter troops donning white uniforms, but alongside the khaki previously ubiquitous among all armies, the *leopard* pattern led us into a world of contrivance where it was now a question of complete confusion, sometimes even to the point of trying to pass for the enemy. *From 'national' uniformity to invisibility, we pass to fusion and confusion.* Soldiers disguised in vegetation exemplify this movement not only where the animal body has disappeared but also where the combatant adopts the most diverse elements from the ambient milieu, branches and seasonal vegetation, the whiteness of snow.... But we also witness various military elements: the troop disguised with the uniform of the enemy at times assumes the role of espionage, the Brandenburg battalion, like a real chameleon, gradually came to look just like their enemies....

One no longer knows who is who, or rather, by a transformation of sight, one can become whoever, wherever. Ultimately, and this is what is being prepared, one could totally do away with the combat uniform – too suggestive – and replace it by a sort of civil suit, doing what the police had done elsewhere a long time previously. *We have come full circle, the dematerialization of the fighting corps is as advanced as its deterritorialization;* every soldier is an 'unknown soldier', the warrior has become a phantom, but a phantom of transformations, nothing more than a servant: serving as a police presence, the replacement for striking workers (dustmen, postal workers, air traffic controllers ...) where the military and civil proletarizations merge spectrally. In sum, first the *mise en scène* and emphasis on the colours of the theatre of the war of the *ancien régime*, then brutally concealed as the soldier merges with the milieu in industrial war, the fighting body has completely disappeared under the disguise that dissolves its formal reality in a false appearance that already suggests the disappearance of the distinction between 'civil' and 'military', a most disastrous political confusion.... Let me add as well that this deanimalization of the body of the soldier is closely linked to the mechanization of the army. If the fighting body disappears in the khaki uniform of the infantry, in the shroud of the alpine chasseur, or in the leopard outfit of the paratrooper, it disappears also in combat vehicles, the deanimalization and deterritorialization of the warrior glory here in the 'wrapping': the body in the shroud and the pilot in the cockpit of his Mirage III or his Phantom ... the latest combat outfit tends to be nothing other than a technological prosthesis that represents an updating of the armour of the chevalier, *the most evident sign of the resuscitated fighting body, it is the vehicle or more precisely its speed,* he wears it a bit like the passenger in the 'time machine', the modern combatant dons only his speed, he passes by just as he passes away. The modern war is no longer the art of the fighting body, it has suddenly become the art of the fighting motor.

The invisibility of speed has replaced that once provided by the mask, the shield, or the wall.

The new military order is a speed order, a *dromocracy*. Much more than the equipment of the corps, it is the armament that specifies and establishes the hierarchies of the combatants, but by 'armament' we must understand 'the various means of penetration' through space, through obstacles, through bodies. Just as General Fuller said: 'When the warriors threw javelins, the initial speed of this weapon was such that one could perceive it in its trajectory and fend off its effects with his shield, but when the javelin was replaced by the bullet, the muzzle speed was so great that there was no parry possible'. With the generation of the 'motorized-combatant', the parry becomes the great circus of war with its various types of apparatus, where the warrior is enlisted into the kinetic power of the projectile as with that Japanese 'human cannonball', the kamikaze, or indeed, the human torpedo, a true pyrotechnic apotheosis where the subject-projectile disintegrates along with his target.

These are thus the weapons that must be concealed from the enemy. The vehicle, like the old combat uniform, is going to be subjected to disguise. Its silhouette is going to disappear under a complex camouflage: for the armouring, the chromatic range of grey-green, sand yellows, and sometimes multi-coloured materials that simulate dimly lit undergrowth; for planes, two colourations that integrate it into the terrestrial and aerial elements, on the belly of the plane, a clear grey that the observer on the ground confuses with the luminosity of the sky, on the other hand, on the top, a greenish tint that attempts a match with nature while it is superimposed on the ground beneath. But this same landing terrain is, in its turn, disguised, the hangers are covered with camouflage nets and patterns. The magic trick, the disappearance from view, this time, of place, of the territorial body:

In no time, the airfield has effectively become a forest or a meadow, a lake or a village.... The dream of rendering oneself invisible is obviously not close to being realized; however, the art of evading view has nonetheless been considerably extended. Today war demands mimesis, it is a question of not only rendering oneself invisible for a short period as in a game, but even of concealing gigantic objects of vast extent for long spans of time. This task represents a science in itself, and the one who is responsible for this must possess a keen sense for unforeseen danger and above all the improbable. The architect in camouflage is the contrary of the propagandist; whereas the latter wishes to show clearly to everyone the issue he is addressing, our illusionist does the opposite, we entrust to him the task of changing the world, he works at this.

Twenty-five years after the First World War, this article in the German revue *Signal* in 1943 indicates the extent of the principle of concealment and camouflage. Total war had extended to the battlefield, the extension of the range of weapons, the scope of activity of war machines, led to the diminution of their tactical 'dimension' and the increase in their strategic and logistical dimensions.

As von Bulow wrote: 'Strategy is the science of war movements outside the *field of vision of the enemy*, tactics within this field'. Henceforth the strategic domain will expand with the very rhythm of various disappearances: of vehicles, infrastructures, cities exposed to bombardments, even entire regions as border zones, one great *black-out*.[4] Henceforth, nothing escapes the planning of destruction, and the territorial disguising [*maquillage*] is the clearest sign of this extension. *To disappear in the moment in order not to disappear for good*, this, it would seem, is the new military alternative. The overpowering impact of explosives and the hyperspeed of vehicles leads to this total mobilization where the speed itself of the intervention precludes the use of flags, of standards, as earlier national uniforms were left behind. The pilot's outfit or that of the conductor of trains is nothing more than an undergarment of the cockpit....

During the time of row battles, the shimmer of clothes, banners, and oriflammes had something of the same significance as a signal radio, they served to intimidate the enemy and communicate with one's allies. With the various recent means of communication, this protocol comes to an end, or nearly, 'radio jamming' or 'electronic counter measures' come to renew the physical disguise [*maquillage*]. Finally, it is all the strategy of speed: the Blitzkrieg that runs counter to the preliminaries, there are no longer any signals, everything plays out the instant war is declared and even more often before it is declared. Here again, speed

and the aeromobility of the forces dispel the conventions of war along
with the finer attire of the corps. As in the nineteenth century, where
we see the birth in France of the new *secret police*, today we find in
regular armies the movement that leads to the 'civilian soldier' and
where the mere performance of its means (of communication and
assault) disintegrates the civil military. The civil war slogan comes to
be adopted by official forces: *the front is nowhere to be found, the enemy
is everywhere*. The speed of mechanized conflicts dissolves not only the
warrior's face, the form of his weapons, the silhouette of his buildings,
it has caused the front itself to disappear. Over the centuries, the *battlefield*, the *domain*, even the *front line* have all been superceded; with
the Blitzkrieg, this last schism is no longer quite as General Guderian
declared: '*There where we find the tanks, there is the front*'.

In other words, there where we find the war machine, there is the
war. But in reality, with respect to what specific site can we make
reference to a machine of assault? War is everywhere, but the front is
nowhere, and the offensive of armoured vehicles is nothing other than
motorized guerilla warfare, a strategic recuperation of the combat of the
poor, of the attack of minorities that is necessarily surprise and secret.
The Swedes, for example, are currently training their soldiers to become
partisans, the State is planning what is called *free war*, another name
for the old guerilla war, but this time of a total guerilla, of a majority
guerilla, *in fact war is liberated from all conventions, from all rules,
and from all restraint*. If, for strategic forces, the nuclear submarine is
currently the most formidable vector, it is less because of its power than
the impossibility of locating it, that is, of *making it visible*. Continuously
undetectable, it represents deterrence as such ... the unknown of the
weapon repeats the unknown of the soldier. The perceived, the visible,
are subsidiary tactics; the secret is power, it is in delocalization that
we find the parry. A supreme effort at disguising [*maquillage*] but this
time a geostrategic disguise [*maquillage*] where the cosmic renews the
cosmetic ... the fate of women in make-up is shared by that of a world
concealed beneath its arabesques traced indefinitely by the weapons
of war so as to remain 'strategic', that is, invisible, that is, 'innocent'.
The peaceful coexistence of nations has the discreet charm of a fabri-
cated naiveté [*ingénuité fabriquée*], the political artificiality of the globe
repeats that of geography, this geometry applied to the representation

of different lands, with its border rings, its colours, and its cartographic lines that are no more territory than foundation makeup [*fond*] is the radiance of health. Did not the Saxon Marshal recently declare: 'I am not for battles, I am convinced that a skilful General can make war all his life without imagining himself obligated to it ... it is, so to speak, necessary to dissolve [*fondre*] the enemy'. The events that followed would prove him right, the world faded away beneath the features of the activities of war, from cartographic pinpointing to electronic teledetection, passing through the scars, the tattoos, of war marked out by the infrastructure of railways, or main roads ... the straightness of these routes recalls the history of celerity, *the straight line is the fossil of violence*, of the violence of the cannonball in the boulevard or the armour on the Reich-Autobahn....

The disappearance of characteristics of bodies in uniform goes along with the disappearance of the body in the unidirectionality of speed. Generalized mobilization is the last form of the disguise [*maquillage*] and the traces of the railway and main roads are like the traces of camouflage on the wall of a building; they conceal the singularity in deference to conformity. France disfigured presents the face of a body excessively fitted out, extravagantly disguised by its means of communication, from the aerial cables up to streaks of jets in the sky that crisscross the blue expanse.

Thus increasingly we lose our direct view on things ... the map in place of actual territory, statistics in place of facts, as Winston Churchill wrote in 1948: 'In the wars of old, decisions arose from events rather than tendencies; in modern war, tendencies are infinitely more important than events'.

Dissolved, confused, blurred, conflicts seem to reveal an aesthetic of disappearance, indeed, right up to the supreme authority: the conductor, the war leader, officer or strategist, all become the semiconductors of an abstract process. As was the case with the soldier, and then the army, this time it is the objective that becomes unknown. For the captain, for the commander of a missile-launching submarine, there is no other memory apart from the calculation of fire, the unwinding of the magnetic band concentrates the trajectory of the missile to the point of its target, just as the Roman roads condensed the power of the Empire through the movements of its legions.

Rolled up on its spool or unrolled in the plain, the straight line symbolizes the infinite because it is always like itself; first military glacis, the straight line is the projection of violence, but of a non-sanctioned violence where movement is everything and the end without value. As is the case for the courtesan, its success is nothing, all that counts is the pursuit; its seduction at first tempts, its innocence is the snare of the trip, attracting, it leads toward the horizon like the prostitute leading the soldier to her chamber.

From the Site of Election to the Site of Ejection

> Thus my people will be deported
> for want of intelligence.
> (*Livre de Malédictions*)

Can we speak here of architecture? If our discourse is governed by nostalgia, yes, surely. Recently I have been looking at some snapshots of Berlin, more precisely of Alexanderplatz; spanning the years at regular intervals from the thirties to the present, these photographs serve less to exhibit the state of these places than the rate of their disappearance, effecting a cinematic dissolve. Can we attribute this sudden acceleration of the urban image to war? Perhaps; but if the consumption of European towns did indeed have its origin with the consumption of space, on our continent it is only from 1945 on that the design [*dessin*] comes to be animated, or rather that the designs [*dessein*] of decision makers and other directors [*metteurs en scène*] upset the urban décor and, beyond that, the entire territorial body. The instincts for conservation of historicists who seem today to be hoping for a renaissance of the old models, in les Halles of Paris as elsewhere, amuse me nearly as much as the so-called innovations; the novelty is henceforth celerity, no longer the change or renewal of forms but the very acceleration of the cycle: tradition/innovation, pure speed. The stylistic periods of the ancient and modern unfold so quickly before our eyes that they are already no longer anything more than sequences in a generalized defection of the architectonic, to the point where today we would need Marey's chrono-photography to perceive the structural form of the undoing of the city, not just of Berlin but even Paris or New York....

The megalopolitan failure is only the harbinger of a much broader collapse. In fact, these are the myths of concentration and integration that disappear with the hyperfrequency of the diffusion of groups throughout the overall territory. Ten years ago, the fact that construction permits could no longer be obtained in Manhattan except on the express condition that a 'demolition permit' be simultaneously procured was presented as a success. The cadence of fixed architectural images was thus limited to twelve years. The phenomenal kinetics of the urban did indeed have its theoreticians, especially in Japan: the *Metabolists*. We mustn't forget that this sort of disappearance had been visited – in less than ten minutes – upon Hiroshima and Nagasaki.... Today, one of these theoreticians, Kenzo Tange, records his complaints in specialized journals regarding the next disappearance no longer merely of architecture, but this time of the architects themselves – he who wished to transform them into magicians finds himself to be the rabbit in the hat or rather like a Japanese shadow. Accelerated obsolescence, this aesthetic of disappearance seems something quite other than an effect of 'industrial design'. As if the revolution of transportation, less than a century ago, had been the West's last cultural revolution, we begin to catch sight of the profound similarity between the emergence of the railway and the cinematograph of the Lumière brothers. During the 'belle époque', as the train from La Ciotat enters the station, everything moves and is animated, all becomes trajectory – speed and projection of the image, but also of artillery and aerial projectiles. Finally in 1905, a scientist advances a thesis that would soon allow a more complete evasion, he entitles it the 'Electro-dynamics of the mobile body', its author is named Einstein. But this movement, today quite perceptible in its extent and historical significance, also corresponds to a total mobilization, that is to say, to a distancing in and through speed.

During a 1973 exposition in the Museum of Decorative Arts, views taken from the inner suburbs of Paris some 70 years ago were presented. Juxtaposed with recent photos, this exhibition exposed the breakdown of the urban infrastructure. What was most striking, beyond the disappearance of vegetation and the change in the level of the buildings, was, in the recent views, the apparent absence of inhabitants of these suburbs which are, however, very densely populated. But this sudden void was only an effect of the speed acquired since the beginning of the century. The population was indeed there, but it had always either just arrived, or was just about to depart. These 'images of time' in a desertified urban landscape amounted to a perfect illustration of SPEED [*VITE*] as the new VOID [*VIDE*], the presence–absence of the fleeting immured in vehicular dissipation, isolated by the violence of the driving energy, the resident closed within the distance of an accelerated trajectory, less 'inhabitant' now than survivor, less 'a member of society' than a temporary resident.

For example, eighty per cent of the inhabitants of the 19th arrondissement of Paris are in fact simply passengers and it is, moreover, important to remember that this figure does not take into account the flood of those who pass through the city entering or exiting Paris by the Portes d'Orléans or de Châtillon. The inhabitants considered are those who dwell in these blocks, to the exclusion of those who circulate through the arteries, the first important distancing. Nevertheless, among the number of those who supposedly live there, eighty per cent do not stay there, even if they remain there to work without lodging or if they lodge there but leave each morning to work outside and often at a great distance ... examples of a gyrovagy that has been called 'alternate migration' and that has definitively dissipated social localization.

Where then is the citizen? What is his last refuge? Does he still live somewhere when he is not pinned down to his bed in infancy, old age, or illness? When we ask these commuters, some will sometimes naively respond: 'I live in the bus, it is there that I find myself again, it is where I get my bearing between my workplace and my apartment'. Others speak of the train from the suburbs where they pass several hours each day and where they strike up friendships while on their way to their destination. They isolate themselves in order to restore themselves or to sleep nightly in their domiciles. The residential quarter no longer has anything to do with any sort of municipal arrondissement, it is nothing more than a distended digitation. In this new topography, if we also take into account those who flee for the weekend or more distant vacations, the space is even further divided up on the level of the country or even the continent. The air of the fleeting, of the temporary citizen, arises thus like a field escaping all localization. The distancing effected by transportation and dispersal is thus quite characteristic of our era even at first glance, the urban concentration seems more important than ever, the megalopolis can only be identified with its 'population density', at the risk of further increasing the social dissipation, the distancing in the violence of accelerated displacement that renews, unbeknownst to us, the old segregation of walls and fences. We often hear of new cities ... if indeed there were any such new cities, we'd know about them! One more city here or there, and nothing but a tautological repetition surrounding the capitals: in London or in France, we mark out urban nebulae but innovation is the failure of the welfare metropolis, what is original is the unheard of development of sites of transit (sic transit), airports, and other sites of ejection that progressively replace our old sites of election. In fact, the end of the North American service metropolis is already leading to the end of the myth of urban areas as sites of the social integration of the peasantry of migrant proletarians, it is here that we find the beginning of a great *disengagement* comparable in many regards to decolonization. Hyperconcentrated in these terminal points and other control and surveillance points, the anational State prepares to cast off its moorings with urban populations, its milieu is henceforth the non-lieu, non-place, of speed, the non-territory of an essentially vectorial politics where the pre-eminence of Time replaces that of Space, to the point that in France we have begun to envision very seriously the creation of a minister of Time Management....

Let us observe the strategy of the two multinational East–West blocs: besides the will to control of the ocean (Mediterranean Sea, Indian Ocean, etc.) and therefore of certain ports and certain islands, the towns are no longer anything more than what is put up as stakes, as targets that it will be unwarranted to protect. There indeed is the New City, at once an open city [*ville ouverte*] and a city offered up [*ville offerte*], the stakes of a terrorist equilibrium where it now serves merely as a hostage in a Generalized deterrence. An anecdote will illustrate this point: during a meeting, the architect and computer scientist Négroponte told me that the Pentagon possessed a planisphere of a new type, fruit of the updated assessment of global resources by spy satellites. Alongside the control of the increasingly diverse movements, the military are updating the state of cities each week: as soon as an edifice is completed in a certain quarter, thus modifying the relief of the urban zone, it is logged in the American army's worldwide cadastral survey, and this for each city of each nation. They take a census of what is built; just as yesterday they drew up the topographic maps of conquered territories, today they redraw the metropolitan morphology ... just in case!

There we have it, the famous 'de-urbanization'! Just yesterday, when one built a bridge, it was necessary to prepare and calculate its destruction in the case of war. Only ten years ago, in New York it was necessary to file a 'demolition permit' in order to obtain its opposite; with nuclear geopolitics, the destruction permit is prepared on the scale of vast global nebulae[5] patiently, inexorably, while the end of cities is inscribed in such perspectives. In the past, the city was a fixed pole of power, a pole of resistance with the citadel–State and its ramparts, but now it is only useful as a civil offering to the militaries of the two camps … a bit like those cheap trinkets that one pawns off on 'barbarians', the city is reduced to nothing more than a shop window to be destroyed. West Berlin reproduces this schema rather well: already ruined, it had been rebuilt merely as a display window of the West. Having lost its status as a capital of the German State, it had lost also a part of its urban reality, a spectacular metropolis, open to the East, a place of transit for fugitives, a terrain of adventure for an architecture of international expositions more or less provisional; more real as symbol than as a place to live, such is the new status of Berlin. Today, the crisis of New York very much resembles Berlin's, the eastern façade of the United States, an immigration port and old display window of the American dream, the great metropolis has also lost no less of its economic and political substance to the benefit of Washington or rather to that of the terminal of Western civilization, the Pentagon. In the eyes of those who control modern geopolitics, two cities alone still remain, Moscow and Washington. Only they posses a credibility on the level of the two anational States, these cities are the last still to possess, for a while, an intact political reality.[6] This congruence is not adequately perceived on the level of its practical consequences: the fading away of a structure at once social and spatial where the synechism reproduces its effects indefinitely, from the decline of cities with the rise of the City State up to the decline of the cities of the provinces with the appearance of the capital of the Nation State. Today, the transnational reduction affects each metropolis, each capital in both the East and the West; already they are nothing more than the place of a subaltern politics where each is almost imperceptibly losing its prerogatives. This is also the case with normalization, Prague being only one brutal example among others.

We are witnessing the reorganization of the political geography:

an industrial redeployment extending to the Third World, an international division of work with multinational businesses, etc. Here indeed the famous regionalization advocated by those who support a global political order! In the great process of the terrorist coexistence of a nuclear peace, the demography of cities is less important than their geopolitical situation, there is no longer much difference between New York, London, or Paris, nor any longer elsewhere between Warsaw, Prague, or Leningrad; all that remain are the two solitary citadels: Moscow and Washington. The uniformity, indeed identity, of the oriental urban architecture in the Occident should have nevertheless alerted us to the phenomenon, for 'the identical' always indicates a profound disappearance; a balancing of the signs of diversity and disparity announces also a cultural and political disaggregation. When Mao Tse-tung presented contemporary conflicts as an immense city/ country opposition of global dimensions, he did so based on an outdated notion of the perennial status of cities, of their power to abide. If cities had indeed accompanied the historical ascent of the Western State, the industrial revolution marked the beginning of their dissipation, and their growth during the course of the past century has completely deceived us when it comes to their capacity for survival. Military-industrial, this revolution would soon reveal its final product: the mobile force, the speed of the projectile. The industrial project was this and nothing other. In fact, the urban concentration was nothing more than a gathering, an episode in the levy en masse of populations reunited before the assault, the dispersal.[7] The nebulous shantytowns of the South American continent suggest to me the outlines of the future project: immense abandoned zones, remnants of the illusion of self-management of a rising penury, as in Villa Salvador near Lima that numbers more than 100,000 inhabitants ... a haphazard site for a fragile mass auto-construction, with various capitals in transition here and there, ports or airports, transport cities, like Manhattan once was, destined to assure the perpetual movement of a political, economic, and cultural delocalization, an incessant intermingling of the social body destined to assure its alienation, a prelude to a global biopolitics.

Certain theoreticians celebrate these practices as a 'return to power' of the people over their immediate environment without perceiving, however, it would seem, the significance of such a split between politics and the environment. The metabolist utopia and the euphoria of a conviviality among autoconstructors is found again therefore at ten-year intervals, but what was previously taken to be the technological progress of construction with Tange, Isosaki, or even 'mobile architecture' with Friedmann, has suddenly become pauperism, miserabilism....

If the port was never a city quite like others, the airport is nothing but a projector, a site of accelerated ejection surrounded by prohibited areas, rendered uninhabitable by the noise and pollution where the particular individual [*particulier*] is less an inhabitant than a simple particle [*particule*]. It is enough to appreciate the intervening evolution in their architecture since the mid-century, in France just as in the United States. Let's take the example of the Bourget airfield: constructed in the thirties, with a central control tower and a waiting-hall arcade comparable to that of any of the great railway stations. Ten years later, Orly was essentially the same, still a palace, a palace of rectangular glass with advanced highway access ... then came Roissy, an embarkation machine, a circular exchanger with its peripheral satellites where one gains access, as if by miracle, to the plane.... In fact, between the automobile, the escalator, and the plane cabin, we pass from one technological vehicle to another without any significant transition. We see the same change across the Atlantic with Kennedy Airport and the more recent Dallas Airport which resembles a computer. It covers a surface comparable to that of the Parisian centre and will allow for the turnover of an equivalent population, ten to fifteen million passengers per year. 'Airport architecture' must, therefore, be as significant for an urbanist as 'airport art' is for an ethnologist conscious of the decline of cultures. If we wish to accurately judge architectural modernity it is necessary to look here and to the highway and industrial landscapes; support of the animal dynamism, the static vehicle, architecture tends to lose itself in the cycle of motorized prostheses. Already, the distance between the lift, the underground, or the train is bridged by the moving walkway ... tomorrow, from one machine to another, there will be nothing but vast, vaguely inhabited terrains. Subjected to the vehicular system, architectonics will be reduced to just so many more or less gigantic precarious instruments, 'works of art' as one says in order to save face in an epoch without a civil architecture, and soon to be without art.

According to the futurist Marinetti, a racing car was more beautiful than the Winged Victory of Samothrace ... perhaps, but in the shorter term, it suffices to consider the new 'Formula 1' racing cars and the rapid evolution of aerodynamics since 1910 in order to guess that a vehicle is nothing other than a larva of speed, the embryo of a constantly deferred becoming, the provisional figure of a defection the final outcome of which is perceptible only with the emergence of another machine, one of even greater speed.

The grandeur of speed ... what is the meaning of such a phrase? We are not able to perceive very well that one speed is superior to another, but its 'grandeur' ... such nonsense masks the fact that the superiority of speed reduces to nothing every other measurable grandeur. As Heidegger declared in paraphrasing Plato: 'All grandeur is in the attack', but it is a question here of an intoxication, an intoxication comparable to that of the depths, the intoxication of a grandeur that tells the metaphysician that it is necessary for us to flee from here below up to the heights as quickly as possible, for the 'here' is now composed of the matter of the body (animal, social, territorial) cast in the form of a flight that is to be likened to a generalized repulsion, to the point that the aesthetic of disappearance passes abruptly into the disappearance of the aesthetic.

In 1976 there was a celebration of the previous 80 years of art. No one suspected, however, the fateful character of the 'entry into the station of the train from La Ciotat'. Yet, at the same time, the first spectators seemed to fall back as they saw the locomotive looming up ... reflex, premonition, where will we fall back to tomorrow? Maybe here, where precisely nothing, or almost nothing, moves, underground, within the thickness of a layer where the last colonization begins, in the solid world of the lithosphere, where penetration is only possible by underground architecture, in these networks of galleries in China today, vehicles of a populating of the shadows.

How are we to interpret the many international conferences on disarmament that have been held since the end of the Second World War? Is it a question here of one of the necessities of coexistence? Of a great plan of universal pacification? Or, rather, is it a question of a new type of manoeuvre, a sort of last strategic game where the great

powers continually strive to unveil their batteries in order to develop
their advantage all the more safely, by constantly diverting the site of
conflict?

After the banning of biological weapons, after the limitation of
strategic weapons, it is now a question of the interdiction of meteorological war and of its corollary, geodesic war. The great game continues,
but it is no longer a question of moves on the chessboard as it was
previously, the symbol of divisions, the mark of armed groups; today,
it is a question of constantly changing the terrain or rather the theatre
of operations. In this *war-game*, which has suddenly become a *peace
game*, the partners resemble adulterous couples who set up in advance
a series of different meeting places in order to evade their spouses!
With this *strategy of the beyond*, it will be necessary to seek out the
stakes in the margins of the game, in what is never mentioned. In
fact, we have seen that what is unveiled is demobilized; with the
dialectic of the weapon and armour, the visible is already lost since it
evades the intelligence that is the rule of the strategic game. All that
escapes the reconnaissance of the enemy, or simply that which is no
longer visible, constitutes the *fitting out* [*armement*] in the maritime
sense of the term: the preparation for departure, for casting off. Let
us try, therefore, to guess at what conceals the great treasure hunt of
total peace. It is more than likely that the double *anti-city* and *anti-
force* strategy merely represents a simulacrum destined to deceive the
enemy; as for the current 'hardening' of different means of combat,
this only illustrates the illusion of the rampart, the remnant of the
principle of fortification, a great trick destined to lend credibility to the
peaceful character of the famous Russo-American adversaries/partners.
... There is much said in technical discourse of the miniaturization
of explosive charges, of precision-guided weapons ... it seems we are
handing over more autonomy to these vectors, more of the adaptability
of response to the missiles ... we now produce the full spectrum of
weapons and munitions from the commando's dagger all the way up
to intercontinental ballistics, passing through assault tanks and ground
assault planes.... Publications on the subject of weaponry proliferate,
becoming more and more popular, military exhibitions and demonstra-
tions are multiplying. For example, at the fair of the Tuileries or that of
Bourget, 'children' no longer need lead soldiers, they can play with real

ones at the many weapons shows. They are displayed in the arsenal, in the barracks, *they sell the secret of the means at a bargain to better keep the secret of the ends.* Here and there, 'war museums' are reopened where the paraphernalia of the past or more recent times are piled up, submarines from the First World War are floating again, and armoured vehicles from the Second are unearthed to be put under glass, the winged fortresses make their entrance in the open air museum, the aircraft carriers in the sea museum, families visit the battlefields, or in Great Britain actual reenactments of battles.... The televised spectacle of the 'great battles of the past' delight the French, while in West Germany, a certain Karl-Heinz Hoffman maintains a little private Wehrmacht which he puts on manoeuvres each weekend to the great delight of nostalgia buffs. Associations of past battles gather for various public festivities, some organizing convoys of old materiel and parading down the Champs Elysées, others repeating tirelessly famous *Kriegspielen*.... It's all a great carnival of glory, but must we be fooled by this? Does this announce the return of cohorts of joyous assassins marching to the sound of the fife? Will we see again the rush of Panzers, as recent conventional conflicts in the Near East seem to indicate? Surely not, *wars of just a few days, even of a few hours, are themselves museographic*; despite the disasters they engender, they are already no more than 'representations' played in all their grandeur by miniature actors that have little effect on totalitarian peace. In fact, these theatres of operations are merely military–industrial 'trial runs,' and nothing more.... If once we tolerated the death of a test pilot in order to refine a weapon, now we will accept with few scruples the extermination of 'populations of pilots' in the Golan, or Lebanon, in order to improve the electronic counter-measures of the Phantom or the precision of SAM missiles, but the most important thing is elsewhere, hidden in plain view. Contrary to the First World War, the Second World War effectively extended to the whole globe, inaugurating what would come to completion in 1960: the conquest of space. In reality total war constituted the end of world war and since that time, regardless of Korea or Vietnam, war has lost its terrain. Like the all-terrain, amphibious, and aeromobile vehicles that it uses in great numbers, modern war is at once delocalized and deterritorialized, and we should no longer be surprised to see different opposed forces abandon, bit by bit, their advanced bases, with the exception – that proves the rule – of some points of transit, ports or airports. In the past we could still speak judiciously on the subject of armies conducting 'field manoeuvres' [*manoeuvres en campagne*] and identify etymologically the camp [*camp*] and the campaign [*campagne*]; currently, however, if the manoeuvre remains at all, on the level of the great military pacts, it no longer has any need of terrain, of the country [*campagne*]. The invasion of the instant succeeds the invasion of the world, *the countdown has become the site of conflicts*, the last 'frontier', the war of time has renewed the war for territorial space, it is the reason for which the two great blocs can so easily proscribe geodesic and meteorological wars.

The main issue of the Strategic Arms Limitation Talks (SALT) in Geneva is no longer explosives but rather vectors (cruise-missile, backfire …), the *delivery vectors* as they are called, or, more precisely yet, their performance, their speed.

If 30 years ago the *explosive* (nuclear) brought the war of space to its logical end, at the end of the twentieth century, the *implosive* (the vector) inaugurates the war of time that lies beyond acquired territories. In full coexistence, without declared hostilities, and with more certainty than whatever scientific explosive, the celerity of vectors releases us from territorial space. If, as Sun Tse wrote long ago, *speed is the very essence of war*, it is necessary to recognize the obvious: today speed is war itself, the end of time. Here we find therefore this *ecological war*, this war on the habitat that is characterized in only one of its aspects by the 'anti-city strategy'. But let us turn back to the decisive moment in the Cuban missile crisis of 1962: the delay of advance notice of nuclear war was *fifteen minutes* at the time, but with the implantation of launching sites of Russian missiles on Castro's island, this warning time would have been reduced to *thirty seconds*, and this President Kennedy could not accept. We know what followed, the installation of the direct line of the red phone…. Ten years later, now that the 'normal' delay is already only a few minutes (between five and ten minutes), the SALT 1 accords between Nixon and Brezhnev aim less than the acronym seem to indicate at the limitation of strategic weapons than at the conservation of the 'human' political power of the protagonists. Meanwhile the constant advance in the rate of the vectors risked, sooner or later, bringing the warning delay below a minute, and thus *definitively abolishing the possibility of reflection and thereby the power of decision of the chief of state* (both in the East and the West) while serving only the advancement of an automation of war that belongs henceforth only to the strategic computers of the two camps.[8] Let us recall as well that the most sophisticated missiles only move at *3km per second* while a laser beam moves at *300,000km per second*. For the record, we should note as well that the greatest emphasis of electronic research is currently geared toward laser weapons projects.... From *the state of siege* of wars of space to the *state of emergency* of the war of time, it will be only a few decades before the era of the State diplomat [*l'homme d'État*] will be succeeded by the era of the State machine [*l'appareil d'État*].

It must be conceded that, after the state of blockade of the City State and of the Nation State, *the state of emergency is the new city.* The end of the world or rather the twilight of sites. It will be the Palestinians who will first measure the effect of its weightlessness, 'a people without a land', as hijackers are forced to understand the suicidal character of the *air-terminal.* After art, after architecture, here we see the advent of *airport politics* ... but this time, of airports that will no longer have the relaxed atmosphere of leisure that the travelling bourgeoisie conferred upon it, instead they will have the tragic character of the extermination camp. Air-terminals, terminuses, and ports of the anti-city that opens on the nothingness of a territory disappeared; site of ejection that one occupies temporarily to buckle the empty buckle of an accelerated wandering; the air terminal, a spectroscope where popular shadows file past, migrants, phantoms in transit, postponing the last revolution, *the revolution of the eternal return....* Here indeed is the anti-city strategy, where entire masses are kidnapped, where abduction becomes the essence of the *transnational* political game, beyond the old practices of sequestration, of the ghetto, and *national incarceration.*

If the Hughes Aircraft Corporation magnate, before dying in a jet, chose to finance both the aeronautics industry and the film industry, it is because the one, like the other, conveyed the same cinematic illusion. For 'citizen Hughes', proprietor of a large aeronautics company, the world was already so limited that he had to acquire several dozen houses, so-called second homes, spread out around the globe. In each, the same furniture, the same newspapers, and even the same meals served simultaneously at a regular time. All this in order not to disorient the master of these sites.

A premonition of the end, of the end of the world? Today, when travellers (already quite numerous) buy an airline ticket in Roissy France for Roissy France, what remains of the trip? Would the last nomadism be one of time? Of the time that passes? Here as elsewhere the embarkation is nothing but a 'one-way ticket', [aller-simple] an *abrupt departure* [*aller en vitesse*] and no longer a real departure [*s'en aller*], since elsewhere as here, in this city of transit, passengers await the vector of their disappearance, in this 'hall of lost voyages' that recalls quite closely the waiting rooms of the old cinemas where one waited, in the heroic epoch when the cinema was not yet *permanent*....

Although the projection of the apparatus of travel is not always permanent, it is still constrained by the departure schedule, and those who wait for the departure in order to return (without going anywhere) are hardly different from cinemaphiles. Thus, those 40 Americans who disembarked for Paris on 31 December 1976 for their New Year's Eve party, to take Concorde and to party on board, arrived in Washington and partied at the French embassy ... a bit like when one stays for a second and then a third showing of a film.

'You have made a city of what was a world!' Such was the reproach of the Gallo-Roman Namatianus of Rome, but this was as yet merely a Mediterranean goal, a Marseillaise joke ... soon, it is promised, Dallas Airport will accommodate more than 100,000,000 passengers per year, thus handling itself twice the population of France. This phenomenal facility will not only be the model in all its grandeur of the anti-city, but also, and above all, that of the anti-nation. Its transient citizens registered in the boarding lists will not necessarily be different individuals but still subjects of an annular identity, 'passengers in rotation', time-zone denizens, a topological state of being that was perhaps best modelled in 1971 when Sarah Krasnoff, who, in order to escape her psychiatrists, boarded KLM's planes, crossing the Atlantic Ocean more than 160 times with practically no stopovers for five consecutive months, before being found dead, utterly wasted, in room 103 of the Frommer Hotel in Amsterdam.

Third Part

Dromoscopy

> The first victim of war is the truth.
> Rudyard Kipling

Movement governs the event; in making transparency active, speed metamorphoses appearances. In the accelerated enterprise of travel, a simulacrum is at work that renews the *trompe-l'oeil*. Like an embu,[1] the ground [*fond*[2]] of the landscape rises up to the surface, inanimate objects are exhumed from the horizon and come each in turn to permeate the varnish of the windscreen, perspective becomes animated, the vanishing point becomes a point of attack sending forth its lines of projection onto the voyeur-voyager, the objective of the continuum becomes a focal point that casts its rays on the dazzled observer, fascinated by the progression of landscapes. The generative axis of an apparent movement materializes suddenly through the speed of the machine, but this concretization is totally relative to the moment, for the object that hurls itself upon the layer of the windcreen will also be as quickly forgotten as perceived, stored away in the prop room, it will soon disappear in the rear window.

Let us disabuse ourselves of any illusions, we are here before the true 'seventh art', that of the dashboard. Opposite to the *stroboscopy* which allows us to observe objects animated by rapid movement, as if they were in slow motion, this *dromoscopy* displays inanimate objects as if they were animated by a violent movement.

To 'mount' [*monter*[3]] a machine is at once to mount on board and to leave the border (of the pavement for example), but it is also for the director of the movement to set himself up before a sort of easel composed of the screen of the windshield and the control panel of the components of the motor-projector. Arranged before the eyes of the driver, this *instrument panel* forms an ensemble, the director of the movement must observe both the approach of objects in order that they not hit the glass (images but also even insects, gravel, birds ...) and the various movements that trigger the gauges and computers. With this fascination of directing, a double game of sighting both within and in front unfolds, with the assistance of the steering wheel and gearstick, the director-composer of the trip will in effect compose a series of scenes *of speeds* that play surreptitiously through the transparent screen of the windshield. With the monotonous sequence of the scenes from the route, each object perceived in the depth of the field, in the progress, is identified with the moment of a deferred collision; in the driver's seat, the driver at the wheel simultaneously seeks out and dreads these all-too-unreal precipitations because their suicidal character holds the director back from advancing. In fact, the dromoscopic simulacrum obscures the telescopic violence of the road, its false images assure and reassure the pilot as he goes. If by its aerodynamism the vehicle is only the embryo of a constantly deferred becoming, through the development of forms that create the least resistance, it is also the figure of a generalized cancellation, a larva of speed with a development that is not perceived except in the emergence of a better form allowing for even greater speed. It is the same with the dromoscopic figuration triggered by the starting up of [*mise en route*] the motor, every control panel represents nothing more than a snapshot of the mise en scène of the film of the windshield, the precipitations of the landscape are only a cinematic hallucination: the opposite of the stroboscope, in the dromoscope the fixity of the presence of objects comes to an end, deceiving the travelling actor-spectator. In the speed of the movement the voyeur-voyager finds himself in a situation that is contrary to that of the film viewer in the cinema, *it is he who is projected*, playing the role of both actor and spectator of the drama of the projection in the moment of the trajectory, his own end.

The art of the control panel therefore appears, on the one hand, like a substitute for the hunt and for its scenes, but on the other hand like the duel and its feints. The gearshift and the steering wheel function respectively like sword and shield; the weapon of speed projects the assault mechanism beyond the scenery of the lands passed over, and the movement of the steering wheel evades, in turning to avoid them, these features which seem to be cast forth by the opposing horizon. In the mirror of the windshield, the windshield wipers and washer maintain the play of the transparency, the transparency which is every bit as necessary for the dromoscopic driving of the images as the thorough clearing out of the road is for that of the automobile. Despite its window, the opening of the passenger compartment is not a simple garret, it is a stage [*scène*] where the signs of the places travelled through move past in the mise en scène of changes in scenery from the change in the rate of speed. Shrinking its passengers' field of vision, the frame of the dashboard gives rise to an increase in acceleration of the sequencing that reinforces the effect of the acceleration of the vehicle. The dromoscopic simulation results from this double reduction: that of the distance-time of the trip and that of the narrowness of the frame of the sighting of the dashboard.

In reality, the driver's seat of the automobile is only a *simulator of landscapes*, elsewhere, in certain supersonic vectors, direct sighting of the surroundings is often abandoned to be replaced by electronic images of the 'flight synthesizers'. Moreover, if, in flight training school, *the flight simulator* gives the pilot the illusion of flight, driving schools employ a cinematic projection. In observing the unfolding of sequences of driving films, the driver prepares the imaginary display of the dashboard of his future trips. In these scenes of the road through the windshield, the world becomes a video game, a game of transparency and transpiercing that the director [*metteur en scène*] drives as he sets off on the route [*de la mise en route*], the ability to control is identified with the ability to move, that is with the *driving test*.

The mastering of the dromoscopic projection assures the security of the trip, in other words, the continuation of the immobilization of the travellers in the comfort of movement; on pain of death, the brutal truth of their situation must never be revealed to the passengers, those who partake of the violence of driving must remain as controlled as the images, immobilized by the straps recalling the restraints of youth, they can only impotently observe the exposition of the scene of scrambled colours passing rapidly before their eyes. So long as the dromoscopic simulation continues, the comfort of the passengers is assured, on the other hand, when the illusion comes to its brutally violent cessation in a collision, it is as if the voyeurs-voyagers are projected like Alice through the looking glass windshield, a death jump but above all a jump into the truth of their trajectory where the gap between the theatre hall and the stage collapses, the spectators becoming actors: it is this *fleeting insurrection* that the seat belt is designed to prevent.

With the dromoscope, it is absolutely necessary, in order to avoid more severe consequences, to follow each of the phases of this movement; as opposed to the cinemascope, the change in speed demands that the director-driver cause each sequence to pass in sequence on the windshield: from the point of acceleration, to coasting, to the *fixed plane* once stopped, and then reversing while parking.

This retrogradation of images in the progressive stopping of the projection is similar to that of the gears in their box; the sequence of phases is one obligation of celerity, one never jumps over the stages of the course – first, second, third, fourth – for the director-driver must maintain the dromocratic order of the dictates of movement.

In this course-continuum the landscape is not so much traversed as perforated, *seen right through* [*percé à jour*], the driver is only the inspector of this perforation where the real is turned inside out like a glove. In going and returning, the journey is only a tunnel where the significance of distance is overturned. With the change of scenery arising from the variation in speed, the informative content of places evolves, each state of movement of the automobile corresponds to a stage in the significance of the environments passed through, by its dromoscopic figuration each speed appears a bit like a *region of time*, of the time of passing through. The framed opening of the windshield is not therefore a window but rather a window-door through which passengers pass without stopping, a window-door through which the voyeurs-voyagers surge forth by the attraction of the destination.

Comparable to the vertical axis of a carousel, the screen of the windshield functions a bit like a *door-tunnel* where the horizontal axis would be the vehicle and the wipers would be the landscapes that follow one another around. In this obscene reversal, the landscape exposes its underside, in turning up its landscapes the territorial body incites the one who masters sites [*maître des lieux*] to the violence of speed in inciting him to the violation of spatial extension [*l'étendue*]. But the transparent screen is also a sort of dial, a gauge that makes visible in its dromoscopic simulation the violence of the course; where the warning lights and other indicators on the panel indicate the *state of the engine*, the glass of the windshield indicates the status of the journey. Dromoscopic vision presents, in the double transparency of the window and the route, the evolution of the physical world; the simulated deformations of the visual field of what is traversed provide invaluable indications regarding the *state of the sites*. With the gallery of the dashboard of everyday mobility, the cultural revolution of transportation is publicly exposed. On the screen of the automobile trip, the precipitation of images amounts to an evident telluric movement where the epicentre is situated at the blind spot of the arrival; the vector of transportation is here, therefore, only an implosive, and those truly experiencing this ambulatory catastrophe are less the privileged ones who contemplate the route than those subject to the routing of the surroundings. With the speed of the continuum it is the goal [*objectif*] of the voyage that destroys the road, it is the target of the projectile-projector (of the automobile) that seems to trigger the ruin of the interval, it is the fleeting desire to go right to the end as fast as possible that produces in the opening out [*écartement*] of the travelling the tearing apart [*écartèlement*] of the landscape. The irresistible attraction of the course dissolves the time of the movement – the *distance-time* – along with the fixity of the objects. Indeed, the cognitive distance of space remains somewhere, but it tends to become the memory, the recalling of the old barely mobilized roads of the route; the other end of the landscape comes closer and closer but the consistency of these places has disappeared in the aesthetic of speed; an optical phenomenon, the end of the voyage acts like a *shutter*, the dashboard controls provide for a hold over life, the abrupt passing of the trees, the instantaneous appearance of houses, views of hills in succession that mark off the route. The excessive attraction of the destination changes the passenger's view like the *aperture* of a camera lens, controlling the exposure.

The fast motion of the camera that captures these dromographic views corresponds to the progressive closure of the windshield; the will to reach the destination as fast as possible limits the field of vision of the voyeurs-voyagers, the *depth of field*.

Today, the means of transmission no longer simply produces, as it did previously, the transportation from one point to another (like a sort of bridge), the means of rapid transport also produces the fleeting figuration of the transfer. In simulating the fleeting nature of things that abide, the means of transmission makes evident the improbable reality of an end of space, the dromoscopic simulation makes the falsehood of a contraction of the world plausible.

The animation of the dashboard misleads voyagers regarding the cataclysmic movement of the end, regarding *the destination of the end*; like a magical mirror, the windshield allows us to view the future. In fact, such dromovision (automobile media) simulates the fleeting well before television (audiovisual media), simulates proximity ... up to the moment hardly imaginable where instantaneity and ubiquity will abolish space along with the interval, making the dromovisual apparatus the perfect equivalent of the audiovisual in a single stroke!

Automobile embarkation will certainly therefore become the occasion for an *exploration by projection*; a bit like the way one enters a laboratory, we will need to mount on board in order to attempt to decipher an enigma: that of the incoherency of motorized roaming, an attempt to guess the logic of this abandonment that propagates the travelling.

If in the history of architecture the window initially appeared in places of worship before being incorporated in common residences, it is because its opening allowed one to *contemplate the sky without touching it*, that is, to contemplate the surroundings of the temple. Later, this time in pictorial history, the frame of the *painting* [*tableau de chevalet*] allowed for the renewal of this critical distance established scientifically by geometric perspective. Today, it does indeed seem that the screen of the *dashboard* [*tableau de bord*] repeats this false proximity; with the rear window, with its windowed doors and its front windscreen, the automobile forms a *quadriptych* where the travel lover is the target of a permanent assault that recalls the perspective of the painting; the illusion is the same, but it now extends to the surface of the world and no longer solely to the surface of the canvas. Driving [*le conduite*] replaces coating [*l'enduit*]; the director (driver) sweeps the amateur (passenger) along in his train in the transparent coating of his driving; if in the past the painter attracted the gaze of the art lover through the illusory depth of the painted work, today the dromoscopic work attracts both the driver and his passenger through the depth of the entire landscape, cast forth toward the light of the destination, they occupy together the soul of a sort of translucent shaft where the passing landscapes compose the calibration of the trip.

In the driver's seat, the immediate proximity matters little, the only important thing is that which is held at a distance; in the continuum of the trip, what is ahead governs the progress, the speed of propulsion produces its own horizon: the *greater* the speed, the more *distant* the horizon. The philosophy of the windshield demands a prevision far more than simple vision since the latter is distorted by the advancing movement, it is the future that decides the present of the course. In the accelerated itinerary the past is passed over, the landmarks are in essence those of the future. Thus, the dromovisual apparatus functions above all as a *means of exhumation*, as a *means of transmission*; it only transmits what is to come, in the unidirectionality of the trip, what abides has already long ago disappeared in the archaeology of the departure. For the driver-prospector of the trip, the driver's seat is a *seat of prevision*, a control tower of the future of the trajectory. Inversely, the control tower of the airfield is, for the air traffic controller, the driver's seat of the airlines. Whatever the apparent movement of landscapes in the windshield may be or the real movement of airplanes on the radar screen, what counts for the controller of the trip is the anticipation, the prior knowledge.

The technology of vectors thus comes to replace the tactics of bodies, just as soon as this vision of a lost world is perceived it is identified as well with a *victorious vision*, to the point that the game of the dashboard comes to seem rather like a misunderstood form of the game of war. Let us remember that in the warrior dialectic, he who is revealed is demobilized; the visible is lost since it is lost to the foresight that is the rule of the strategic game, just as on the roadway, the prevision of the movement of the opposing horizon is for the driver similar to the prevision of the movement of the enemy for war leaders. A sophisticated form of *Kriegspiel*, dromoscopy would be in some ways a video game of speed, a *Blitzkriegspiel*, where the military practices of the major state are continuously perfected, every high-speed vehicle would be essentially a vector of command, a 'command car'.... It is meanwhile revealing to consider the historical evolution of the various 'driving seats': if yesterday we still flew in the open air in contact with the atmosphere, hearing the sound of the motor and the wind, and sensing the vibration of the machine, we could also note that the excess of speed has contributed to a progressive enclosing of the driver, first behind the screen of a simple glass windscreen, then the full windshield and enclosed cabin.

'Driving by instinct' has given way to 'driving by instruments' and then to 'automatic driving' anticipating what will probably be the full automation of automobility....

In fact, the flight deck of warplanes offers a political image of the future, the control panel exposes to those who wish to see it the foreseeable evolution of power, veritable crystal balls, the screens and dials make clear the otherwise hazy course of the politics to come. The new 'war machine' takes up the past 'lookout machine', the two of them are now as one. There is no longer anything like the past dichotomy between the function of the weapon and that of the eye, the assault machine is bound up with the vision machine and the destruction of vision contributes to the destruction of life. Unfortunately, dromoscopic accidents [*accidents dromoscopiques*] are less spectacular, it seems, in their immediate consequences, than collisions [*accidents téléscopiques*], no wreck remains and nobody is 'visibly' concerned about the security *of vision*. However, faced with this vertigo that affects the passenger while he dives into the depths of the landscape, we should pause to reflect; this *intoxication of grandeur* that drives us to pass certain levels of acceleration is formidable. The grandeur of the world, its spatial extension is suddenly confused with the will to power of those driving: it is *the assault that divides up the course.* Territory no longer exists except by the violence of the advancing movement; it is progress that leads to the twilight of place through the attraction of the destination, the voyeur-voyager no longer needs, like his sedentary brother, to stand behind the keyhole of a centre of panoptical convergence, his course is nothing more than a long look where the place [*le lieu*] and the eye [*l'oeil*] are etymologically confused.

As Martin Heidegger decreed in 1933 in complicity with the philosophy of the Führer: 'The beginning is already there, it is not behind us like what was long ago, but it stands before us. The beginning burst in upon our future, it rises up far away like a distant disposition, across from us its grandeur which we must rejoin'. Since then, a number of *drivers of peoples* and other *great helmsmen* have followed behind the dromoscopic screen of absolute power, but it does not seem any more reassuring to consider the army of their progeny: motorcyclists, motorists, *family drivers* who reproduce in their everyday getaways the dromocratic order of the great invasions. In this sharing of the power of the violence of speed what sort of political repercussions may be expected? In the driving of the motor, what democratic illusion is at work? What liturgy?....

Just as the catastrophe of the shipwreck was introduced by navigation, where the vessel disappears in its element, so also has accelerated traffic triggered and developed a new catastrophe, the collision: that is, the disappearance of one vehicle into another. *A mirror of speeds* that reflects back the violence of the trajectory on the object and the subjects of the movement, the catastrophe of the collision thus amounts to the shipwreck of speed. If we consider meanwhile the term 'télescopage'[4] we note that it is itself composed of two meanings: 'examine what is at a distance' [*télescope*] and 'mix indiscriminately' [*télescoper*]. The optical illusion of the telescope consists of approaching what is distant in order to examine it, and that of the automobile of mixing indiscriminately what is close and what is distant. This accelerated traversal is linked, therefore, with a certain problem of perception; the course becomes an excessive joining of what is distant with what is close, and the function of high-speed vehicles consists less in transporting the passenger than in causing physical reality to slide by, that is, to modify as with various lenses the surfaces of visual experience.

Progressively doing away with our awareness of distances (cognitive distances), speed, in its violent approach, distances us from sensible realities; the more rapidly we advance toward the terminus of our movement, the more we regress until *speed becomes, in a certain way, a premature infirmity, a literal myopia.* So if in the complete clearing of the field of vision (deforestation, desert, glacis) *what is distant visibly approaches*, with accelerated travel *the connection creates physical distance* until the horizon no longer recedes into the distance. Where the 'look-out machine' [*machine de guet*] (spyglass, observation tower) brought the horizon close by the domination of altitude or the optical properties of lenses, the 'machine of war' [*machine de guerre*] (vehicles, various vectors), in propelling the passenger toward the horizon, separates him to the point of being in an adjacent world, so much so that we could consider the play of the vehicular proximity to be a detaching, a recoiling, a literal retreat.

Here, propulsion by reaction seems symbolic of the movement under way since the transportation revolution. Thrust dromologically replaced the draw of the propeller, in the high speeds of aerial propulsion, the vehicle depends upon the ejection of a certain quantity of movement (product of mass times speed) *in the opposite direction to the forwards movement*, the assault results therefore in the retreat of forces, it is the *speed of the recoil that pushes the vehicle* as if it is what is expended, the loss of energy that produces the violence of the course....

In the projection of the accelerated voyage, territorial space is thrown back, left behind in the wake of the trajectory, *territory is exploited by the acceleration of displacement*, as if the consumption of space and time follows upon and repeats the consumption of raw materials, as if the dimensions of the world stem from its exploitation as a field of action.

Meanwhile, with heavier-than-air vehicles, the vector is propelled by its speed, the speed of its trajectory opens its path; the high speeds of propulsion determine the infrastructure of high altitude travel. In triggering the takeoff of the vehicle, *speed takes the passenger to the sky*, it is no longer only the opening out of the depth of field, the path, that allows the passage, *it is speed* [*le vite*] *this time by which we cross over the void* [*le vide*].

As a 'speed factory' *the motor produces the entrance way*. It is an excess (of speed) that produces the access to the atmospheric volume above the surfaces of territorial space. However, it must be noted, the exploitation of the world as a field of action has its limits in the curvature of the planetary horizon, to the point that the violence of excess speed is inevitably only a regression, an eternal return (to the port or the airport) that brings its passengers back to zero. *Each trip functions like a countdown*, the new catastrophe of collision [*télescopage*] arises from the fact that the arrival seems to counter more and more frequently the departure: faster than the sun, the supersonic jet reaches New York before having left Paris.... Where there were once still the three terms of the departure, the trip, and the arrival, there now remain only two: the departure and the arrival. With the transportation revolution, the interval has progressively disappeared in the progress of acceleration. With the airlines, for example, the 'distance-space' (in kilometres) has been replaced by the 'distance-time', pure temporality where the milieu is done away with as a field of action by the violence of the progress of the machine. But this contraction-collision continues, each augmentation of mobile power reduces this *line* of aerial trajectory, tomorrow no doubt there will no longer be anything but arrival, *the point of arrival*, the departure will have itself disappeared in the instantaneity of the projection [*projet*]. Such is already the case with audiovisual communications where the observer and the auditor are matched up before the screen, *the departure for the meeting has come to an end, it is replaced by the arrival of images* on the screen or even that of the voice in the earpiece. In telephonic communication the two auditors listen attentively for the arrival of the voice of the correspondent; the negation of the departure results precisely from the negation of the spatial and temporal distances of the dialogue. Here, the symmetry of the recoil is obvious: each of us remains in our own place while awaiting the arrival of the transmission (telephonic or televised), indeed, the archaeology of departures has come to an end, *with the speed of the assault, the wait has renewed the retreat, the recoil.* Dromoscopy is, therefore, paradoxically *the wait for the coming of what abides:* the trees that file past on the screen of the windshield, the images that rise up on the television ... all substitutes for reality, these apparent movements are only simulacra. But here it is a question of returning to the notion of visibility and therefore to light, *since the visible is the effect of the apparent movement of the sun rising and setting on the horizon*, it is the dromoscopic illusion of its course that organizes our vision of the ambient world, the movement of the star in the sky or in the window is therefore the perfect equivalent of that of the objects that rise up on the windscreen, *to the point that the distant horizon toward which the voyeur-voyager is directed is itself only a panoramic screen* where celestial objects file past astronomically to be seen in the (daily) instant of the (annual) trajectory of the planetary vehicle that the passengers occupy, or rather in which they live, for a time....

A cinematic illusion, the course of the shadows on the ground, translates before all else the rotation of the earth, like the setting of the sun, the awakening of the ground, the ascent of the distant horizon;

the visible would thus be the apparent reality produced by the atmospheric
screen with the transparency of gaseous lighting

It is meanwhile revealing to consider the intensive production of these 'artificial skies', these dromoscopic screens constituted by the large bay windows of contemporary houses, the success also of the (totalitarian) ideology of social transparency and the multiplication of audiovisual procedures in an ever-increasing number of different domains: control of movement, teleguidance, diverse means of surveillance. With the excess of speed, vision [*la vue*] becomes progressively the way [*la voie*], the entranceway [*la voie d'accès*], to the point that *daily life seems to have become an 'optical watch' where vision* [*la vue*] *replaces life* [*la vie*], as if, in waiting to arrive without physically leaving, each is now content to remain waiting in front of the audiovisual device, hoping that the dromovisual device will attain in its turn the instantaneity of ubiquity....

In fact, there is henceforth only one mediation, not that of the vector, of the vehicle, but that of its speed; between the audiovisual media and the automobile (that is, the dromovisual), there is no difference; *speed machines,* they both give rise to mediation through the production of speed, both are as one since the functions of the eye and the weapon have come to be confused, linked up, since the transportation revolution.

Here, the euphoric illusion of Macluhan's 'message-massage' is evident, mediation is not the product of the means of diffusion and the communication of language, of the word, or of the image, more or less effective than the manuscript of the printing press, mediation is the business of speed and the bringing of interlocutors into contact, the diversity of various means of communication (audiovisual, automobile ...) finally matters little since all have become the 'means of communication of extermination'.

But let us return to the violence of speed: if alacrity is the very essence of war and if, as Kipling explained, '*the first victim of war is the truth*', then it is indeed necessary to state that *the truth is the first victim of speed*; it is this that we learn visibly from dromoscopy, it is also this that Sun Tse explained when he indicated that 'military force is regulated by its relation to appearances'. War being a privileged form of the enterprise of appearances, *force, that is, the violence of military movement, is subject to the regulation of appearances* and not only through dissimulation, ruses, or camouflage, since *weaponry is itself the product of the event of movement*, what the specialists call 'logistics'. It is meanwhile a question of harking back also to an error in judgement: neither the *projection* [*jet*] of ancient weapons nor the *firing* [*tir*] of modern ones ever had as their essential objective the death of the adversary or the ruin of his means, but rather the ruin of his *projection* [*projet*], it is always a question of deterring him, that is, of *checking his forwards movement*, whether this be an attack to contain the opponent's attack or whether it be an invasion hardly matters, *it is movement that governs the event* (*of war*) *and it is movement that produces the weaponry*, as Napoleon made clear in his decree: 'The capacity for war is the capacity for movement'. If yesterday alacrity was the essence of war, it is necessary today to state that it has become its absolute form. With the industrial revolution of transportation as a 'factory of speed', indeed more than as a 'factory of machines', speed becomes war in its pure state, pure war.

A state of undeclared war, the state of emergency is a state-surprise (in other words a 'pure arrival') that pertains, due to the negation of space and time, as much to departures as to declarations of intention. Pure intensity, this surprising state of war on the world as a field of action abolishes along with the truth of its material the reality of its dimensions; an absolute war or rather a last war, speed amounts to the end of the physical world as dimensional truth; state of war vs. state of fact, speed triggers the defeat of facts [*défaite des faits*]. Then, like something dear to us that we forgot through the course of a long voyage, we discover the world is absent; after the nostalgia of images of the past, we founder in a nostalgia for a present world become purely imaginary.

If the dimensions of the physical world resulted from its exploitation as a field of action, and if speed resulted in the negation of these dimensions, what then is a dimension?

In his book, B. Mandelbrot responds that it is a matter of the degree of resolution and that the numerical result (from zero to several dimensions) depends on the relationship between the object and the observer, that is, the distance between the observed and the observer,[5] *spatial dimensions being hardly more than fragmentary messages that geometry will never cease from interpreting*, the true 'dimension of the world' would then be not only a matter of the degree of resolution of the image (geometric, geographic) but also that of its speed, the value of the dimensional mediation never ceases to metamorphose (according to Mandelbrot, to alternate) dromoscopically thanks to the progress of the speed of observation, *the means of communication of dimension*, vectors or vehicles (surveyors, lenses, microscopes, telescopes, automobiles, satellites …) being simultaneously the *means of extermination of dimensions*. The ultimate traffic accident where, at the speed of light, the apparent reality of the visible world comes to an end, implosion, dimensional collapsing [*télescopage*] that would see the disappearance of appearances in the dazzling light of speed.

Since the visible is only the surface effect of the alacrity of the luminous emission and since, meanwhile, what happens more and more quickly is perceived less and less distinctly, it is indeed necessary that we recognize the obvious, that what we see in the visual field is such thanks to the mediation of the phenomena of acceleration and deceleration in all points identifiable with variable intensities of illumination. *If speed is light, all the light of the world, then what is visible derives both from what moves* and the appearances of momentary transparencies and illusions. The dimensions of space, are themselves only fleeting apparitions, in the same way that things are visible in the instant of the trajectory of the gaze, this gaze that both is the eye [*l'oeil*] and that defines place [*le lieu*].

The various sources of speed (generator, motor) are, therefore, indeed sources of light and sources of images, images of the world when it is a question of its dimensions. Triggering the appearance and development of 'high speeds', the dromocratic revolution contributed to the development also of a great number of shots [*clichés*] that treated different types of physical stature with the new representation; the transportation revolution also set off the industrialization of the traditional enterprise of images, *a factory for speed* and, therefore, also for light and images, this suddenly becomes *a cinematic projection of reality*, the fabrication of a world, of a world of artificial images, *a montage of dromoscopic sequences where the optic of mobile illusion renews optical illusion*.

The historical function of geometry seems, therefore, to have been the progressive and progressivist reorganization of 'movement-power' [*pouvoir-mouvoir*], the development of a sort of generalized logistics or *chronologistics*, applied, not only to the visible domain – since this domain is only the appearance of reality produced by speed – but also to the totality of physical realities. By the constant renewing of the relations of semblance to movement, geometry leads to the regulation of different forces of penetration; by the updating of appearances, in revealing matter as perspective, that is, as dimension, as objective, the geometric enterprise accelerates its dissipation, to the very rhythm of the extermination of its dimensions, speed finally provides for a crossing over, without any problem, of the distance between the physical and the metaphysical.

The Light of Speed

All that appears appears in light.
Paul de Tarse

What will we wait for when we no longer need to wait to arrive?[6] To this question we can now respond: *we wait for the coming of what abides*, such is the apparent result of the light of speed, in other words, of the staging of the transportation revolution. With the appearance of the motor, another sun rises, radically changing vision, and its lighting will increasingly change our life. Thanks to the double projector, at once the producer of speed and images (cinematic and cinematographic), everything is animated; the disintegration of vision begins, preceding somewhat the disintegration of the matter of the physical bodies that appears with the first studies of the forms of least resistance (aerodynamics). Here *speed and the elements combine to give form to the appearance of the mechanism* [*l'apparence de l'appareil*], while the field of its course is entirely recomposed (and we witness nuclear disintegration ...). The wind erosion doubles from this point on with that of the relative wind of speed that sculpts both the vehicle and landscapes, while also acclimatizing the passenger. Although we can no more mask the light of speed than hide the sun with our hand, *the disintegration of the transmission of the (cinematographic) image and of the transmission of the (cinematic) body* will quickly be completed, to the point that soon no one will any longer be surprised at what will be, nonetheless, spectacular disturbances in vision triggered by this alacrity. *The locomotive illusion will thus be considered to be the truth of vision, altogether as though the optical illusion will appear to be that of life.*

How were we able to fool ourselves to the point of dissociating the optic of cinematic illusion from the cinematographic optical illusion? *To the point of identifying the sequencing* [*le défilement*], *the sequence* [*le défilé*], *with truth?* ... perhaps because for a long time now the logistical history of geometry has occulted the relativity of vision by training us – through the artifice of *successive dimensions* taken in perspective – to take vision to be truth, the visual to be the real ... *To consider appearance, solely appearance, and thus to neglect movement and to observe movement only while neglecting its celerity, is to participate in this 'fixism'* that we find in play through the full course of cosmogonic and geographic history, from Copernicus to Wegener passing through Galileo and others. Today it seems we live less in our own habitat (its field having practically disappeared) than in the habit of velocity; assimilated to reality, its verisimilitude alienates us to the point of eliminating the optical effect of celerity, thereby normalizing the blurring of perception caused by acceleration.

It is the last form of anthropocentrism, a new and original form that appeared with the emergence of the second sun that is the motor, the focus of speed and images with respect to which the 'voyeur-voyager' becomes repeatedly *refocused* to the point of being *focused* in the most total inertia since it corresponds finally to the axiality of the geophysical extension comprised in the moment of the gaze: *the motor arbor* [*l'arbe moteur*] *becomes the tree of life* [*l'arbe de vie*], *the axis mundi.* Ever exposed to the speed of solar light, we are henceforth overexposed to the light of vehicular speed produced and projected by our machines. The enigma of movement doubles now with that of the cinematic simulator; where previously the dromoscopic effect of the setting sun (like the moon) on the horizon produced along with *geocentrism* the greatest possible optical (cinematic) illusion and undermined all anthropocentrism, the industrial proliferation of sources of speed doubled and infinitely echoed its egocentric simulacrum.

With the scenographic revolution of speed, 'hunting by chase' transforms into a sort of 'hunting by ambush' where *the equipment of the course* renews *the weaponry of the hunt.* Repeated, the accelerated displacements project a last *imago mundi,* constantly displaced, the passengers displace the world in the projection booth within the automobile, as in the dazzling whiteness of the screen. Thanks to the performance of the vehicle, the black chamber doubles as a white camera, the driver's seat becomes for the voyeur-voyager the sepulchral chamber of the exposition of the trip, a passageway for display of the landscape. The world travelled through becomes pure representation, but a forced representation since all is distorted by the forwards movement, this movement that is nothing more than the expression of the extermination of temporal duration and spatial extension. Where the *Orient* and the *Occident* had once signified the departure and arrival of the course of the sun and marked out the geopolitical organization of the earth in *exploiting the Occident, that is to say, the sign of the destination but also of decline, playing down the Orient and, therefore, the departure*, we can now state that, having reached its destination, this same Occident tends, with the industrialization of speed, to *institutionalize urgency*, that is, *the pure destination* that annihilates finally the departure, all departures and all the Orient, in an instantaneous circumnavigation. Twilight of the sites of a universe overexposed to the light of speed, the decline of the Occident thus implicates the decline of the physical world since, as one of the strategists of intensive motorization, General J. F. C. Fuller, noted: '*The offensive carries* a priori *in itself a fatal germ, it weakens itself by its own success*'.

With the industrial revolution of transportation, the appearance of the motor-generator could for a long time be compared to the morning of a day of progress, to the *rising* of a shining star, but the increasing acceleration of mobile technologies will soon lead it to resemble its *setting*, in the withdrawal, the retreat, of the real. But here, it is necessary still to specify that it is not quite right to speak of the 'exposure' of the world to the light of speed; rather, the geophysical field is the object of an *overexposure: as in telemetry, the effect of the real results from a double sighting and from the henceforth permanent superimposition of exposure to solar light and the engaging of vehicular speed*, so much indeed as perhaps to herald the dawning of the 'paradoxical day' where the luminous addition will trigger a night of excess light, of excess speed, *the last (stereoscopic) collision* [télescopage] *where the occidental state of emergency will be identified less with the eternal return than with a non-return, that is, with the definitive negation of what comes in what comes again, since all will abide entirely in no longer ceasing to arrive.*

The instantaneity of the arrival will drop what remains, rest will thus have become the greatest of long distance voyages, the diurnal/nocturnal alternation will itself have come to an end since night will be identifiable through the full course of the days, in the greatest possible light.[7]

The positions of sites, of things, is interchangeable indefinitely thanks to the overexposure of acceleration, each pole will become interchangeable, to the degree that in this sort of instantaneous autocommunication the means of communication will appear finally what they have never ceased to be: weapons, means of extermination.

Put into contact, or rather brought up to the brink of this twilight moment where *beyond the semblance that has disappeared forever, things continuously collapse in the haste of what moves;* speed initially conceived to oppose the effect of the ground, of weight, will become itself a sort of *alternative gravity*, a weight adjustable at will, the ultimate triumph of logistics. Thus, the dawning of the paradoxical day of the motor 'sun' – the propagator of light and images – will succeed the incidental influences of a second gravity that will produce in its turn *a double fall of the body: after that of the mass in planetary attraction, that of the absence of the mass of light in the instantaneity of vehicular attraction.*

The transportation of the body at the speed of light, previously precluded, will finally dissipate the old propriety of mass that consisted in resisting all acceleration by reducing the magnitude of movements, by braking; beyond the nuclear disintegration and the explosion of fissile materials, we are helpless witnesses to the vehicular dissipation, to the implosion of all mass and of all matter in the ubiquity of the excess of the light of speed. Thus, at the heart of this *critical mass* that has attained the point of no return, where temporal duration and spatial extension will have been evacuated by the final reconcentration of the physical field, *all surfaces will be face to face, overexposed in a single interface*, the absolute triumph of the geocentric illusion where the Occident will have finally come to its complete expression.

If the sun dial was the first dromoscopic computer of speed, it seems that soon the screen will replace the mirror. In numerous athletic disciplines, field and track, soccer, or horse-riding, the video recorder and closed-circuit television allow the participants to see and review themselves with just a slight delay. Thus, in the cavalry school of Saumur, a tele-video network allows the rider to analyse his movements on one of a dozen 'monitor-receivers' that encircle the manege, without even needing to leave the saddle. . . . These recording technologies thus offer to each the possibility of observing himself in deferred time, or even *live* as in a mirror, and this, as many times as he wishes, thanks to the *replay*, until the details of his movement become familiar. In allowing the chronological chain of these movements to be judged,

TV recording can also reconstruct them for him in *slow motion*, as if the speed of execution, which is, however, one of the objectives of this competitive training, becomes a handicap to a clear self awareness.

This curious doubling of the personality is affecting more and more other professions, as if *auto-control*, the direct result of the rise of technical automobility, has become a new ethic, as if *the optical watch* has progressively supplanted immediate action, *life becoming imperceptibly a piloting by the viewing of a foreign body.*

In the sports example, the stereoscopic effect is striking: it is no longer satisfactory to learn a sport or riding through training and the repetition of certain movements, certain postures, chosen with the assistance of a teacher or *trainer* [*moniteur de sport*], it is now necessary that the athlete learn to gaze at himself in the mirror of the screen. At once actor and telespectator of himself with the aid of a *TV monitor*, his dynamic lived experience is suddenly identified with the sequencing of a remote object; the subject finds, and invents, himself as he is engaged – or entranced – by the spectacle of his feats and as *each of his movements rises up before him as the horizon of his action.* An introverted tourism, the movements of his being appear and disappear in their dromoscopic rhythm, like landscapes in the continuum of the trip. His body is broken up into a series of sequences, the actor turns back upon himself in order to hunt down his errors and his imperfections; *hoping to attain himself as the target, he never takes his aim off himself,* memorizing, he hopes, certain reflexes, the results of an 'image of the body' doubled by the artifice of the vehicle. A new type of ostracism, the actor possesses himself henceforth in the measure to which he accepts being dispossessed of his immediate consciousness for the sake of the sole sense of vision, but a vision which is remote and distant.

Like the 'image of the world', that of the body undergoes thus the metamorphoses of accelerated transport; at a distance from itself, in the stereoscopic distancing of his (televisual) contemplation, the actor acquires a power over his movements in the instant when he considers himself dispatched like *an expeditionary force.* The illusion of (audio-visual) optics and the (dromovisual) optic of the locomotive illusion are nothing more than one and the same illusionism. *Through a telecommanded autism,* athletes increase the performance of their movements in exactly the proportion to which they take their own image for themselves and as they exchange their mass, their volume, for the two dimensions of a silhouette, for their shadow on the screen. Here, the television that is originally used to establish a link between separated poles in making instantly visible what lies beyond the field of vision (as in the captain's seat of a ship, where the controls are doubled by the screens of an optical-control panel, making visible the blind spots of the enormous mass of the vessel, and thus avoiding collisions) is now used conversely *to give the athlete a distant view of what is closest to him*: *his own body*, as if proprioception had suddenly become a disability to be overcome by televisual technology.... Overturning henceforth the range of proximities, audiovisual and dromovisual systems no longer respect any of the elementary limitations of the body or of territory, falsifying relations to mass, to spatial extension, to matter, and, therefore, to action; various 'shots' and other 'recordings' hunt down every perspective in infinitely multiplying them, as in a mirror.

The movement-power [pouvoir-mouvoir] becomes thus a phenomenon of generalized dissection in which nothing can any longer remain as it is. It is not only the procession [*défilé*] that is the truth, for the staging of the distancing [*mise en scène de la mise à l'écart*] becomes, in the dromo-scopic decomposition of vision, a kind of a sacrifice. With endoscopy, for example, the trip becomes the introspection of the organs that compose the body itself. Penetration to the centre of the living matter, movement across the full length of the arteries all the way to the heart, the trajectory of the gaze is no longer limited to exterior territories passed through on the route of the automobile, but, this time, extends to the perforation of flesh, *the perfusion of the intimate dimensions of one's being* where clinical observation violently breaks in in a kind of flaying where the organs without a body appear bit by bit like so many *obscure zones* of life. Under the scalpel, the thickness of the flesh appears a bit like another subterranean world that the dromoscopic vivisection of the endoscope renders in its impulses, its ebb and flow. The voyeur-voyager thus engages in the most complete topological reversal possible: from immediate proprioception of the body to the mediated appropriation by the (stereoscopic) distancing of the video screen, up to this forced introversion of the gaze where the viscera become suddenly the region of a sort of itinerary of physiological disengagement, *an intimate deviation where what appears in the endoscopic sighting is what remains of life.* After having reduced to nothing, or nearly nothing, *temporal duration* and the geophysical *spatial extension* by the acceleration of transports, it seems that the vivisection of speed now attacks the very density of masses, as if the objective had suddenly become the *durability* and thickness of the physical body as a whole. We can meanwhile verify this with the recent perfecting of the scanning electronic microscope that allows us to see instantly, in relief, and from different angles and powers of view, the opacity of matter down to the exploration of its 'ultimate crevices', but also, with the development of the (civil and military) subterranean facilities, the lithospheric colonization of the depth of the earth that today succeeds the more traditional development on the surface.

Since the transportation revolution, the remote has become so close that the resistance and the opacity of matter seems to take on the attraction of a new exoticism, *the distancing is no longer so much the result of the temporal duration and the spatial extension of the course, as that of the durability and solidity of the material.* A new vertigo, the solidity of the world under our feet, attracts us like the plane once attracted the nomad and the rider, secretly we will desire, it seems, this fall of the body into solids, the (totalitarian) ideology of transparency catches up here with that of the transport and demands to be brought up to date, the opening of the tunnel. After the abandon to the (colonial) intoxication of continental expanses, we sink into the intoxication of subcontinental depths.... Tomorrow, we may be certain, with the extreme intensification of different speeds of penetration we will wear out the density of matter – of this compact matter that presented an obstacle to our exploitation – just as we have worn out the geophysical dimensions and geographic distances. *Ever faster, ever higher, but also, ever deeper*, the pathways of subterranean transparency (territorial and animal) will constitute the forced reversion of the accelerated transport. Preoccupied with *creating a void*, we will not tolerate much longer the density of matter; already having seen right through the earth through seismographic, radar, sonar, and laser instruments, we will soon do away with the screen of the territorial body; latter-day troglodytes, we will besiege the mass of the planet as yesterday we conquered and developed its surface. Thanks to the logistical geometry of networks, we will turn now to colonizing the depths.

The planetary depths will thus appear like the last horizon to be settled, *but a settling of the shadows that will finally prove to be only an aftershock, only an effect, of the underside of the conquest of space, the retreat, the recoil of space into the centre of matter.*

Just as the actor and the orator fashion their acting style [*jeu de scène*] with the use of audiovisual technology, various 'rules of the game' [*règles du jeu*] are subjected in their turn to the impact of broadcast technology, to what may be called *audiovisual pressure.*

Let's take the example of the first winter Olympic games televised worldwide in Grenoble: with the help of the time difference, there were 400,000,000 telespectators who witnessed the triple victory of J.-C. Killy live, this publicity winning for him considerable prestige across the Atlantic ... after having assisted in the training of the athlete, television now influences the game, the (atmospheric) pressure of live broadcasting is exerted not only upon the athletes and the referee (whose calls are often discredited when his angle of view is inferior to that of the telespectators), but also upon the crowd of those who assemble to witness the event in person.

The presence-absence of millions of voyeurs and the (economic and political) stakes of this liturgy do in effect weigh down with all their weight on the action. The thousands of spectators actually present lose their value in the face of the millions of absent telespectators, each alone in their own homes. Let's verify this one more time: *those who remain in the wings prevail from a great distance over those who are present.* A certain supremacy might thus seem to be established solely to the advantage of the audiovisual vector over the automobile vector, but this is still, and will always be, the same cinematic optical illusion; for, in fact, paired with the proxemic perturbations to which they give rise, they are inseparable.

The advantage of the vector over the vehicle does not arise from its instrumental and functional characteristics, but only from the current superiority of the speed of transmission. A geographic spacing still remains between camera shooting, the camera's recording, and the transmissions to the control monitors of the technicians and finally the sets of the telespectators; this gap arising from the spatial extensions of the visible world must be offset, compensating for the absence of the telespectators, by a displacement of the camera crew, to the degree to which there are not always – despite our geostationary telecommunication satellites

– camera networks installed in fixed position at the four corners of the globe, as is the case for major urban intersections. If we now have at our disposal numerous command posts to govern the flow of air, train, and road traffic, and even if there are different types of control posts for the traffic of information (production of images, and mixing boards), there is no *universal monitor* transmitting live and continuously the integral vision of a world without a blind spot, without a horizon, and without antipodes....

Despite the teledetection systems of the armed forces (such as NORAD identifying all flying objects 24/7), the practice of the telecommand which is applied to the majority of large vehicles is not yet applied to the largest among them: the celestial objects on which we are all passengers and where the *shadow zones* are still decidedly the greater portion and which therefore demand the use of a means of transport with the *logistical support* of the means of communication, the physical displacement of operators, the mission of this other expeditionary force comprising broadcast technicians.

'To be superstitious is to believe that our thoughts are in things and that they move them', wrote the philosopher Alain. *Would driving then be an act of superstition?*

In Houston, in October 1977, the laboratory using instruments of telemetry left on the moon by the Apollo missions ceased to function, one by one the control screens went out and then nothing would move any longer on the dead star.... The old maxim of astrologists was confirmed: *'He who knows, commands the stars'.*

The movement of celestial objects renewed by the movement of fleeting images, dromology becomes the astrology of technological objects, the means of communication consisting of simulators of the space passed through. Motors, generators of speed and images, are therefore less the means of transporting the passengers than of dephasing and desynchronizing him, to the point that he must now learn to pilot not only images, as in whatever sort of television production, but also learn to drive visible telluric movements, since henceforth, it would seem, it is *the earth that comes upon him more and more quickly....*

What do the mechanical or electronic characteristics of vectors matter, since all that counts finally is their power of propagation, *this speed that is the cause and not the effect, since it dilates time just as it contracts space?*

There is nothing more left for us to do except forget the specious distinctions between the propagation of images or waves and the propagation of objects or bodies. *Since temporal duration is measured in intensities, distances are the most important product of the technical mode of existence;* this is moreover confirmed by the recent changes in the means of production, of which the most important and least recognized was probably this production of the end of the world, this extermination of the backcountry by the acceleration of mobile technologies, this *dromocratic geocentrism* of which we are far more the witnesses than the beneficiaries.

This extremity tests us; it is not, as we claim, a conjectural phenomenon, but a cultural and political event that raises – beyond ecological questions of limits and of the exhaustion of resources, and those resources of residual proximities which are no less essential – the dromological question of the exhaustion of distances.

So if, in 1848, Stuart Mill could still declare: *to produce is to move*, later, the formula is reversed; it is transports and transmissions that command production, to the point that *dromology appears today like a science whose theories take the form of vehicles.*

The study of the course and of its different means through the ages thus revealed itself as the discovery, the archaeological invention of vectors and vehicles, considered, then officially recognized, as veritable 'visions of the world', veritable logistical theories of the movement of people, what Stendhal guessed in writing: '*The novel is a mirror that strolls down a great boulevard'.*

In this sense, each new means of communication would appear a bit like a 'travel journal', a new novel of spatial extension and temporal duration, or more exactly, a final state of advancement of the world toward its loss. Here, each vehicle considered would be an incident along the way, in the manner of an *accident of the transfer* opposed to the substance of the world in a given moment of its history, where each of the means of movement would be simultaneously perceived not only as 'a means of transport and transmission' but also as a *means of producing special effects* in the space-time of the passage, the movement of the transient objects and bodies but also of landscapes, a deportation of distances where we must recognize that the *high-speed vehicle produces the accident* (*visual telescoping or the 'telescoping' of collision*) *at the same time as it triggers the movement.*

In fact, the wreckage and injuries suffered in a traffic accident are only external signs, the visible recording of imperceptible traumas suffered through the course of a journey by the passenger and the vehicle in this generalized withdrawal that propagates the trip, this special effect of traffic which was verified by film, by the cinematographic artifice of its sequencing, in the unexpected invention of the first of these 'special effects' by Georges Méliès: 'I was filming', he recalls, 'the Place d'Opéra when my camera failed to function. You would think that during the time it took me to inspect the mechanism the people on the road would have changed! Suddenly, without even thinking, I succeeded in turning my reel.... But once I developed the film, what a surprise: *I had begun by taking images of a bus that was passing on the Boulevard des Capucines and when the vehicle arrived at the Boulevard des Italiens it was transformed into a hearse'.*

If this comic episode is useful in illustrating the optical (cinematographic) illusion, it is equally so for testing the locomotive (cinematic) illusion. A means of dephasing the field of action, but also of desynchronizing action itself, the vectorial dynamics of the vehicle are here clearly underestimated since they give rise both to a transformation in the dimensions of the passage and a permutation of the passenger, of this traveller suddenly become the accidental visionary of a chance Beyond like that recorded by the craft of Méliès in 1900, with repeated special effects, from his *Voyage dans la lune,* or even from his *Déshabillage impossible,* where we can see a traveller attempting to undress without ever succeeding, his clothing being instantly put back on. The victim of the phenomenon, the character tries to take hold of his speed costume, yet as he takes it off, faster and faster, his clothing reappears.... A bit like water refilling in a bottle or demolished buildings reconstructing themselves violently, tomorrow, if we don't watch out, telluric acceleration will render travelling itself impossible.

A phenomenon of pathological adhesion, the uselessness of the departure will soon apply to all action; from edge to edge, no longer any distancing, the extreme proximity of things will alienate us to the point that the celerity of vectors will result in a transmutation of spaces probably as ridiculous as those phantasmagoric scenes of an Émile Cohl or a Méliès.

This notion of 'the special effects of cinematography' was to be extended by those masters of the spectacular illusion, the Lumière brothers. Indeed, none before them had aspired to the realism of cinematic sequencing, the animated chronophotography of Marey represented only a preliminary effect of the so-called truth of movement; its decomposition in successive stages did not disrupt the postures and movements that sketch out the movement of the body, it could be called thus a *cinema on this side*. With Méliès and the animation artist Émile Cohl, we have the *cinema of the Beyond*, beyond this so-called veracity of the light of speed of film that seems to restore the sensible unity of life and that is nevertheless nothing other than a *vision*.[8]

On this side of and beyond the Lumière brothers, special effects don't exist, or no longer exist, simply because no one makes claims for the *truth of the sequencing*, that is, for the objectivity of the sequencing of images; all that remains is the illusion of 'special effects': the effect of the splicing of a single movement in Muybridge and Marey, the effect of the splicing of a series of sequences with Méliès and Cohl. These two will meanwhile push the filmic sequencing, not to the absurd, as has been suggested, but to its limit, the limit that is the transmutation of the subject and not only its transfer, its transmission. With them, it is no longer a question of *putting the image of man into motion* as it was with Marey, but rather of *putting the series of sequences of man's comportment into absolute speed*, so much so that all that finally matters is the acceleration and deceleration, the 'movement of movement' that becomes thus the actual subject of Méliès' films, no longer in the manner of a Louis Lumière, as a pretext to deceive the spectator regarding the efficaciousness of the truth of the images of life, but in order to entertain or frighten him by the imaginary irrealism of speed.

A theory of representation in which the procession, the way [*la voie*] and the convoy [*le convoi*] sketch out the projection, the unwinding of the film constructs and deconstructs the world in the flash of an eye: it constructs it in managing the time and space of a 'false-day'; it deconstructs it in destroying it *in extremis*, in displacing the subject of the trip, this observer of the *arrival of the end*, this old traveller who is now little more than a 'gazer' [«*regardeur*»] (Marcel Duchamp), a sort of

arriviste, a parvenu, in a dromocratic society where the waiting rooms
have replaced, following the nomad's tent, the cinema [*salle obscure*] of
sedentary peoples.

D. H. Lawrence was mistaken when, in *Apocalypse,*[9] he expressed bitter
nostalgia for the time when 'man lived in close contact with the cosmos
and observed the celestial movements with a profound and impas-
sioned attention'. We have probably never paid so much attention as
today, we have undoubtedly never been so attentive to the *cosmody-
namic* movements, but these are transfigured by a subliminal light, it
is this light and no longer the light of the solar star that extends across
space in a *compensated time* which is no longer exactly that of Kronos,
but rather that of the energetic ruse of motors.

If in the past each city in the Orient was symbolically situated at
the centre of the world, this centre has subsequently been displaced,
displaced ceaselessly and more and more quickly, since its axis has
become the engine, the mobile performance of these *vision generators*
that are the speed machines invented in the Occident. The theory
of a 'movement-power' [*pouvoir-mouvoir*] which is always opposed
to the exclusive pre-eminence of 'knowledge-power' [*pouvoir-savoir*],
dromology is a hidden science (that of speed), both a logistical
complement and supplement to the science of life. Chronologistical,
that is, no longer solely chronological, it is not the fictional story of
historical facts, but the remembering of the invention of the effect, of
this *appearance of the real* [*effet de réel*] made possible by each vehicle in
its time.

As the sublimation of the hunt [*chasse*], the art of the course would
thus become progressively *the recording of the putting into motion of
space, the history of the putting into play of time by the means of movement*
(messages, people, goods) where territory itself is progressively done
away with [*chassé*]. Giving rise to the physical body as *dimension*
through the exploitation of the course, the industrial exploitation of
speed thus exterminates the animal body at the same time that it does
away with [*chassait*] the body of territory, thus reducing to nothing the
spatial extension of the geophysical field.

As Nadar wrote in 1863: 'It is folly to seek to fight against the air
by being lighter than it. To fight against the air, it is necessary precisely

to be heaver than air; *in aerial locomotion as elsewhere, one rests only on what provides resistance,* it is up to air to yield before man, and it is for man to extinguish and control this insolent and abnormal rebellion.' These military terms are clarified by the words of the first photographer to have captured aerostatic perspectives; but if we only depend on what resists, what resistance and *what rebellion is in play in the innovation of various means of locomotion?* The hunt by pursuit yesterday, the hunt by ambush today, it does indeed seem that the dimensions and different mensurations have themselves been invented by the science of geometry as with so much weaponry, that is, so many means of eliminating the resistance of time in the movement and rebellion of space.[10]

Fragmentation, arbitrary partitions destined to assure the reign of the one who passes, the power of the one who moves, *the system of movement of reality and matter* and not, as one thinks, of recording, geometry proves to have been the hidden face of this 'movement-power' crafted by the Occident since antiquity. So, if to produce is first of all to move, *to measure is to displace,* not simply to survey – to displace in order to execute measure – but rather: *to displace territory in its (geometric, carto-graphic) representation.* Its geophysical reality is deported in a geodesic configuration that possesses only one entirely relative anthropocentric value. Consider what B. Mandelbrot describes, after L.-F. Richardson, regarding the measurement of a coast, the coast of Brittany: 'If the coast were straight the problem would have been resolved, but since this wild coast is extremely curvy, we can imagine a person walking its length, striving to travel the least distance possible and measuring the distance he covers; then we begin again in rendering the maximum distance on the side of the smaller and smaller. At a certain point we must, in seeking exactness, imagine a mouse in our place, then a fly, and so on. The closer we are able to come to the coast, the greater the distance covered, *the final length would be so great that we can for all intents and purposes consider it infinite.* Anthropocentrism intervenes therefore in one way or another and the apparently inoffensive concept of *geographic length* proves to be not entirely "objective" since the observer inevitably must intervene in its definition.'[11]

To set dimensions is thus to dephase, to dephase with respect to the observer, this geometry, this 'voyeur-surveyor' who produces the measure at the same time as he causes its displacement. But this productive movement of magnitude and length can be accelerated by the use (assault) of whatever 'means of movement'. This is what is omitted in the study of the variation of approximated length of the coast of Brittany, and what is also concealed in the statement: '*If the coast were straight the problem would be resolved*', the temporal aspect of mensurations. The figures of man, the mouse, or the fly who survey the Brittany coast are only (anthropomorophic and zoomorphic) aspects of a specific speed of displacement: that of a living body that moves in space and time. Let us imagine for a moment a vector of rapid movement to accelerate each of these subjects, and everything is metamorphosed yet again: *from one side, the length tends toward infinity*, this is the morphological aspect of the problem, *from the other side and simultaneously, the distance tends toward zero* because of the very acceleration of measurement, and this no matter what the 'nature' of the surveyor, since this nature is inseparable from the speed of its movement.

Since the beginning of the century, we have witnessed the progressive disappearance of 'kilometric distance', and more recently we have witnessed, with the rise of supersonics, the allegedly progressive disappearance of 'distance-time'. The measure of the world is henceforth a 'vector of release of movement', the means of locomotion that desynchronizes the time and space of the trip, just as yesterday geometry or the surveyor had themselves *dephased* its geomorphological reality in attempting to *set its dimensions*, thus subjecting the earth to the systems of displacement of a geodesic representation.

Currently, the systems and instruments of measure are less *chronographic* than *dromographic*; it is no longer the time of the passage that serves as the standard in a space passed through, but rather speed[12] has become the privileged measure of both time and space. In the supersonic vehicle, the speedometer no longer counts *kilometres*, it only measures the intensity of the acceleration, a '*machometre*' which is nothing other than the relationship of the speed of a moving object to that of sound in the atmosphere in which it is moving.... But this 'unit of measure' is not a true *measure of speed*, for the speed of sound is proportional to the square root of the absolute temperature! The only unit of measure is therefore absolute speed, produced by the absolute temperature: *the speed of light*.

A latter day solar cult, the ray of sun becomes the measure of all reality, *the light of speed illuminates the planet at the same time that it provides for representation,* but a representation where the violence of its fusion and the power of its emission have replaced the course of the sun from rising to setting.

In fact, night and day no longer organize life, in this 'false- (dromo-scopic) day' where sunrise is equivalent to sunset, speed gives rise to life and death, indifferently. As Léo Szilard suggested bitterly on the subject of the nuclear threat, '*The earth is perhaps not the most important planet in the solar system …*'.

Fourth Part

The Negative Horizon

What we see arises from what is not apparent.
(Paul de Tarse)

An inverse firmament, the desert is the sky of visible speed. Contrary to their precursors who ardently wished to soar to high altitude, those seeking to break records today attempt to attain the greatest acceleration on the surface of the earth. The horizon once again defines the ideal of conquest, *the desert is desire, desire for a body of absolute speed.*

A surface of performance, the void is no longer an absence, but the presence of an extreme rite of passage, giving rise to the search for extreme sites [*sites insolites*] possessing properties conducive to the demands of extreme speed: desert plateaus, salt lakes, ice surfaces, endless beaches, *sensitive panes for the recording of record speeds*, like the impressive Bonneville desert, west of Salt Lake City, fossilized site of an evaporated inland sea, *a layer of salt and sand for speed trials* where for nearly half a century short-lived records of horizontal acceleration succeeded one another.

In fact, *deserts are the projection screen of the light of speed*, and the progressive desertification of various surfaces (territories, bodies, objects), the consequence of an increasing illumination.

The pedological horizons hold perspectives unheard of until now, speed becomes a form of advance Aeolian erosion, *salt of the terra firma, the desert increases with the onrushing dromological rhythms.*

A sublimation of the hunt, the course imposes a cleared surface; a sublimation of war, the speed record demands a pure surface. Devoid of accidents, of relief, *the ground becomes the mirror of acceleration.*[1] To the abrupt telescoping of the trajectory is added the reflection of the ground: 'an effect of the ground', inseparable from the aerostatic

levelling of the terrain, automobile speed still depends upon the aerodynamics of the machine, the desert increases in depth. After having
caused the linear and planar rectification of routes, acceleration imposes
the perfect interface. Early on Caesar would assert that 'the greatest
glory of a state is to make its frontiers a vast desert'. A smooth levelled
surface – is the desert not the first transfiguration of the states of
matter? – such as Herschell indicated in his time: *an object illuminated
in the light of the sun on the horizon acts like a mirror....* The illumination of the horizon serves to transform non-polished surfaces into
reflective surfaces, as we see verified with dromoscopic illumination: *the
accelerated perspective acts like a luminous source*, the anamorphosis of
the trajectory produces an effect of accentuated depth, followed by an
optical rectification similar to that of light on the horizon. The vehicle
transfers its vectorial properties to the objects that run along its route,
and we may assert, therefore, the same reversal as that which occurs in
the darkroom or the mirror: on the one hand, the reflected objects seem
to recede even though they are fixed and the automobile is advancing;
while, on the other hand, the closest surfaces have what seems to be a
rapid movement even though more distant surfaces seem immobile....
In reality, most images, whether mobile or immobile, arise from
the capture of the visible domain by *a process that puts into play the
interaction of light with the surfaces of reflection or of recording* (natural
elements of reflection, photosensitive emulsions ...) and according to
the same principle as the inversion of the image. The perception of
relief and the estimation of distances (space and time) being inseparable
from the stereoscopic acuity, binocular visionaries, we only perceive
the third dimension when one of our eyes receives an *image temporized*
through its relationship to another (this is what is called the 'Pultrich
effect'). For the object in accelerated movement, this temporization is
further reinforced by the polarizing effect of the windows of the vehicle,
in other words *by the artifice of the horizontal illumination of speed inter-
fering with the nearby or distant surfaces of the environment.*

A forced cinematic reference, the line of the horizon is the necessary
condition of acceleration. *Visible on the level of the surface, speed appears
thus like an optical phenomenon of reflection of the ground.* A surface effect
in constant (advancing) 'telescopic' and (accelerated) 'dromoscopic'
transformation, acceleration is in fact only a form of hallucination.

A perversion of vision, a cupidity of the eyes, he who gets behind the wheel of a racing car saddles a new 'mount' and completes his natural stereoscopic vision with a new type of prosthesis of vision capable of providing him with the *mobile illusion of a kinetic transformation of his field of vision*, the optical illusion being perhaps here only that of an alleged 'relief' of perspectival space.

The (aerostatic) aeolian erosion of the terrain, caused by the meteorological wind and (aerodynamic) aeolian erosion of the relative wind of the machine, results in *the abolition of the relief of distances* (the mobile illusion); the progressive effacing of the interval of time of the route is finally similar to the wearing away of the rough edges of the object through research into aerodynamic forms. The accelerated perspective of the course (the optical illusion) being only a cinematic representation of the morphological mutation of surfaces (of the machine just as of the terrain), *would not aerodynamics be a particularly misunderstood figure of anamorphosis?* A geomorphological mutation of the terrain, aridity of a soil calcined by the salinity and speed of the wind; a technological transformation of the profiles of the machine to improve the coefficient of penetration through air: *research into limit-speed passes first through a series of telluric and technical deformations affecting both the means of transport and its support, in order to produce the fleeting hallucination of a champion....* As one of them explained: 'To roll in complete freedom and depth on a beach is far more exciting than passing through a delimited course'. *Exiting the frame* of the two dimensions of the painting, as was already explored by the *trompe-l'oeil* painters of false perspective, exiting the three dimensions of the stage of the speedway, this is the constant objective of those attempting to break the record for absolute speed. Contrary to vertical speed that requires a *lightening* of the components of the aerial vehicle, horizontal speed imposes an extreme *lengthening* of the terrestrial vehicular system (road and car), as well as a considerable increase in the weight of the machine in order to assure the hold on the road.[2] *In order to reduce the trail of the aerodynamic flow and thus to shorten the time of the trajectory, speed lengthens the object*: the rectilinear line of the road and the streamlined fuselage of the car, the route and the machine are constantly elongated, *space is distended to the rhythm of the retention of the time of the trip*. It took a distance of about three metres for the first automobile to exceed 100 km/h (Jenatzy's 'Jamais Content') and nearly eleven metres for the first vehicle to attain a surface speed exceeding the sound barrier (Stan Barrett's 'Budweiser Rocket'). But this extension of the line, *this distortion of the outline of the machine, doubles that of the terrain*: 3 or 4 kilometres for the avenue in the park in Achères, site of Jenatzy's record in 1899; from 20 to 60 for Pendine Sand and Daytona Beach, sites of the Seagrave and Campbell trials during the thirties and forties; and finally, more than 150 km for the Utah salt flats, site of J. Cobb's, C. Bredlove's, and A. Arfons' records. *To shorten the distance of time and reduce the relief of the trajectory, the false perspective of speed lengthens the spatial distance of the object* (machine, terrain), an aerostatic erosion either natural or reinforced by the *surface* of the trials, an aerodynamic erosion of the accelerated perspective of the trajectory; with this *generalized anamorphosis* we are in the presence of a transmutation of types arising from the kinetic and cinematic energy of technology.

'*I see nothing but becoming*', said Nietzsche.... In this optic, we could add, since *space is that which prevents everything from being in the same place*, the conquest of speed is the pursuit of this 'parking of deterrence', of this last 'place' where objects and their features would no longer be solely *isomorphs* but *holomorphs*, that is, interchangeable at will, rendered *homogenous* and *dromogenous* by the artifice of the instantaneity of ubiquity.

An apocalyptic land, surface of reflection, *the desert receives the image*, the optical illusion caused by the overheated atmospheric strata, *the image of the mirage*.

Before Herschell's discoveries (1809), well before the Bitumen Judaicum of Niepce's photosensitive plates (1816) or the silver salt of photographic film, *the sands of the desert were the materials of a perfect holographic revelation*.

In fact, the hologram is not the sophistication of a false perspective, the realization of a perfect image, but the opposite: *the exhaustion of relief, the extermination of all perspective*.

Henceforth, what is 'false' is no longer anamorphosis but the depth, the length, the distances of time and space perspective. *The attainment of the horizontal 'escape velocity'* [«*vitesse de libération*»] *liberates us from the alleged reality of the third dimension*. In allowing us to escape the time span of the trajectory, *speed actually liberates from the 'volume' of the object, from places [des lieux] as from the milieu.*

No more delay! No more relief! There is no longer any significant difference between the real and the effect of the real.

'We only go fast on the level of the earth, speed is the modern form of gravity.' This statement from Paul Morand dates from a period when upward speeds were low, and escape from the earth's attraction was difficult for the pioneers of rocket engines to imagine. Today speed has totally rid us of gravity and, therefore, from weight; in other words, it has done away with inaccessible heights. Today, with the attainment of escape velocity at ground level, what is at stake *is the abolition of depth, the end of expanses of time.* Following the vertical escape that metamorphosed altitude into cosmic distances, horizontal escape aims at transmuting the greatest 'lengths' of planetary space into a pole of inertia. *Pure speed becomes both height and length, the alpha and omega of absolute power.*

'Just as the rays of the sun unite at the focal point of the concave mirror in a perfect image and produce there the maximum incandescence, the energies and the contingencies of war unite in the principal battle to produce there a supreme and concentrated effect' (Clausewitz). This exterminating concentration is henceforth completely assured by technology. The metaphor has become reality: both a means of instantaneous destruction and a means of sophisticated projection, *the speed of physical light becomes the absolute weapon and the light of speed produces the perfect image, the hologram of pure power.*

If the course was once a sublimated form of the hunt and its acceleration – a sublimation of war (Blitzkrieg), maximum incandescence – *pure speed is now the supreme and concentrated effect of a war beyond battles, of a pure war requiring the focal point, the pure surface of the desert.*

No more delay! This apocalyptic injunction also signifies the suppression of any excrescences capable of giving rise to any turbulence. From the most minute roughness of the ground up to the level of the greatest territorial proportions, surfaces become screens, mirrors of the azimuthal projection of distances, the holographic representation of surfaces of the old geography.

Since the desert expands with the rhythm of speed, the question is no longer one of knowing whether the cinema can do without a place (projection room or television), but rather whether places can still do without the cinema of the horizontal illumination of speed.

Adverse surfaces, the mirror of conquerors, the desertified expanses have attracted generations of prospectors, those who seek remnants, buried treasures; the last of the genre, the racing seekers of the vertiginous, of ultimate speed. This is how Art Arfons, the old world-record holder, put it: '*We conquered the vast interplanetary spaces, but we know so little about the means of moving ourselves over our mother the earth*'.

Compared with the antipodes of the spectacular character of spatial conquest, this re-entry into the atmosphere seems paradoxical. After the unbridled pursuit of vertical speed, this sudden revival in research into the greatest horizontal speed seems enigmatic: *recourse to the desert, cult of the mother surface?* ... We might have been surprised in the thirties to see a pilot of the Royal Flying Corps, Malcolm Campbell, abandon the aerial adventure to enrol in a course of land records and to use aviation only to fly over the European and African continents in search of *dromogenous zones* conducive to speed, desert plateaus, mineral cemeteries, where speed trials would no longer be dependent upon wind and tides, like those previously carried out on the hardened sands of Pendine or Ninety Mile Beach ... in the same way we might today wonder at the renewed attraction of *negative horizon.*

After the countdown of the launch of vertical rockets, it is now that of horizontal rockets capable of breaking the sound barrier on the surface, like Stan Barrett's Budweiser Rocket, the first vehicle to have exceeded MACH I, *with the assistance of a Sidewinder missile, provided by the American military,* on Edwards Air Force Base in December 1979. Curiously, it is this same base in California that Charles Yeager flew over on 14 October 1947, when he first broke the sound barrier on board the BELL.X.I.

This experimental fighter, equipped with a Reaction Motor with four rockets, had a wingspan of 8.54 metres, but its overall length was not much less than that of the Budweiser Rocket at 10.85 m, as opposed to 11.57 m for Stan Barrett's vehicle.

This similarity of performance between the terrestrial and aerial machines 32 years apart is perplexing. The strategic objective of interceptor aviation is to pass as quickly as possible through atmospheric space. It is easy to understand the goal of the BELL.X.I, even though the goal of 'missiles of the road' remains strangely unreal.

Today, the protagonists of supersonic performance report that '*the most difficult thing is quite simply to find a suitable stretch of land*'. Since the first trial in 1979, where the vehicle attained 1,027 km/h on the Utah salt flats, the operation 'Speed of Sound' had to be slowed and then postponed *for want of a good site*.

As it turns out, the deterioration of the surface, the use of this layer of salt that is worn away year by year, the very limits of the terrain and climatic vicissitudes of the area make attempts at speeds beyond 1,000 km/h more and more difficult.

The aeolian erosion combined with that of the relative wind of the vehicles that have been running on the Bonneville Speedway for nearly half a century are ruining the salt flats. After every running of the course, the tyres need to be changed and often even the aerodynamics need to be changed; eventually it will be necessary to *change the location, to change the terrain....*

For supersonic trials, Hal Needham's team had explored Iran, where, near the town of Quom, there is a dried-up lake bed with a good surface, ideal as seen from the sky, but lacking a practical means of access for heavy equipment. They also explored the Andes (with fond memories of l'Aeropostale[3]), however, without success ... *thus they were led to seek the assistance of the army and chose the old lake of Muroc, part of the military base of the US Air Force in southern California.*

Since weather plays a considerable role, to break the sound barrier on ground level it is necessary that *the wind, the altitude, and the ambient temperature* be taken into consideration, *in other words, that the atmospheric pressure of the terrain be taken into consideration, without which the 'atmospheric pressure' of the machine cannot be correctly calculated....* On the course at Muroc, at the end of 1979, the sound barrier ranged from 1,171 km/h at −9°C, to 1,192 km/h at 0°, and climbing to 1,214 km/h at +10°. As nights in the Mojave Desert were particularly cold, they would tow the Budweiser Rocket to the departure zone at four in the morning.

With this type of vehicle, all systems are controlled externally by a computer in a mobile trailer. In the event that the pilot was unable to cut the engine, the computer would release the first braking parachute at 1,000 km/h and the second at about 480 km/h, while the hydraulic brakes could not be used until 240 km/h. A deep sea diver of the desert, possessing a totally autonomous air supply, the pilot is linked to the control technicians by an onboard radio system.

On 15 December 1979, at 7.25 a.m. and at −7°C, Bill Frederick gave the order for ignition. *The time to launch the cameras and the vehicle had already filed past the electronic eyes of the timer situated four kilometres from the starting point.* The negative horizon exposed, 'Sliding home' became reality.[4] Stan Barrett had indeed attained the speed of sound. But the official confirmation would come from the sidereal sky, where three of twenty fixed position military satellites over the West Coast recorded to the nearest decimal a speed of 1,190.300 km/h. The sound barrier at this place, time, and temperature was 1,117.800 km/h; *operation 'Speed of Sound' (SOS) ended in complete success.* As its promoters would say a bit later: 'We proved that it was possible to attain, without excessive risk, a supersonic speed; this was enough, the record and its ritual were no longer of interest to us'.

We might justifiably be surprised at the choice of a speedway to avoid taking flight, or at the release of parachutes, or even, as the last element in the stage, at the orbital control of a terrestrial performance by observation satellites.... Indeed, the pursuit of a greater velocity has always proved to be the pursuit of a greater fusion/confusion of elements and types. Later, Stan Barrett announced that his next attempt would be to attain *1,000 miles per hour* in the vicinity [*banlieue*] of Los Angeles ... the site of exiles [*lieu des bannis*] thus becomes again the glacis, the trial run for the excess of speed. But let us return to the starting point, in 1889, to the central route of the park in Achères, where, for the first time, a motorized wheel turned at 600 revolutions/minute in contact with the ground, and what a ground! It was in the middle of a field of manure in a Parisian suburb where Camille Jenatzy had just won his 'speed duel' with the baron of Chasseloup-Laubat, in surpassing the 100 km/h mark on board an electric vehicle, the 'Jamais contente'.

During this period, *the trials all took place in one direction on open roads,* the length of the Nieuport canal in Ostende, Belgium, on the straight line of the Ablis, on the first *official route* recognized in 1902 by the 'Automobile Club de France', in Dourdan, on the national highway.

The Americans did not at that time have a network of major roads; Henry Ford found himself forced to use the *racetrack* for horse racing in Grosse Point, Detroit for his trials, before breaking the record, in 1904, with a speed of 147 km/h on the ice of Lake Saint-Clair, *his workers having covered the mirror-course of Anchor Bay beforehand with cinders....*

On the beach of Ormond at Daytona, in 1906, Fred Marriot surpassed the mark of 205 km/h with a steam-powered vehicle, the 'Stanley Rocket'. In 1907, the test track became an instrument: the speedway in Brockland in Great Britain, first of its kind, and in 1909, in Indianapolis, a suburb with no city, a closed circuit, the motorway, looped around the horizon. In 1910, the Association Internationale des Automobiles-Clubs Reconnus locked up the round-trip tests, stipulating that: 'Only the tests that ran in two opposed directions, launched over the same distance calibrated both in miles and kilometres, would be recognized'.

Later, the *autoroute* would repeat this feedback, and the German pilot Bernd Rosemeyer would kill himself in undertaking a trial on the Frankfurt-Darmstadt section of one of the first 'Reichautobahnen'.

This sudden negation of the objective horizon is also the negation of any sort of arrival at the destination. The quest for pure speed becomes the negation of the trajectory; the functioning of timing devices and the silent functioning of photoelectric cells only serve to record one type of project, that of an instantaneous round trip. Symptomatically, as with capital executions, the coolness of the night favours acceleration, attempts at speed records always take place at dawn; the rising of the sun serves as a guiding light for the dawning of the day of the light of speed. In 1924, on National Highway 20 near Arpajon between midnight and six in the morning, the police stopped all traffic. Trapped, the drivers were transformed into spectators of the Eldridge trial: 234 km/h, *the last record on an open route.*

A bit later, not far from there, in Linas Monthléry, following Great Britain and the United States, France finally built its first permanent speedway: *Autopolis,* a motor city, complex of the eternal return that would initially reunite within the enclosure of the speed circuit all the necessary equipment for research and for auto sport, driving schools, laboratories, test tracks, hotels, museums, etc. The architecture of speed would seem to have a beautiful future; after the autostradas, didn't the Italians build a factory for Fiat under a test track in Turin that served as a rooftop terrace?

In 1928, on the line of sight of Ormond at Daytona Beach, Major Seagrave launched a revealing procedure in installing on the hood of his 'Golden Arrow' a double telescopic sight on the axis of his windscreen with an aim like a shotgun: 'After having installed at the starting line a red light and, 20km further at the finish line, a second light source, he climbed into his machine and then lined up in his direct line of sight the light indicating the start. Well before having crossed the finishing tape, he placed the beam of the distant light in his telescopic sight.'[5]

We must compare this experience with that of the physiologist E. J. Marey, who also used a hunting scope for his first chronophotographic 'shots' which allowed, let us not forget, the invention of the cinematogaphic recording chamber. With Major Seagrave's *teleobjective vehicle*, it was no longer a question of recording the sequence of images of a gull's flight, it was rather a question of becoming *a ray of sun on a beach*.

Contrary to Marey, who wished to fix the rapid sequence of the beating of wings, Seagrave sought to link together as quickly as possible the reference points of his course. On his line of sight installed on the hood like a gun barrel, the fury of the mobile power caused the optical illusion of telescoping: *where the chronophotographic gun recorded the ballistics of the bird, the telescopic lens recorded the trajectory of beacons.* The automobile acts like a measuring instrument, the racer [*coureur*] becomes a *cursor* [*curseur*]. While a concurrence is suddenly established between the progressive illumination of the morning horizon and the accelerated perspective, the light of the finish rises to the zenith for the adept of limit-speed; *the course becomes a hunt for the sun.*

After having successively sacrificed space to time, and then the distance of time to distance-speed, the vector becomes the last dimension of a world that is now reduced to the *desert of the moment*. In August 1935, completely absorbed in piloting his plane by eye, and with no system to allow him to read the control panel during the course, Malcolm Campbell decided to mount on his 'Blue Bird' a mobile camera that could film his instruments.... Later still, in 1947, his son Donald would instal a *telemetric system* set to transmit the data from the dashboard indicators to his technicians *on the ground....*

Guided by its driver, teleguided by its controllers, the vehicle has in effect become a *moving chamber*. Closed into his pressurized cockpit, unable to look down, transfixed by the onset of the finish line, the pilot is now the plaything of a hallucination: *the sensible horizon fast shrinking away, he understands that war has come, the pure approach of the arrival of the end*. Thus, during a torrid summer in 1938, light became the enemy of the speed record.

Captain Eyston, adversary of the record holder John Cobb, had just surpassed 558 km/h at Bonneville, but the stopwatches did not respond: 'Reflected by the metallic body and by the dazzling surface of the salt lake, the brilliant light beaming down, the photoelectric cell at the finish line did not register the passing of the car ... no record, no ratification. They would thus paint the 'Thunderbolt' black so that it could interfere with the ray of the cell'.[6]

Appearing like the effect of a sequencing, *the optic of the locomotive illusion is analogous to the cinematographic optical illusion*. At the height of desertification, the fascination with the negative horizon amounts to exhausting the last resource of space: the void. *The will to power is here, therefore, the will to arbitrarily increase the density of the depth of field*, by changing the objective horizon into a 'wall' [*mur*], into a screen, for the inscription of the effects of the light of acceleration. In this architecture, the narrowing of the aim signals the completion of a site; the sound barrier [*mur du son*], 'wall' of heat, thus Sliding Home impatiently built itself up, the refuge of exile for those who covered space with their tombs [*tombes*],[7] these record-breakers [*tombeurs de record*] who, not content with the desert of the ground, secretly aspired for opacity, for the *desert of the sky*.

The speed cage is excessively reduced, the frame of the windscreen closes on the atmospheric depth. The resistance of the air to the progress of the automobile causes the hardening of the sky, *the crenel of the course becomes the rampart of the limit-speed, the wall of light*.

Massive, translucent, the desert thus gives birth to the last figure of the Bunker, a singular reversal takes place here: *the void of the ground causes the fullness of the sky*, of a sky with a polish that is reflected in the reduced silhouettes of the vehicles.

'In order to fight against the air, it is specifically necessary to be heavier than air. In aerial locomotion as elsewhere, one is only supported on what resists', declared Nadar in 1863.... But this resistance is no longer, the conquest of space has taken control over this insolent rebellion of the elements and distances of time; space has become totally *dromogenous.* Indeed, this *accelerated aerodynamic perspective,* this science of anamorphosis applied to the objects in movement, goes back to the beginning of the century. Twenty years before the first aerodynamic successes, going back to the years immediately following 1910, the conquest of the air by heavy weights was hardly enough for the engineer Henri Coanda. With the assistance of a chronophotographic camera measuring the movements of air around tapered forms, he experimented with the very first forms of aerodynamic casings and advanced a 'theory of the vacuum' according to which it would no longer be a question of seeking to conquer air resistance with the aid of a motor, but *rather to create before or above the vehicle a vacuum into which it would rush forth....* It was, therefore, no longer sufficient to fight against the air by relying upon what resists; now it is necessary to create the vacuum from the atmospheric void. The propeller motor gave way to the vacuum of a jet's turbine. The aspiration for drive ends in a suction, the wish to attain the horizon as quickly as possible corresponds with a profound inspiration.

The atmosphere is succeeded by the dromosphere, anticipating the sidereal orbit; the circuit of the racetrack and the circuit of the speedway is succeeded by the *centrifuge,* a stadium for a single man, ocular witness to the *anamorphosis of a speed body,* a peripatetic figure where the weighty mass sustains a series of grotesque deformations caused by gravity. Let's remember here Lieutenant Colonel John Stapp's face, the first to attain a surface speed of 1,016.888 km/h, on a jet sled, twenty years ago.

If the world is merely a false semblance that time sweeps aside in a single blow,[8] *speed is the air, the wind, of time – a relative wind that instantly sweeps away the desert of bodies.*

'Every surface is an *interface* between two spheres constantly governed by an activity in the form of an exchange between two substances in contact with one another.'[9]

The screen replaces the mirror. Bonneville Speedway, 10 September 1962, Glen Leasher's 'Infinity' breaks up during a live broadcast to millions of spectators; his shimmering shards reflecting through thousands of cathode ray tubes scattered across America....

Some years later, seated behind the broad pane of the windscreen, a female broadcaster embellishes her performance, killing herself at the light speed of televised images. In 1967, Donald Campbell met his death on Lake Coniston during a high speed trial on water. Fifteen years earlier, John Cobb disappeared in Scotland, at the bottom of Loch Ness, as if the absence of depth of Utah's dried-out lakes left him unsatisfied....

To appear, to disappear too fast, to project oneself too far, with too much élan, toward death; a catastrophic challenge where the one attempts to put an end to his days in abandoning himself to the performance of his prosthesis, while the public looks on anxiously hoping to witness his fate. In the past, great men went to their death facing the sea, at the bounds of the open sea, but now we plunge into the black chamber of televised mourning to make our mark, albeit a negative one that will resuscitate us in recorded images and sometimes, paradoxically, in slow motion.... Thus, throughout the sixties, the contest for the absolute record would become the object of a publicity war. The least attempt requiring an unprecedented concentration of capital, no automobile company could afford to invest hundreds of millions in a single prototype, for the purposes of a commercially useless title, *the techniques employed being more applicable to aeronautics than to the automobile.*

With the aid of large tyre companies, oil companies would thus assure the changeover. The fruit of an aberrant technological mix, these vehicles would become true *rolling laboratories.* Their pilots where no longer wealthy amateurs, professional racers, or aviators, the new champions all came from the American Hot Rod Association, in other words from a sporting school composed of three large categories of modified cars: *altered, stock,* and, especially, *dragsters,* capable of attaining the greatest speed over a 400-metre strip. Art Arfons, record holder for speed in 1965 at 875 km/h, was himself an old champion from the drag-racing world. His 'Green Monster', *equipped with a jet that came out of a surplus F104 fighter,* had the front drive shaft of an old 1937 Lincoln, the gearbox of a 1935 Packard, and an ignition system for the parachutes comprising a 12-gauge shotgun! As for his arch rival, Craig Bredlove, also a 'hot-rodder', *the turbine of his 'Spirit of America' came from a B47 bomber.*

A fusion, indeed, confusion of genres, publicity platforms piloted by showmen. *If, from the sixties on, speed always sells, we might ask ourselves what does it sell?* ... The limitation of the power of turbines and other extra rockets, caused the tyre companies to lose all interest. After the *600 revs/minute* of the Michelin tyres on Jenatzy's machine in 1899 and the *2,600 revs/minute* of Campbell's Dunlops in 1931, in 1976, the wheels that revolved in the desert between *6,000 and 7,000 revs/minute* where made of a special aluminium alloy.... After the oil companies and the natural gas company sponsored Gary Gabelich's 'Blue Flame', the last attempt at the title at 1,014 km/h, the *professional stuntmen*, Hal Needham and Stan Barrett took up the wheel of rockets sponsored by Budweiser.

Human sandwich, human projectile, finally for them *the message is the speed of release.* To the aerostatic and aerodynamic desertification of surfaces is added the desert of an economic redeployment: if it was once necessary to seek the funding of sponsors to acquire and capitalize speed records, today we see a reconversion, *the last post-industrial resource, acceleration exceeds accumulation,* indexed on the 'distance-speed' of sound and light and no longer on the old 'distances of time' of matter, *the escape velocity* [*vitesse de libération*] *becomes the equivalent of profit.*

The sound barrier [*mur du son*] is akin to the standards of gold or silver. The reference is no longer the *material standard* of the stock exchange or the standard meter in iridic platinum in the Pavillon des Mesures, but the concrete radiance of vacuum speed. A latter-day solar cult, the laser becomes the *light standard* of the world.[10]

The Driving Within

The automobile vehicle is not a 'machine' like others since it is both a stationary machine and a vehicular machine. Stationary: the motor on its test rig, or its chassis; vehicular: the drive system, wheels, or tracks, that take the vehicle over various surfaces, tracks, roads, highways; the pairing of the driving wheels and the road engages the production of the effects of speed, artifacts specific to each vehicle as it races along in contact with the ground or in its immediate proximity. The automobile machine is not, therefore, a simple means of transmission, 'a speed machine', it is more the means of transmission of speed as such. The habit of identifying speed with the movement of transportation has misled us regarding the nature of the 'movement of movement'. As a quantity, speed possesses both a magnitude, the number of kilometres covered per hour, and a direction; but it is also, therefore, a vector, and, just as the automobile industry produces the vector-vehicle, so also does it manufacture and produce vector-speed. As we remember from physics: 'Every movement can be resolved into one single proposition: force and change in velocity are vectors that have the same direction'.

Thus, the automobile vehicle (car, boat, plane) is composed of two vectors: both the mobile force-vector as well as the speed-vector of movement, which is a consequence and direct product of the first, but also of the ambient milieu and the particular element (earth, water, air) of travel.

The drive of the automobile vehicle and its acceleration (positive or negative) are thus both effects of the surface and atmospheric conditions, or, if one prefers, of the type of resistance to progress. The functional and instrumental nature of the surfaces of contact of the infrastructure (roads and highways) as well as the forms of least resistance of the vector-vehicle contribute to making the speed-vector the essential characteristic of automobile movement, or, even more precisely, one of its *dimensions*. In effect, speed only becomes one of the 'dimensions' of movement in so far as it can be conceived of as constant through the course of the time and conserved through the course of the movement. Meanwhile, this constant magnitude, secured in the past (with difficulty) by the extreme rectification of the line of the surface for wheeled vehicles and thanks to the profile of vehicles, is maintained today by the electronic artifice of the on-board computer, a true speed programmer.

After the innovation, a long time ago, of the Greek and Roman public road networks – and there is a half century of experience with the highway infrastructure also contributing to affirm this – that is, after the spatial and geographical innovation of the unidirectionality and unidimensionality of the vectorial pairing, innovation now lies in the 'management of time and movement', thanks to the electronic control of the speeds of the course.

By this means, the vehicular complex composed of the 'small dynamic vehicle' (auto, motorcycle) and the 'great static vehicle' (road, bridge, tunnel) produces negative or positive acceleration like a new dimension of the world, or rather, like a constant renewal of its dimensions. Ceaselessly reprogrammed by technological advancements in the control of vectors, this renewal is not only perceptible in the shortening of distances of time, but also in the system of appearances, in the vision of passengers. 'A speed machine' and not solely 'a transport machine', the production of the vector-vehicle gives rise to the projection of a sort of illumination, the pairing of motor-wheels engages the pairing of car-road; between the departure and arrival, the country and its landscapes unwind like a drive belt. This artifact, disregarded like an optical illusion, is nevertheless no more illusory than the shrinking of the distance of the time of the course. One might just as well consider this rapprochement in time as a mobile illusion, since the geographic distance separating the point of departure from the destination, the distance in space, does not vary any more than the landscapes move in the dromoscopic vision of passengers travelling at speed....

We are, therefore, in the presence of an unsuspected dimensional production that is identified with an integral cinematic projection. 'Automobile', the means of rapid transmission, appears therefore equally to be 'audiovisual', since its passengers are the prey of a gnosis,[11] both visual and auditory.

For them and them alone, the car plugged into the network of roads produces an illuminating energy, a visionary experience [*voyance*] distinct from that of the pedestrian. An entire projector in itself, the speed machine thus produces the emission of an indirect illumination, the diffusion of a light that, although not the speed of light, nonetheless does cause the instantaneous redefinition of the image and spatio-temporal dimensions of the territory passed through.

Similar in this way to the electronic improvement of the broad-casting of the televised image in the accelerator of the cathode tube, the motorist's vision is not an incidental aspect of the subliminal comfort of travel, but one of its principle axes, which the more or less panoramic opening of the windshield and the side windows only serves to enhance.

'Voyeurs-voyagers', the pilot and his passengers find themselves in a spectacular situation that arises from the synoptic character of their movement. *Motor-handicapped*, slaves to [*asservis à*[12]] a locomotive prosthesis, they are still just like the *voyeur-handicapped* subjected to the fascination of a representation of the world where the means of automobile transmission [*communication automobile*] participates (directly or indirectly) in the ensemble of different 'means of trans-mission', and not solely as a means of transportation. In fact, *the future of the automobile enterprise passes through the progress of the enterprise of appearances*, that is to say, through the linking and fusion of audiovisual and automobile media, forming thus an interconnection technologic-ally founded on the pre-eminence of *information* over *transportation*.

A style of experimentation or style of execution, scientific knowledge and technology are bound up with the political and cultural pressure of different epochs of history.[13] In fact, what one calls 'style' is probably only the (scientific) *genre* or (technological) *mode*[14] of a period of knowledge....

Electronic technology is not exempt, we need only decipher its strategic origins.

I

In the past, with the power of writing and in light of the little available data, the accent was placed on the transport of information: the metabolic transport (runner, horse, pigeon ...) or technological transport (signals, chariots, ships ...). The power of the pontiff was at first identified with *movement-power* (promotion [*promouvoir*]). His palace thus served as a sort of 'inertial guidance centre' of the information of the country. Political and police power, in that it was based on *knowledge-power*, therefore arose directly from the power of withholding information by a privileged caste of messengers (charioteer, enfeoffed runner, cavalier...) capable of getting information from the furthest lands – 'general information' [*renseignements généraux*[15]] necessary for the withholding of taxes and therefore, indirectly, for the strategic and economic control of the country.

As the value of a message was identified with the speed of its delivery, we may easily imagine the importance of this 'courier service' (this Roman *cursus publicus* whose principal would take on the imperial purple).

Let us recall the feudal privilege of the nobility and the wealthy to posses a dovecote, the fastest courier system. After the static system of optical signals of antiquity and the progress of the telegraph, the advent of the transportation revolution is sudden. The train follows upon the mail coach. Indeed, this revolution in the means of movement is only the logistical outcome of the effort of several millennia, efforts that consisted in placing the principle accent on maximum load and transport capacities (by river, sea, or land) to establish the economic and strategic power of various dominant powers. At this stage, information is only of quite secondary benefit, given the repercussions of the technological evolution of the means of transport (galleys, then sailboats, chariots, and horse relays, stage-coaches and postal relays, telegraphic and rail systems ...). It is necessary, meanwhile, to consider that during this epoch in history, public power was built upon the physical force of the infantry as much as on the invasion force of the cavalry; despite the artillery, no advanced technology totally supplanted this metabolic force of the mobilized corps on the ground (from Caesar to Napoleon, the measure of speed was always that of the relay horse).

A true cultural revolution of the modern West, the transportation revolution actually introduced the 'information revolution'. With the proliferation of the means of 'communication'[16] (train, automobile, plane, radio, telephone, television) made possible by the industrial revolution, the power of information increased with the same rhythm as the information of power. Now we are in the era of 'press agencies' but also of the scientific and international development of the police, that is, of 'intelligence services' (both civil and military).

Today's computers and data communications systems only serve to complete a cycle sketched out a century ago with the telegraph and the railway system.

We are thus witness to a phenomenon of 'disanimalization' followed by a phenomenon of 'dematerialization': not only the animal (the pack animal, the draught animal, the race animal) disappears to the advantage of the machine, but the technological vehicle of transmission tends to disappear in its turn with the rising importance of the message transmitted, leading ultimately to the instantaneity of radio and radar signals.... By-product of the steam engine and in spite of the electric motor, the automobile will have to wait for half of the twentieth century to participate in the 'information revolution' as radios and televisions make their way into the cabin along with the tentative introduction of TV. Since its mechanical and thermodynamic (Cugnot) origins, and in view of the very lively concurrence of the railway and commercial aviation, it must be stated that with the automobile, the principle of the autonomy of transportation continued to mask that of the information of transportation.

With electronics, we enter the period that is coming to completion today.

II

With the increasing inflation of the new means of remote communication and transmission, we witness a spectacular reversal: automobile information comes to dominate the attraction of autonomous transportation, without actually doing away with it. Let me be clear, however, that it is a matter here of a mode of information specific to the indicated means of transportation that knew neither how to repeat nor totally reproduce that of other mass media. Indeed, there are two sorts of 'means of mass communication': audiovisual (press, radio, TV, computer, telephone ...) and automobile (the means of terrestrial, air, and maritime transportation and movement ...)

Each of these conveys [*véhicule*] what amounts to a specific informational content, a type of information linked to its own nature. Vector of transmission or vehicle of transportation, both possess the property of modifying the intrinsic content of the 'messages': transmitted messages (radio, TV, telephone ...) or the transmission of the trip (train, car, plane ...).

The course (travelling) is a discourse (message), since it is always a question, in both cases, of conveying sense [*sens*], in the one direction [*sens*][17] (going) as in the other (returning).

Discourse-course, feedback of the trajectory, the history of audiovisual and automobile mediation brings us back to the problematic of direct vs. indirect information.

All technological innovation involving vectors or vehicles must, therefore, return to this 'informational logic', in other words, to the logic of sense (object/subject [*objet/sujet*]) just as to the logistics of sense (trajectory [*trajet*]) – as is especially true in the sphere of electronics.

Let us not forget that each thing (object/subject) is simultaneously space, time, matter, a formation of sense and information from the milieu, and, more precisely, in connection with time, essential in the example of the round-trip (automobile) or of feedback (audiovisual), relativity teaches us that time is contracted in matter and that a violent movement increases matter's density while expanding time.

Even if this physical property is only spectacularly verified in the extreme violence of the high velocities attained by aerial and space vehicles, it is not, however, useless to note that the message (informational content) is not exactly the massage (vehicle) but the vector, that is to say, the movement of movement, the speed of the means of transmission [*communication*].

Finally, whether we consider the acceleration of the telematic transmission of data (millisecond, bit-second) or of the supersonic transport of people (km/h or mach) matters little, since, as we have seen earlier, speed is the message, the last message of movement; it makes sense to analyse the cinematic nature of transmitted information, and this no matter what sort of vehicular performance (subsonic or supersonic) of machines or instruments of transmission (audiovisual or automobile) may be involved.

Even if the most spectacular effects of the real are now reserved for sophisticated instruments, it continues to be the case nonetheless that each vehicle possesses the vectorial property to transmute through its speed the objective reality of the course as much as the informational content, even the meaning of discourse.

III

Direct information is the immediate result of sense, vision, hearing, olfaction, and touch as much as *muscular sense*, that is, capacities for *motility* in place and *mobility* in the space of 'one's own body', which is, let us not forget, our first means of locomotion.

Let us also note that the physiological properties and the psychological faculties of our five senses result from organs of vision, hearing, olfaction, or taste, but also, and above all, from the movement of displacement or change of position of the body in space-time. Peripatetic pedagogy of the itineraries and course of the body, psycho- and sensorio-motor exercises, an initiatory and formative 'voyage', corporeal displacement is the urgent imperative of the acquisition of information. The gesturality of the 'sport of (physical) transport' is the very condition of the formation of judgement, before, well before, linguistic or scriptural mediations (consider the function of the preverbal communication of mime and dance). Modes of indirect (or mediated) information apart from language and writing, the well-known bases of all advanced social communication; it would seem it is the media of literature and the press (written or broadcast) as much as that of the iconic medium of, first, the fixed image (graphic, pictorial, geometric ...) and, then, the animated image, the cinematic effect that reproduces indirectly, that is, mechanically, electrically, or electronically, 'the apparent reality [«*l'effet de réel*»]' of displacement, in other words, the direct information of the 'voyage'. In the original cinematographic example, the 'picture' and 'sound engineers' act, in effect, as the assistant to the spectator, the cameraman is the voyeur-voyager, the forwards agent [*corps expéditionnaire*[18]] of the sedentary-voyeur [*voyeur-sédentaire*] in the cinema. To reiterate, the fundamentally cinematic character of the data of judgement is at the centre of the information problematic: in the case of immediate information, it is a question solely of the locomotive organs of the subject, while in the case of mediated information, the motor organs (electric, electronic) of the object come into play.

Natural or artificial, locomotion introduces the notion of the vector of the sequencing [*défilement*] of the image, images of the landscapes passed through or cinematographic images of the film viewed on the screen, where both the frame of the 'tracking shot' and the framing of the 'point of view' of the spectator or telespectator are similar in every way to that of the windshield of the automobile.

In fact, speed is the common denominator of direct and indirect information.

In the case of 'metabolic (or animal) locomotion' it is the vitality of the subject of movement that allows the subject to be effectively informed (being alive [*être vivant*] is being lively [*être vif*], in other words: being-speed [*être-vitesse*]). In the example of 'technological locomotion', it is the speed of the mobile object that transmits the informational content, the meaning of the unfolding [*défilement*] of the sequences, that is, the semantic structuring [*enchaînement sémantique*] of sense.

Thus, metabolic speed and technological speed constitute the vectors of the 'message'; information proving to be the final (terminal) product of a particular sort of illumination of the real (speed of light and light of speed) as well as of an intensive illumination, the increase in the speed of displacement equivalent to the darkening of sense. Thus, just as, on the one hand 'excess light' dazzles, and, on the other hand, the superimposition of increasing luminous intensities results in darkness, 'excess speed' corresponds to a progressive loss of informational content, of its value. If yesterday, as we have seen, the value of the transmitted message depended upon the speed of its delivery, today cumulative instantaneity tends to separate the message from its value or at least, to accelerate its obsolescence. That which is easily verified with information from the stock market or with that of military espionage is also verified, unfortunately, on the level of the informational content of countries and landscapes passed through, with its corresponding despondency and stress.

With the going just as with the return, the benefit of time saved must be measured against the loss of value of the space passed through. The rapidity of automobile trajectories only increases at the cost of the meaning of places, that is, at the cost of the direct information of those travelling through; the automotive vehicle behaves like any other 'audiovisual media' in transmitting an informational content relativized by speed itself. With its demand for the disengagement of the depth of its field and of its immediate surroundings, the 'media automobile' contributes as well to accelerate the impoverishment of the milieu (tracks, roads, highways, and specialized racing circuits).

The telling poverty of discourse [*discours*] illustrates the unidirectional uniformity of the course [*parcours*] (the infrastructure of trajectories), and thus it is not difficult to conclude from this that the acceleration constant is equivalent to the fusion of the means of communication, to the mixing of the audiovisual and automobile, that is, to the spontaneous generation of a new machine, or rather, of an entirely new vehicle.

IV

From travel to transfer, from transportation to transmission, we have thus, recently, with the advent of electronics, witnessed an undifferentiated mixing of genres, quite different from what we once saw with a simple association of elements. Applied to the functioning of the propulsion of the vehicle just as to the transmitter, electronics introduces a definite technological mutation. If there is a radical difference between the pigeon and writing, and if there remains a certain distinction between the crystal radio set and the automobile, this difference is in the process of disappearing altogether. The best example of this mixing of transmission/propulsion is without doubt the on-board simulation used in American military aviation, capable of simulating not only simple movements for landings, take-offs, or various emergency scenarios (as with commercial or private simulators), but also far more complex scenarios, like those associated with fighter planes, for example.

We should note that what were previously ground-training simulators are now on board: the C5 Galaxy thus possesses two coupled flight decks, the traditional flight deck in the aerial space which guides the trajectory of the jet, and the flight deck which governs the flight systems. This rather specialized 'co-pilot' no longer observes the sky, relying instead solely upon monitors, screens that provide continuous indications of the effects of the flight on the airfoil, any technical deformations or perturbations affecting the airframe, circuits, or the function of its engines.

In the absence of any actual problems, this 'test pilot' simulates accidents and malfunctions; in order to test response, he pushes the system – including the other pilots – to the limit of its technological range.

In the past, the pilot alone managed these controls, monitoring indicators and warning lights on his control panel. Subsequently, the gigantism and increasing complexity of the mechanisms brought about a transfer of responsibilities from the pilot to the simulator (whether this would be inertial guidance or a human expert matters little in the end, since the outcome is identical). The Galaxy is both 'guided' by its in-flight pilots and 'teleguided' by its in-flight simulator, where the latter takes over more and more control (see on this subject the first flight of the Rockwell HIMAT in July 1979). Thus we see it verified again that indirect information is supplanting direct information in all domains. This is, moreover, confirmed in actual practice, as the hours in the simulator are tallied along with actual flight time....

Beyond the literal 'policing' dimension of the piloting of the vehicle, that is, the control of its flight, the purely 'ludic' dimension of the electronic game finds here its first official validation. Economic factors come to support this analysis: on the one hand the cost of the vehicles and of the fuel fully justifies the validation of the simulator hours as equivalent to actual hours in flight, on the other, and more importantly, we now witness the dissociation of the fares and the distance effectively traversed (consider here the recent deregulations: yesterday it was telecommunications, today international aviation ...). As the new economist Gary Becker explains: 'The only thing that changes in the end is the price of time'.

Space is being continuously devalued, we state one last time that the message is no longer the movement of the vehicle but indeed, as indicated above, the movement of movement, in other words, the speed-vector.

Thus we come to better understand the fusion of various means of communication and telecommunication, the progressive erosion of differentiation between the remote transfer and transportation: the measure of the value of both the message and travel no longer depends upon the technical specificity of the audiovisual or automobile machine; it is instead the celerity and intensity of the transit (see on this the subject of transmission networks, the notion of the 'packet switching' and 'access protocols'), the quite recent fusion/confusion of computers and telematics that allows us to take the theoretical and practical measure of these issues.

V

Since the 'message' is no longer the autonomous movement of a vehicle, but rather the movement of movement, that is, the vector, it matters little what is moved (an object) or transmitted (data, or images); all that matters now is the vectorial power of the transfer. Electronics is defined today as being the most powerful means of putting vector-speed into play.

Let us consider now the sophistication of modern fighter planes: enslaved to[19] the machine, incarcerated in the closed circuits of the electronics, the combat pilot is motor-disabled. When he takes hold of the stick, the sensors measure his movements and transform them into signals; this original signal is sent to a calculator which receives information arising both from the gyrometers and the accelerometers. The computer of the inertial guidance system directs the combining of the different signals and then processes an outgoing signal wherein the future movement of the vehicle corresponds to the pilot's intended control law.

Since the servo-commands are analogous, these automatically controlled laws give the pilot the feeling that the plane which is actually aerodynamically unstable in its centring is stable, homogenous, and easy to manoeuvre. The strategic necessities continuously require increased mobile performance of the system, the distortion between reality and fiction is thus continuously increasing, resulting in the definitive abandonment of mechanical systems of transmission and the increase of electronic relays.

A means of remote penetration, the means of autonomous transport becomes thus a transmutation of types. This is, moreover, confirmed by the research on telepiloted drones (RPV: Remotely Piloted Vehicles) and above all on the future of highly manoeuvrable aircraft technology [HIMAT], where the control of lift must be entirely, or almost entirely, governed electronically, the planes of the airfoil losing their ability to support and provide lift in order to serve in the directivity of the flight trajectory (this technology having been drafted by variable geometry); the plane is fundamentally unstable, flying at great speed, constantly out of sync (in altitude and direction) and thus constantly needing to be re-equilibrated.

Even if this state-of-the-art technology is still experimental, it does nonetheless indicate the future of vehicular electronics. With the HIMAT, electronics supports both the vehicle and the power of its propulsion. If the combat plane of the future (ACF) is supported in space by the speed of ejection from its nozzle, it is also supported, no longer by the fixed planes of the airfoil, but by an extremely complex central guidance system that maintains the equilibrium in flight through a series of sensors distributed over the skin of the plane. These interchangeable elements possess a controlled flexibility (in a fashion similar to the vibratory membrane of dolphins).

The instantaneous feedback of the flight data effects the immaterial support of a plane practically lacking an aerofoil. This programmed instability, or rather, this constantly deferred accident of what is in effect a controlled stall, provides for a manoeuvrability unprecedented in the history of supersonic fighters; the coupling of the speed of ejection of the jet and the speed of information of the guidance system provides for a telematic control of lift, totally freed from the mechanical airframe of the traditional airplane (wings, fuselage, flaps, ailerons, and stabilizers ...).

If the computer has disappeared in the telematics, that is, in the instantaneity of its remote transmission (as in networks of telecommunication satellites), we note here that it disappears also in a restrained object. The end of the great *distances of time* exhausts not only the meaning, the geographic dimension of the world, but also the technical dimension of the system, its very configuration.

After *distance-speed* (millisecond, mach ...), the body of the locomotive machine undergoes a pressure analogous to that of the territorial body: the technological object undergoes a deformation inherent in the speed of the transfer of information. The speed of data transmissions acts ultimately in the same way as air resistance on the form of the machine; we witness a conjunction of the telematic and aerodynamic, to the degree that we may name this type of vehicle no longer 'super' or 'hypersonic', but rather teledynamic, since the speed of information is far closer to the speed of light than sound. In effect, just as television results in the telespeed of luminous particles accelerated by the cathode tube, so also, the perception that we have of the actual form of the supersonic machine is really nothing more than a hologram arising from the excessive dynamic of information, that is, from the capacities of the informational teledynamics.

Even if research into the electronics of the future car does not pertain to this high technology of aviation, it is nonetheless the case that research into the aerodynamics of the effect of the ground presents several points of comparison with this prospect of the mutation of the vehicle (we should recall here the principle of the aerodynamic profile of Formula 1 racing cars). More and more attention is paid to the relationship between *support* (tyres, undercarriage) and *surface* (trajectory, course ...), and there is a tendency to assimilate the space between the moving object and the ground to a motor, to a nozzle blowing 'relative wind' (wind of speed, meteorological wind, or artificial wind of the wind tunnel ...), in other words, once again, to combine in coupling two previously distinct elements, no longer by a simple modification of the road (of earth, asphalt, or iron), but rather by *the technological mutation of the interface*.

The fusion/confusion of the mobile and immobile thus results in an entirely new economy of the trajectory of the object.

VI

If we consider chronologically the evolution of the technologies of transmission (command and support), beginning with the mechanical means, then electromechanical, electromagnetic, and finally today's microprocessors, what do we find? An ever greater miniaturization of components and processes; in other words, a certain statistical tendency to fade from view, to conjure away the mechanism and the machine....

In itself, this movement is very revealing of the recent trend of technologies and, especially, of electronics. We saw above that if the speed of terrestrial displacement triggers the impoverishment of the sites of movement (tracks, roads, highways, or racetracks) in smoothing them out and tending toward a uniform trajectory, and if the high speeds of air transport result in the increasingly excessive refinements of the aerodynamics of vehicles, we may assert that the instantaneity of the transfer of information also results in the extreme miniaturization of components, and finally, in the sudden disappearance of the technological object itself. Thus, we may note, this threshold of vision is of immediate interest, as is the usage and attraction of the instrument or machine. Beyond a certain critical threshold, the technical object is assimilated to a new combination, a new device which in its turn becomes the buyer's or user's instrument, his target of interest.

It is not a question here simply of marketing; the enterprise of appearances is not concerned solely with the acquisition of the instrument, but also, and above all, with its usage; the very utility of the technical object (vector or vehicle) is the reason that it seems essential in the case of electronics to consider the nature of the display (number, analogue, image ...) rigorously. In effect, the more advanced the miniaturization, the more important the display becomes; in any case, we can prophesy without risk that electronics will probably disappear in opto-electronics, as the computer is in the process of disappearing in telematics, that is, in the screen of the terminal of the remote display.

We can thus verify, once again, that mixing is an integral part of the most up-to-date technologies; it may even be that our current technology is only a particular form of fusion and of fission (of materials, species, disciplines ...), in other words, a hidden figure of catastrophe and of catalytic accident. An aspect of the crisis of dimensions, miniaturization seems finally to be one of the axes of scientific and technological development; but here also we witness an acceleration of the processes of slipping out of view. So, if in the past every technological object was subject to a progressive diminution of its size, this has played out across long periods of time. Today, the will to clear away obstacles, the lightening of components, results in an accelerated depression of forms and volumes; the technological object need no longer simply arise from imperatives of usage (mobile performance, economics ...), it needs now instead to inscribe itself within a miniaturization sequence at play in the technology of production, one analogous to what obsolescence is to the economy of consumption. Its ultimate dissolution in a new combination being the same as what was in play at the outset, aerodynamic research, the 'form of least resistance', is no longer applicable only to air, to relative wind, but applies foremost to the time-space of technologistical development that will inevitably lead to the *absence* of the advanced element.

Mark it well, if computer technology disappears in telematics it is because the giant computer itself has dissolved into the flea of the microprocessor.... At the same time, if electronics tends to become blurred with 'opto-electronics', it is because the reality of the object is losing its meaning, its value, to the short-lived advantage of the sequences of its representation.

We can now verify these claims with the American research programme into an invisible plane: the Stealth. Here, the aerodynamics of the airframe is no longer geared to improve the coefficient of drag in the atmosphere, but rather to favour a far greater dissimulation to radar reconnaissance.[20] The plane's profile results not only from the speed of propulsion and the instantaneity of its sensors of sustentation (as in the HIMAT), but rather from the speed of detection by radar waves....

The supersonic configuration is, therefore, the fruit of a double dromological performance: that of the speed of the jets and that of the celerity of the detector, and from this the relative invisibility of the design. All this, in order to enhance the strategic character of an aerial space devalued by its excessive transparency,[21] and with this, the increasing importance of an opaque, and thus deterrent, submarine space.

Thus, the aesthetics of the appearance of a stable image, present by dint of being stationary, is superceded by the disappearance of the image, present by virtue of its flight....

Fifth Part

The Politics of Disappearance

> We must always see ourselves for the last time.
> (Pascal Jardin)

If in the past the first political act consisted in making the form of the city apparent at the same time as the figure of citizenship, and this was the underlying meaning of the rites of foundation and the rites of autochthony in the ancient civic space,[1] it seems that we are now witnessing the premises of a fundamental reversal: it is no longer a question of forming 'autochthonous' (i.e., native) citizens along with foreigners coming from whatever sort of synechism, as was the case in the Athenian city, but rather a process leading to the disappearance of citizenship by transforming the residents into 'foreigners within', a new sort of untouchable, in the transpolitical and anational state where the living are nothing more than 'living dead' in permanent deferment.

The ceremony of the 'folly of May' thus echoed the ancient rites, since it sought to make the disappeared of Argentina *reappear*, by maintaining the political presence of the absent through the presence of their wives in the Plaza de Mayo in Buenos Aires. If the Agora or the Forum circumscribed a *scene* for the liturgy, for the acts of the people, the Plaza de Mayo serves only to delimit a *screen* for the projection of a shadow theatre where the real actors have effectively disappeared. Thus the daily murals of a nation condemned to silence are logically superceded by the procession of a population devoted to absence. So if the *yellow star* singled out the Jews from the anonymous crowd [*foule*], the *white scarf* worn by the women [*folles*[2]] in the Plaza de Mayo evokes the defiance of the work of mourning, the negation of widowhood. The sign of membership is superceded by the signalling of the disappeared, the declaration of absence. The inversion thus appears to be radical: if the political State prescribed a right of citizenship or a national identity, conversely, the transpolitical State implies a loss of identification, the progressive discrediting of all the rights of citizenship. '*Where are the disappeared*?' The slogan of wives and mothers from the Plaza de Mayo signals an innovation, the invention of a new economy of distancing where prisons and detention camps would themselves be on the way to disappearance....

The last form of the 'Nation', extermination will thus have exterminated the camp, that is, the fundamentally political principle of its limitation. Extending to the full range of the living, the transpolitical State would, as the strategies of political war feared, bring about a complete discharge[3] where the invisible *police* of a generalized inquisition supercede the visible polis of a population with rights. As the West German Chancellor recently declared, '*The supreme value is no longer the Nation, it is peace*'. This phrase translates perfectly what lies beyond the political, the civic discharge. *Peace tends to replace the Nation*, the state of total peace supercedes the national State, and from this the concept of 'security' surpasses the principle of 'defence', specifically linked with the geographically limited State. Since the public will to power consists less in assuring the continued existence of a Nation by the defence or extension of its boundaries than in sustaining peace, the politically declared reality of the 'enemy' now disappears, making way for the indeterminacy of constantly redefined threats. So, in describing America as a new sort of nation that was neither imperialist nor sought to expand its territory, Richard Nixon represented the United States has seeking simply to present a 'way of life' for other nations to study and adopt.

We now see that, in this way of life, *pacification replaces nationalism*, the final *citizen* becoming less active than passive; the enemy of the constitution is henceforth less an 'internal enemy' of the national State than a 'threat' to the civil peace, a danger for the *constitution of internal pacification*. In this sort of class struggle, in which the opposition is almost exclusively that between the 'military' and the 'civil', and where the warrior is transformed into the police, we may surmise that *extermination as a superior form of the State of pacification will exterminate death, that is, the delimitation of this transpolitical life* by the menacing threat of imminent disappearance, the innovation of a subject who is 'living-dead' [*mort-vivant*], no longer akin to the Spartan Helot or the Roman slave, but a kind of 'zombie' inhabiting the limbs of a devalued public life.

The Latin American sub-continent seems, therefore, to have become an immense laboratory where populations of guinea pigs serve as test subjects for experiments in transpolitical procedures of a 'military class' exempted from fighting foreign adversaries through the geopolitics of zones of influence. Incapable otherwise of participating in nuclear deterrence and in the development of new weapons, the armies of Latin America seek to advance their means of psychological warfare through the constant innovation of new threats, through the definition of new forces of opposition, in order to perfect their liquidation. After having abandoned, on the orders of the Pentagon, the *principle of external threats*, the principle necessary for the legitimization of 'military' power, they invent all sorts of variants of risks or dangers, and set about simply reactivating the *principle of internal threats*, the police principle *par excellence.*...

Thus, entire countries are progressively becoming sites of social extermination, training zones for armed forces incapable of going beyond their own boundaries, an insidious form of a 'militaro-police' coalition comparable to Interpol, an interarmy conspiracy destined to sacrifice the civic and political power of the people, where in the place of self-sacrifice for the sake of the Nation, these states sacrifice their own population in the name of a state of generalized passivity.... Already, during the era of total war – this war more on civilians than on armed forces (let us recall the comparative count of civil and military victims) – we crossed a limit, that of the battlefield, passing into the era of the mass exterminations of enemy populations. In the (Latin American) total peace, we see the extension of the same logic, but through an interiorizing of these processes, it is no longer in the name of all-out war that we sacrifice civil populations of the enemy and that we accept the sacrifice of our own by our enemy; this time, it is in the name of all-out peace (national security) that we decide to sacrifice ourselves and an increasing part of our population. With nuclear deterrence, the military declares war only on civilians; all who are not directly engaged in the army become a potential threat to the internal stability of the State, and so we see the recent proposal to extend the convention of

1948 on genocide to address this 'state of internal war' beyond civil
war by allowing the UN to intervene against the police engaged in
the systematic elimination of their national population, as was the
case with Cambodia, and as is the case still in San Salvador. It should
be noted that the brutal suppression of civil political power is, in the
Latin American coup d'état, only the first stage [*stade*[4]] of a discharge
of every civil authority, of all opposition, indeed of any hesitation in
collaborating with the police, as is evident in the written statement
from 1977 by the leader of Strategic Zone 232, one of the *seigneurs* of
internal war in the province of Misiones, Argentina: '*The control of the
population must be complete, this is why we will eliminate the neutrals
and even the indifferent, for no one can be 'absent' from this struggle*'. This
explains the fundamentally utopian character of this public pacification
that does not conform to any limit, or to any attempt at applying a
political brake, since '*organized struggle recognizes no limit, neither moral
nor natural; it lies beyond good and evil*' (Lieutenant-colonel Pascarelli).
Thus we are better able to comprehend the principle of the 'complete
discharge' announced by Clausewitz: it is totally illusory to hope for an
end to extermination beyond the limits of the political. The progressive
transformation from real enemy to defined threats and potential
suspects in fact implies a perpetual renewal of final ends, a perpetuation of elimination: older people remember the past, adolescents know
the customs and the language of the country – this collective memory
presents a challenge to the new *masters of time*. Thus, regarding the
elderly Khmer population, the Cambodian Angkar would declare:
'*Keeping them alive does nothing for us, letting them die is no loss*'. And
from this, the advent, beyond traditional *biopolitical* regulation, of a
transpolitical deregulation, the fiction of a 'state of pacification' that no
longer accepts the term of physiological life as the persistence of natural
or moral limits and that is not content solely with killing successive
categories of those in opposition, or those merely hesitating, or even
those outright indifferent, but *that also arrogates to itself the power to
decide who lives and who are the living and who the dead, and who the
'living-dead'*.[5]

   Meanwhile, this military messianism goes hand in hand with a new
attempt, that of favouring in Latin America the appearance of alternative cults largely sustained by the authorities and destined gradually

to supplant Judaeo-Christian monotheism, the last official adversary of the tyrannies throughout the entire sub-continent.[6] Under the pretext of assuring the health and preservation of a 'national identity' against the menace of a generalized subversion through the deployment of 'parapolice' squadrons – a sort of anticorps, as Admiral Guzetti put it – the 'warrior' attempts to take on attributes of the 'priest', giving rise first to the competitive opposition to intellectuals and then to the religious. An adept in an eschatological perspective where security ideology expands the clinical symptoms of the sanitation ideology to the dimensions of the social body overall, to the eternal salvation promised after death, the 'false-priest' substitutes a potential survival where *it is necessary to live in order to die better*, that is, to perpetuate the extermination, the cult of the State, the *statolatry* of a State in its pure state, the monotheism of a 'present divinity' anticipated by Hegel.... As an Anglo-Saxon specialist explained 'the right to death', this variation of the right to disappear: '*People don't want to die, they want to be dead*'.

Indeed, since 1945, if the developed countries have perfected the logistics of the *nuclear state*, the underdeveloped countries of Latin America have increasingly refined the *suicide state*, each striving in its way to surpass and completely discharge the political State, the logic of deterrence develops on two levels: *that of strategic nuclear deterrence and that of popular political deterrence*, constantly reinforced by the legal arsenal of emergency legislation.

This particular vocation of the Latin-American sub-continent can be explained, as I see it, not only by its role in providing a privileged refuge for the old criminals of total war, but especially by the existence in its centre of the ultimate underclass: the Amazonian Indians, who enjoy no political status whatsoever since they are officially considered to be *minors* and since *all sorts of obstacles to contact are placed between their tribes*, in the obvious interests of the land grab of their territories.[7]

The Argentine bill of 22 August 1979 concerning the massive disappearance of people that so disturbed international organizations is not, therefore, in any way, the final solution of the problem, but rather an anticipation of a politics that deliberately worsens the situation for self-interested reasons. *This project aims, in effect, to consider dead every person not appearing before the judge within a span of 90 days, while the only notification provided was by means of the press....* This legislation allowed the families of the disappeared to receive the deceased's compensation, his pension and other insurance monies. The short-circuit established between 'national security' and 'social security', the principle of comprehensive insurance thus extends from the health of the body [*corps*] to the security of the body 'politic' [*corps d'État*].

The *massacre societies* of an archaic past, adept first at ritual, and then at legal execution, were succeeded in the classical era by *incarceration societies*, this stage ranging from the incarceration of the prison and the sanatorium up to that of the Soviet psychiatric asylums of the modern era.[8] It does indeed seem that the postmodern era is now preparing means of obfuscation, with the arrival of the *society of legal disappearance*, an original form of capital punishment where the transpolitical power aims at identifying itself totally with medical power in decreeing not only who is 'dead' and who is 'living', but above all those who are the 'living-dead', citizens with no rights, in permanent deferral.

The current clinical debate on *medical death*, or irreversible coma, finds itself here transposed into the civil plan of the *social death* of the absent, disappeared, or downcast, whichever ... a sophisticated form of ostracism in the post-historical era of the war of Time, beyond the historical era of the wars of territorial space, the project of the Argentine law becomes the outline of a *civil excommunication*, an agonistic figure of extermination without a trial, without an amphitheatre, and without internment camps, beyond every delimitation of law or place. Contrary to the past where the State of law [*l'État de droit*] was identified politically with the (social) State of siege [*l'État de siège*] of the City and then the Nation, the State of non-law [*l'État de non-droit*] developing in Latin America exceeds all limits in a fundamentally delocalized State of 'transpolitical' emergency. It is, therefore, entirely logical not only that the dead disappear, but above all that death cease ... henceforth it is an urgent imperative, an absolute necessity, no longer with regard to a humanitarian end, but from an eschatological perspective: that of indefinitely perpetuating extermination, the ultimate figure of the State.

The progressive generalization of abduction, as with the taking of hostages by different 'terrorisms' (individuals or States), has, for a long time now, prepared public opinion for these types of panic procedures where the disappearances inaugurate a sort of *public magic*, a phenomenon of transpolitical substitution, just this side of every (political) constitution, where the 'social specters' definitively supersede the legitimate subjects in a civic kinetics in which the end is constantly renewed, the fault of always being totally accomplished.... It is in this sense that it will be necessary soon to analyse, in comparison with moral and legal debates on the '*right to die*' (euthanasia or life-support therapies) and abortion, those who will not fail to rise up in support for the '*the right to disappearance*.' So, even if 'the liberation of disappearance' is not yet claimed by the ambient liberal conformism, several precursory signs announce it. On the one hand, the exotic term '*Robinson syndrome*' designates the case of adult runaways who desire to reinvent their lives elsewhere, under an assumed name; on the other hand, the protection of the patronymic name no longer seems assured. For example, a 1966 adoption law allows the falsification of the civil status of the child whose real name is erased from the registers, while the 2,000 children born in France from artificial insemination live without a fully legal civil status. Finally, in the provinces, the disquieting problem of disappearances is left to the judgement of the police: '*Our police structures are poorly organized for cases of disappearance*', admitted an inspector from Vaucluse. '*On the one hand, we are occupied dealing with criminals, while on the other hand, it is very risky to put significant measures into effect, since in most cases we end up with a voluntary disappearance*.' Several lawyers are rebelling against these practices which deprive those who have involuntarily disappeared of any chance of being the object of a deeper inquiry. A committee regarding disappearances has been formed just recently and, as one of its founders states: 'It is a very ambiguous problem – in the name of individual liberties, we are, oddly enough, protecting voluntary runaways. This is all well and good, but we pass over the involuntary disappearances. When we note that no exact figure concerning them appears in the official statistics – over 7,000 people go unfound – I would estimate about 2,000 to be the number of people who have involuntarily disappeared each year in France' (Patrick Giros, priest).

Given that the official figure of disappeared in Argentina falls between 5,000 and 15,000 people, we are right to worry about the estimate of the *Comité sur les disparitions*. For the past six years we have been witnessing a mysterious manipulation in the Soviet Union of demographic statistics concerned with the death rate.[9]

But let us return to our point of departure in Latin America. Before the disappearance of people had become such a widespread means of coercion, information was still available, and it was possible to detect an extraordinary *phenomenon of standardization of those on the social margins left to their unhappy fate* of unemployment and the rise of a self-managed poverty in suburban nebulae – the product of indigenous self-managed construction – accommodating up to 100,000 inhabitants, as in the Villa Salvador on the outskirts of Lima, Peru. Here, in fact, it is a question of an internal pseudo-colonial situation.[10] *The masses become paradoxically the margin*; the classical model of policing becomes inoperative. Falling short of an outright *declared civil war* and, therefore, not constituting a direct threat to the military, the latest approach to oppressed peoples becomes that of a supplement to social order, an extreme 'social worker' enrolled in the special units, 'parapolice' commandos, thanks to the institution of a *state of undeclared internal war* where the self-defence of militias takes over from the self-management of the shelters, favellas, barriadas, and other post-urban shantytowns. (Along the lines explained by the French deputy M. Daillet in his *Rapport sur la defense*: 'Civil defence is charged with assuring the security of the rear and preventing, in the case of a serious crisis, the birth and blind action of political dissent against which military defence is impotent'.)

In these infra-human zones, abandoned to the racketeering of paramilitary and parapolice 'extermination groups',[11] twelve years ago we could already observe the appearance of drug trafficking and then the illicit trade in life substances that would gradually be transformed into an enforced conscription [*impôt du sang*], no longer of the military sort where each mobilized citizen is held to protect, even at the price of his life, the safety of the fatherland, but this time, that of an unjust peace where, for the profit of multinational corporations, the most destitute are forced to supply *blood banks* unregulated by the interested governments, such as those in Brazil, where there are still 700 banks of this sort and where the police continuously refuse to acknowledge the problem, although in certain maternity hospitals in the favellas, new mothers and their infants are not discharged unless they give their blood....

Five million litres of plasma are thus commercialized each year in Latin America by firms realizing profits of 10,000 per cent. These ritual practices of the *liquidation of the living* were not allowed internationally until the invention of a method called 'fractioning' which allows the chemical isolation of each of the constitutive elements of the blood and the innovation of an *industrial plasma* with a long shelf life.[12]

Thus, along with the energy crisis and the exhaustion of deposits of *raw materials* [*matière première*], we have in the destitute countries the *last resource* [*matière dernière*], the deposits of the underclass undergoing an intensive biological exploitation.... Beyond the extensive and migratory exploitation of the work force of a transplanted proletariat that provides for worldwide industrial redeployment, here we find a final form of transplantation, indeed, a 'transpolitical transfusion'.

Left unable to participate in an increasingly sophisticated technological production, the native [autochthone] underclass of South America is effectively 'liquidated' as a source of labour, becoming imperceptibly a final *mine*, the final resource of organic compounds culled for the revitalization of privileged populations. *Isn't Argentina now seeking to import 10,000,000 Japanese?* What a discrediting of the indigenous – and no longer solely the Indians – such a 'professional deskilling' of its national population, brutally clarifying the recent practices of mass disappearances, the organized underdevelopment of entire regions, the strategic zones of a suicide state where the *industrial recession and customs disarmament are the results of a transfer of revenue from all social and economic sectors toward the agrarian sector.*[13]

Return to the past, return to the passive, where *the State of internal pacification* would no longer be solely a transitory militaristic aberration, but the sinister dawning of a slow regression of the Nation, of the extermination of a civil society where the repression of intellectuals and workers and the latifundiarist restoration constitute complementary wings of an implacable and long-term neofeudal tyranny, a *stereopolitics of the worst kind* destined to assume historically the complete discharge of the national state in the interests of a transpolitical and transnational state arising both everywhere and nowhere.[14]

Native [*autochthone*] or immigrant ... indigenous or foreign ... a mythical debate engaging what has become a classical opposition; the notion of native status [*autochthonie*] represents one of the founding myths of the political.

The communal matrix, the *Earth-Mother* of origins, is superseded by the exclusive sex, the *City-Virgin* giving birth, by 'parthenogenesis', to the native [*autochthone*] citizen, born from the democratic soil of the city of Athena, the presiding divinity, at once mother and father of a subject become legitimate citizen of a City-State, of a civic idol built by the hands of men: 'For the philosophers who wondered about the perennial character of the City, *political discourse had already resolved this question.*'[15]

A necessary 'topos' around which the civic imagination of the Athenian 'demos' crystallizes, autochthony is, first, this *empty place* where, beneath political discourse, a discourse on the structure of the kinship of the state breaks through: is one born solely of one or of two? and is one born from the same or the other? In a word, *is one born from the earth or from men*? To this problem the myths of autochthony respond by refusing to decide: one is born from the earth *and* from sexuality.[16]

Later, much later, this debate is taken up again in the argument of social determinisms. With Ratzel's anthropogeography and the social morphology of Mauss, the alternative proposed will be displaced from sex to the society and from the City to the Nation, to entire continents, up to the interpretational delusions of the *Lebensraum* of General Haushofer, the Third Reich's master of geopolitics and of this *Lebensborn* biopolitics theorized by Rosenberg. It is this theory that will, during the Second World War, contaminate the geostrategy of the United States for the famous *doctrine of national security* will arise from the conflict with the German Nazis before reaching the borders of the Andean sub-continent, with the assistance of, first, General Golbery, the inspiration of Brazil's geopolitics, and, beyond that, of a professor of 'military geography' named Pinochet, finally to return to its source with the recent developments of 'l'espace social européen'[17] ...

A degraded form of the 'political' in the old sense of the term, ever refusing to decide between place [*lieu*] and milieu, sociology will engage the persistence of the morphological illusion in omitting *time* in favour of a reference to, and reverence for, history. Nevertheless, contrary to the process of synoecism, *the marshalling of men* from the 'rural demes' in a single city, autochthony appears as a *marshalling of time*, of a time that has nothing historical about it, as it involves instead a perpetual recommencement of the origin. Again, as Nicole Loraux explains: 'In order to have its moment in the history of the democratic city, the myth of autochthony is nonetheless written in a *slowed, repetitive, time*, which, year after year, repeats the same festivals, the same celebrations, thus marking off the space of the City'. A necessary 'topos' of official discourse, Athenian autochthony is therefore, *before all else*, a mythical 'Kronos', a political rhythm, a ceremony leading the panathenaeans up the Acropolis from the cemetery of the Kerameikos, from birth to the public death of these 'sons of the fatherland', for whom *time is annulled in the irrevocable return from the end to the origin.*

An eternal present inscribed in the time of the 'polis', the autoch-thonous myth stresses the 'political' time of the citizen in separating him from his tribal or familial idiorhythms. This process begins with the agrarian origins and proceeds up to the beginnings of the industrial era in which the *dromocratic* revolution will succeed the democratic revolution in innovating an *accelerated time* where the energy techno-logies will progressively eliminate the myth of the territorial rootedness of the state. The 'cult of matter', Earth Mother and Virgin of origins, will be supplanted by the cult of light, where absolute 'substance' is worn out and fades away, giving way to a necessary *accident of the transfer.*

The Athenian erection, at the *chthonian* passage from the origins of myth, will be replaced by the *cryptic* passage from shadow into light. The traditional political enclosure will be succeeded by a great 'trans-political' disorder. An autochthony of *time*, more than of any particular place, less indigenous than photogenous since time is the cycle of light,[18] the subject that will see the day will be born less mortal than *visible*; less a topos than a chronos, this subject will be born in the light of the time of a *chronotropism of the living* where mythical conditioning of the liturgy will give way to technological conditioning of popula-tions exploited in their biorhythms.

In the face of this trauma, the principle of the *geomorphological identity* of the citizen tends to be effaced; less a native [*originaire*] than a member of a society [«*sociétaire*»], there will be no delay in the imper-ceptible process whereby the citizen becomes nothing more than a *stand in* [*suppléant*].

Privileged residents, those entitled to the 'rights of the city' of a
democratic state, are superseded by *visitors*, transitory citizens, tourists,
spectators of a dromocratic state where vision [*la vue*] is life [*la vie*]....
If yesterday, in the unity of the neighbourhood, the other was at once
known and recognized through repetition, the ritual of encounters and
public events, with the transportation revolution, this 'neighbour' will
become a *specter* that one will see only accidentally. The great disorder
will, therefore, do less to perfect exchange than it will serve to give rise
to this *fleeting presence*. This kinetic habituation to the disappearance
of the congener will have the character of a social divorce: passing
[*passant*], fleeting [*passager*], physical presence of the similar will lose its
reality to be replaced by its 'brand image'. The blind spots stretch out to
the point where the diffusion of the body increases and the transience
of people will surround us progressively with strangers. The discrediting of the notion of the *enemy*, to be replaced progressively by what is
suspect and poses a threat, thus signals less the decline of defence than
the absence of allies, the discrediting of civic alliance.

We will thus see the extensive character of, first, provincial and, then,
national definitions of locations succeeded by that of an intense transnational visualization where the long *theories*[19] of the democratic liturgy
will disappear, replaced by the 'unwinding [*défilement*] sequences', an
accelerated substitute for the actions of an absent people.

The art of seeing, of foreseeing, politics does not, therefore, escape
the rule according to which 'Art does not render the visible but rather
renders visible'.[20] In this reconversion of the field of representation, the
City ceases to be a 'theatre' (agora, forum) in order to become instead a
darkened chamber, a *cinema* where visibility supplants all territoriality,
all legitimate location. But let us return to consider the invention of
Athens: 'There is an upper area: *the Acropolis*, and a lower: *the Agora,
the Kerameikos*. There is also an interior, the Acropolis and the Agora,
and an exterior, outside the walls of the City, the Kerameikos where the
Athenian democracy buried those who served. In this public cemetery,
the common inscriptions[21] were consecrated to an idealistic glory: the
polis, the indivisible unity that owes its authority to the *effacement of its
andres, its soldier-citizens, valorous yet identical and interchangeable*'.[22]

Curiously, in this genre of historical heroization a certain site is
missing, namely, the *stadium*, in which the democratic equality of

the City comes to an end with the rise of a momentous dromocratic publicity.[23] Here the civic point of view is inversed: there is an upper area, the levels on which the spectators are seated, and a lower area, the track where the actors file out.... Within this theatre of mobile performances, those present have the view of the gods, while those who pass through are dominated by the insatiable curiosity of the crowd of voyeurs. We are far from the ideal platitude of the equals of the agora, nothing like that, instead there is only the spectral analysis of a population exposed to the disclosure of an elite of movement.[24]

If the public place is, therefore, the place of the demos, the track is, by way of analogy, that of the invention of a dromos where the eternal return of political origins is renewed by the revolution of a 'trans-political' spectacle which bears with it in a germinal state the tyrannies of an empire where logistical ideals progressively replace the political ideologies of Athenian democracy. While the agora and the republican forum will have long since disappeared in the enclosure of parliaments, the 'public place' will survive by becoming the stadium of military processions, before disappearing in its turn into the traffic of the trans-portation revolution. Thus, after the gymnasium, the amphitheatre and the racetrack will have played their role in anticipation of the airfield and satellites installing in orbit their peripheral rites.

According to J.-C. Melatti's ethnology: '*All the Indians of Brazil gathered together in the stadium of Maracana in Rio de Janeiro would only fill it half way ...*'.

Site of a morphological overexposure, the sporting arena is, therefore, not only a 'crater' for the popular irruption, it is also a type of census. In this inventory, *the form is the ground [fond] that rises again to the surface.*[25] Surveillance becomes the last quarter of the eclipse of the community, *the high-security quarter* of the logistical delocalization of power. It is logical, thus, to see the national stadium of Santiago, Chile, transformed into a *concentration camp*, since the enterprise of political appearances gives way to the aesthetic of military disappearance.[26] A reduced model of an abolished civic space, the stadium is without doubt the end of the morphological illusion of the State, the ultimate 'stadium' of the city and, therefore, indirectly, of legitimate citizenship. What plays out in Latin America, beyond all reasons of state, is an argument between the ancients and the moderns, a campaign promise

of the 'postpolitical'. So, if the assault of tanks on the square in front of
the Palace of Moneda ended in a classical incarceration of opponents
in the gymnasia, then in the stadium in Santiago, the weekly ceremony
of the mothers in the Plaza de Mayo in Buenos Aires signals a tragic
disordering, a loss of references. Without destination, without end, *the
'procession of the mad' attempts to find the path again in order to win back
the terrain, the place lost before the seat of the Argentine government.*

Their liturgy takes the place of the hearth of the community, of the
Athenian *cratos*;[27] an agonistic ceremony, their perpetual movement
is situated beyond the death of the 'similar', beyond the political, it
poses for us the question of the *identity of the living.* The 'public place'
becomes at once the cemetery of the political and a 'transpolitical'
forum. If the wives of the interned Chileans would still surrender
themselves to the stadium to get some news of the detainees, if the
widows of the Iranians had to reunite in cemeteries, the widows of the
Argentinean disappeared have no other recourse than to make public
their absence.... Insistently rejecting the uncertainty of the fate of their
spouses, of their parents, the 'mad ones of the Plaza de Mayo' have
invented a decisive interrogation: *we must choose between the Agora of
political identity and the public cemetery, since their common abolition is
made impossible by our presence right here.*[28]

The act of presence replaces the act of birth and autochthony; the
opposition to tyranny is no longer one of ideology, it is that of a life,
of the enigma of the living body mysteriously *present in time.* We
can do away with civic space or eliminate the political capital,[29] but
in abolishing the public cemetery, we simultaneously exterminate all
descendents. The funerary foundation of societies is stronger than the
erection of the city, *the vengeance of presence prohibits the mass grave of
the state.*[30]

The Strategy of The Beyond

It must be acknowledged that from
now on Europe is too small for war.
Hitler, 7 July 1943

Profession of faith, profession of fire, holy war seems to have returned.
With its rites, its sacrifices, the fanatic machine is once again set
marching, marching back toward the night of medieval times whose
bloody confrontation of religious beliefs was the prelude to that of
political ideologies.

In this retrospective, many are those who feel ready to don again the
armour of light to fight the 'good fight', but especially *to resurrect an
enemy which disappeared in deterrence*, in the balance of a terror become
far too impersonal. As Einstein explains, 'The belief in the action of
demons is found at the roots of our concept of causality' (cited by Léon
Poliakov in his essay on the origin of persecutions).

The fundamentally archaic character of a number of recent events
should, nevertheless, have alerted us to this return to the flames of the
stake. The collapse of a political thought corrupted by the libertinism
of liberalism, the redundancy of an illusory materialism constantly
contradicted by the facts, the rise in power of a mode of destruction
coming increasingly to dominate the mode of production, the economic
ravages of a *global logistical strategy* which claims deterrence on all levels:
all of this should normally have warned us of the coming of a sort
of 'transpolitical' eschatology. Indeed, for nearly half a century now,
none have brandished the end of the world without a revival of the
demonology of origins.

Already, at the time of the assault on Mecca, an event of unprecedented gravity, totally underestimated by the political leaders of the
time (consider President Giscard d'Estaing's dispatching of French
gendarmes of GIGN[31] as military advisors), we saw the rise of the
spectre of the *holy war* of believers on the side of the *pure war* of
armaments or, as they are called, nuclear 'vectors of deliverance'.... The

symbolic battle of humanity's salvation by fire or by faith, illumination
of a public extermination of infidels or simply of opponents, in the
name of a false messiah or a real missile, beyond [*au-delà*[32]] political
discourses, discredited, disqualified by the very extremity of situations
for which Libya or Iran furnish foreign models, or right next door, in
Ireland.

The assassination attempt in Saint Peter's Square in Rome[33] was thus
aiming for a new *destabilization*, but of what sort? That of the state of
the Vatican? But this is not Libya.... That of Christianity? But we are
no longer in the time of the *God of Armies* [*dieu des Armées*] of the Old
Testament, the era of the Crusades is over, ecumenicalism falls under
the contradictory sign of a *God disarmed* [*dieu désarmé*] and often even
of a disarming god, let us remember the murder of Oscar Romero,
beaten in the cathedral of San Salvador on 24 March 1980 for having
openly preached *military disobedience....*

In fact, one may be right in wondering if the separation of the
Church and the army has not become the logical complement of the
separation of Church and State.

With the advent of nuclear arms, the old theological doctrine of
the *just war* that associated state powers and the Vatican for so long
has become obsolete. The proof of this is the journey to Hiroshima
after Auschwitz of the one who declared in 1980: 'Nuclear holocaust
threatens. In whose political interest could there ever be a new war?'
If Pius XI denounced in his time the statolatry [*statolâtrie*] of a rising
fascist State, Jean Paul II persisted in denouncing terrorism to the
United Nations, in Ireland, and elsewhere, the cult of Peace by deterrence, *the idolatry of an absolute weapon,* supposedly capable of bringing
about salvation.

It is thus evident that if war tends to be definitively rejected by the
Church, it is because it has attained such proportions as to have gained
the power to obscure divine revelation: *the scientific and technological
apocalypse now screens* [*fait ... écran*] *the mystical apocalypse.*

When one observes today the growing role of the military castes in
the control of sects,[34] the appearance in Latin America of substitute
cults destined to supplant Judaeo-Christian monotheism and supported
by the ruling armed forces, one intuits the nature of the duel which is
taking shape here between the 'priest' and the 'warrior', the anticipation

of a new type of *syncretism* aiming to set up an official faith founded on the primacy of a military-scientist thought become *messianic*, and consequently dominating all political thought, be it secular or religious. The patent failure of disarmament agreements, the practical impossibility of interceding except by an *act of faith* in the adversary, the progress of nuclear force presently results in denying strategy as *prior knowledge* [*connaissance préalable*]. The 'automatic' character, no longer solely of arms, of means, but also and above all of command, amounts to the denial of the capacities of reasoning and, therefore, finally of all 'politics' to the advantage of systems of information and 'transpolitical' decision; systems destined to keep up the appearances of peace in the context of a popular deterrence readily fulfilling the means of nuclear deterrence.

As Karol Wojtyla wrote in 1975, 'The program of our era is to persecute while keeping up such appearances as allow the claim that persecution does not exist'.

The Inquisition is thus no longer what it was, i.e., that of the parochial monitory to the political police and to the contemporary 'secret services'; the obscurantism was imperceptibly displaced from the religious to the secular, then from the 'civil' to the 'military'. Moreover, the events of Poland illustrate this reversal of the tendency as the reappearance of a *tripartition* such that the 'priest' becomes the ally of the proletariat in a state of war where the 'warrior', become policeman, declares hostilities exclusively against his own people, against his nation.

The separation of the Church and army is manifested here by solidarity with the oppressed, in a *peace* which goes beyond that of a State no longer relying only on force, but also on *an internal deterrence echoing the external deterrence* (stemming from the Yalta Accords) that imposes today the use of a categorical imperative, transcending all legitimacy and every political system, *since the dictatorship of the Communist Party in this case resists democracy more than anything else* – blackmail to the integrity of security in which the era of integral nationalism, beyond [*au-delà*] some defence of the homeland, is brought to a close, since the enemy is nowhere and the threat everywhere....

With the Polish Solidarity movement, we witnessed in 1981 an escalation to extremes by the demands of a rediscovered social solidarity,[35] a sort of challenge, *an act of faith* where an apartheid-like dialogue develops indirectly between the militant unionist and the soldier, over the heads of the political ruling class, at first pressing the national army, faced with the demographic development of a union overwhelming the Party, to take on responsibilities, then, in inciting it, *for having dared propose to it the creation of a union in its ranks,* to opt (despite its logistical weakness) between the confrontation with the Soviets or a *coup d'état*. This formidable situation is intensified to the very end, since certain unionists were even contemplating going to negotiate with the Russians, over the heads of those political intermediaries who no longer represent anything, leading to the proposition of a 'national referendum' on the validity of power in Poland.

As repeatedly affirmed by Lech Walesa, *the belief in an external non-intervention was leading to a liberation of the internal debate, bringing with it every risk of confrontation.* Indeed, the defiance of the Christian unionist could be seen as a sort of faith in deterrence; either he misunderstood the singular nature of the nuclear Age, or, he was rejecting its fatalism in seeing his people as *already dead,* that is, as caught up in the throes of a deterrence which prohibits all evolution and hope of liberation through an *act of faith,* a kind of civic resurrection in which not only the union member, the participant in negotiations, takes part, but the opponent as well, the potential adversary.

In fact, what was at stake was only a replica, an intimist reduction of what has been at stake between the geopolitical blocs for more than 30 years, *as if the rift of Yalta no longer really passed between the NATO nations and those of the Warsaw Pact, but had instead been taken into the very interior of each country, of each city, in both the East and the West.*

How else do we interpret the persistence of 'socialism' in numerous countries of the Western world (not to mention those of the Third World) and the growing influence of American cultural imperialism in the countries of the communist bloc? ... This interpenetration of customs and aspirations no longer concerns solely some *hooligans* or *gauchistes,* but rather an entire generation, a *generation of children lost* in unemployment, the slackening or the excesses of a generosity which rejects with the divisions of history the values of the past, a kind of useless avant-garde, or rather an *advance contingent* [*contingent avant-coureur*] of a foreseeable catastrophe: that of a generalized non-development to be shrouded, though not for much longer, by the screen of different political regimes, the progressivist illusion of affluent countries of the 'middle powers' faced with impoverished countries, so that the general tendency is toward the conspiracy of the 'great powers', not only in the domain of the arms race, the exhaustion of different economies, but also in the *non-development of civil society*, within their respective zones of influence.

The desire to abolish 'the Welfare State' that now reunites the European socialists and the new American economists is too similar to a pathological bonding for us not to worry. Moreover, without speaking of the role of Western banks in the Polish normalization, note that if the Soviet Union was inspired by the military–industrial development of the United States, and has perpetuated the underdevelopment of communist civil society, the events occurring in the capitalist world since the Moscow Accords (SALT, 1972) and Watergate indicate that, conversely, the Americans, under the pretext of a *neo-conservatism*, are tempted by exaggerations in the sphere of domestic collapse, the unprecedented strategic possibilities offered by the abandonment of all social solidarity such as was illustrated by the measures taken by Reagan, first 'Pentagonal' president of the United States. The progressive and, for some, alas, progressivist abolition of a political reasoning that yesterday justified the legitimacy of national defence by recourse to the stereotypes of a security now complete, *a conservatism that no longer refers so much to the Nation as to the imperatives of deterrence*, causes our epoch to enter into a 'transpolitical' world-apart [*outre-monde*] where a regime of fatal beliefs dominates beyond [*par-delà*] the ideological rifts, reinforced by futuristic systems that are no longer all that different from systems of incantation of the past obscurantism.

The foremost concern is, therefore, not to 'relearn what an enemy is' (J. Freund), as too many of the French would hope, attached as they are to an illusory 'national force of deterrence' so readily opposed to the Polish unionists and German pacifists, but rather to attempt to discover where the hostility lies, the essence of a threat which until now evaded analysts, probably because it was no longer situated in any particular configuration, but universally distributed, exceeding thus all recourse to traditional 'geopolitical' interpretation.

For several years now, we have observed that 'localized conflicts' surely

are so in space but certainly not in time. Limited wars no longer stop,
but continue indefinitely: the war in Indochina continues in Cambodia,
in Laos, as well as on the borders of China. The Irish conflict is now
more than ten years old, and despite the visit of the Pope, the civil war
lives on with its murders, its attacks, its chain of more or less voluntary
deaths for 'political rights' refused to prisoners.[36] There is more of the
same in Libya, in Syria, in the whole of the Near and Middle East,
where Iran and Iraq sustain a conflict while lacking the will to bring
it to an end. Meanwhile, Israel – after having proclaimed *Jerusalem the
eternal capital* – did not shy away from carrying out the most serious
form of state attack, *pre-emptively* destroying the nuclear-processing
facility of Tamuz[37], before annexing the Golan Heights....

Plunged into a situation symmetrical to the one in Poland, Turkey
is today subject to a 'state of internal war' without anyone in the West
being particularly bothered, the United States playing here the role
of the Soviet Union, in lending assistance to General Evren in social
and union repression. Ever kindled anew, centres of tension ignite
here and there without any of the old ones really being extinguished;
this endemic disease of limited conflicts betrays the imminent decline
of the nation state torn between the demands for internal autonomy
and regional independence and those of an increased 'transnational'
dependence, particularly in the economic and strategic domains. The
question of war is no longer, therefore, as some claim, that of the
imminence of a third world war, of an East/West assault leading to
nuclear confrontation, but that of an *internecine war* in the process of
spreading to the entire world.

*The chronic disorder thus becomes, as before, a state of fact beyond the
state of peace of nations in political accord,* whence the uselessness of the
UN in the prevention, as well as in the solution, of disputes.

The spontaneous recurrence of the significance of religious questions
is, moreover, indicative of the decline of ideologies which have, until
this point, been the underpinning of national realities. Consider Libya,
notably weakened as it emerges from the chaos, or Iran, where *fundamentalist sedition* played the role which would have typically devolved
upon military sedition in overthrowing a regime. The growing influence
of Islamic fundamentalism throughout the Maghreb – not to mention
Poland where Christianity assumes responsibility for the persistence of

national identity – reveals the importance of a destructuring that, in nearly all regions, attains the political configurations inherited from a recent past. As for the southern hemisphere, other than Africa, Latin America develops another phase of the process: that of the definitive abandonment of the *notion of external adversity,* a notion nevertheless important in the legitimization of the public force, but especially of armed forces, ultimate recourse of every 'legitimate' state. Such has been the case, in fact, since the *Inter-American Treaty of Reciprocal Assistance,* signed in 1947 and which permits today different national armed forces to conduct themselves beyond their respective territorial limits in *transnational police forces.* (Did not Argentina support, in Bolivia, the putsch of the drug-general Meza? As for Guatemala and the armed forces of Honduras, did they not participate with the forces of San Salvador, in the heart of the 'iron triangle', in the repression of the Salvadorian refugees? …) The Andean sub-continent reacts in the manner of a new society in which the confinement of each of the countries involved permits the powers to implement a social deregulation where the normalization of the state of internal war comes *de rigueur* to be dedicated to the *state of enhanced national security.* It is as if, since the decline of external adversity, the state of siege ceases to be an exceptional state becoming instead a juridical means socially analogous to what the fortified wall was previously for the city, the system of permanent border defences for the threatened nation, as if in the hour of instantaneous exchanges, the national politics no longer survives except in the shelter of a shadow realm now the norm; thus the *disinformation,* the radio-silence, the interruption of exchanges and communication so often imposed on besieged populations by their own armed forces.… It is from this perspective that we must analyse Brazil's and Argentina's declared hostility to the requests of the United States concerning the creation of a *Treaty of the South Atlantic* which would bring together these countries and Uruguay with South Africa. In effect, *the integral security of the American subcontinent henceforth prevents geopolitical opening, that is, geopolitical extensivity, solely to the advantage of a transpolitical intensivity*[38] aimed at the enslavement of native populations now 'hostages of the state'. This turning in on oneself, this inertia of the South American States, is confirmed by the recent declarations of General Pinochet that 'those who join together to envision a political opening are wasting their time because there will be no such opening', indicating the path followed by the authoritarian or political regimes, the necessary inversion of a public power incapable of facing an *open war* on pain of immediate internal collapse.

It is, moreover, significant that in Central America, as in Southeast Asia, *if one fought in the past against the invader, today one is more likely to be fighting against nationals trying to flee the country.* Vietnamese, Haitian, or Cuban 'boat-people', Salvadorian 'land-people', the progressive decline of democracy gives rise to the circumstances in which all opponents become at the same time *prohibited from abiding and prohibited from leaving,* whence the paradoxical logic of the forced disappearance of people, as a means of pressure, of mass psychological torture of a population subjugated to a permanent 'state of siege'. The political police thus become the instigators of a secular society where the inquisition again takes up its office, advancing an administration of fear which looks at the same time like a protection racket and comprehensive insurance, a cult of salvation without God but not without idols.[39]

Limited in space but unlimited in time, the localized wars of the era of deterrence thus progressively replace the psychological effect of the old delinquency, the crimes and misdemeanours of private individuals against the establishment of the law. The disappearance of the declared enemy promotes diffuse threats and a generalized suspicion with regard to civic populations all amounting to a kind of deterrence of public opinion. *From this point on, it becomes necessary to reconsider 'civil rights' along with the lawful regime,* so that certain irresponsible propositions arise which, as the inverse to what is happening in Ireland, will identify Argentinean political prisoners with those of *common law.*[40] Stemming from the 'Assembly of the Rights of Man', this proposition aims in reality at making the disappeared reappear; nevertheless, even if, today, it seems noble, this proposal still underlines the ambiguity of a humanist opposition faced with the extreme perversity of a society where institutional regulation no longer exists, having been replaced by a deregulation of social behaviours authorized by the abstention, even the assent, of an international community whose powerlessness is obvious.

Finally, everything happens as if the national and international powers no longer have the capacity to come up with lasting resolutions to the important problems, as if, with 'the crisis', the democratic authorities, just barely capable of assuring the management of statistically average situations, had lost the possibility of controlling the excessive situations. Could it be that this is a symptom of a kind of decline?

Nothing remains very long *in the same state* any more, 'geopolitics' would then see itself supplanted by a 'chronopolitics' where intensivity would suddenly take precedence over the extensivity of traditional (associative, federative, etc.) societies of which decolonization marks the decline....

Faced with this stalemate, whose magnitude was revealed by the protracted Vietnam conflict, after the détente or 'crisis of war' a 'war of crisis' gradually arises, an economic energetic war, a war of time, a war of each instant, where from the time of the appropriation of a complete conventional and nuclear panoply, no form of armament, nor army, any longer has the power to decide inter-state disputes, but only *the power to open a field of political destabilization similar to a war that will never stop, not due to any will to power, but this time by virtue of powerlessness.* The protracted duration of a 'transpolitical' powerlessness stems from a sort of chain reaction, the disintegration of the legitimate state, the apocalypse of the state in its pure state, beyond [*au-delà*] the old principle of the inscription of rights and obligations of each in a constitution (an organic law as precise as the geographic configuration of the nation), to the dubious advantage of a 'transnational' administration of time and energies, comparable, probably, in the order of duration, to what was once materialism in the order of history.

Today, if limited conflicts no longer deserve the term 'war', it is because they constitute its *de-generation* [*dégénération*[41]]. Where 'total war' encounters the total impossibility of extending itself spatially due to the absolute character of the new means of destruction, its degeneracy [*dégénérescence*] allows its indefinite extension in time. Thus the era of the great pacification has arrived, not, as one alleges, with that of 'conventional wars', but that *of a non-conventional supra-delinquency,* terrorism of the state beyond [*au-delà*] all political forms (domestic or diplomatic), since it affects indiscriminately the foreigner and the national; blockage[42] of 'real war' to the advantage of the development of *trend wars,* banalization of a statistical extermination where the Great

War becomes impossible, except by accident. Thus, *with the inhibition of the acting out of war, the preparation of a global logistics supplants the perpetration of a world war*, whence the inflation, the research and development of the arms trade, despite the incalculable risks of a destructuring, of an economic collapse, not only of the Third World, but also of middle powers.[43]

Thus the transpolitical inversion of a *relative war* succeeds the fundamentally 'political' invention of a *relative peace*. Succeeding the great invasions, the wars of the conquest of space, of the era of *extensivity* of national and colonial powers, is the imperceptible 'war of time' of the *intensivity* of an anational power, without real representation and which no longer manifests itself except through the repetition of an increased delinquency, 'crimes against humanity' against which no authority can any longer impose sanctions. We must, therefore, lose our liberal illusions concerning *decolonization*, lose as well our euphoria regarding the *decentralization* of certain countries (Italy, France . . .). Deregulation, whose economic and other consequences we are now subject to, in no way announces the advent of a golden age of regional self-management, but presages rather an era of endless conflicts in a world returning not to the epoch of local self-regulation, but to the obscurantism of a *recuperated feudalism* where amateur terrorists will soon be replaced by professionals of terror: heads of state using their armed forces, their personal guards,[44] their paramilitary police like common 'overlords of war'. Having no longer anything to do with some *military engagement* like that of the United States in Vietnam or of the Soviet Union in Afghanistan, the situation would be rather similar to that of the Far East of 'warring kingdoms', the persistence of the localized violations and conflicts announcing a long night of Jacqueries and transnational crusades, anticipation of a *pure state* capable of securing a universal domination, figure of a 'military-scientistic' messianism arrayed[45] with attributes from the last empire. . . .

Everything will probably play out, therefore, through the *proxemic evaluation* of the partners-adversaries, in other words, through the capacity of their global logistics to act *in real time*, with the most extreme precision, on the nuclear as well as on the conventional level. Soviet interventionism, the setting up by the Americans of a 'rapid deployment force' of more than 200,000 men, and the role of the police recently secured by a number of task forces illustrates well the return to a terrorist activism, linked to the appearance of weaponry and new arms with the technical characteristics of sophisticated munitions.[46]

Thus the equilibrium of terror, triumph of the strategy of deterrence, is succeeded by the permanent disequilibrium of a strategy of tension, where global logistics supplants intercontinental ballistics, all this favouring a dramatic reversal of public opinion, the solicitation of the support of the people, a collective intoxication before the probabilities of a world conflict, the imminence of a nuclear war,[47] the psychologically necessary surpassing of the *status quo,* such that we were already preparing the major risks of atomic energy while the *famous equalizing power of the atom* was forgotten, omitted, as had been previously that of the parity of gold and of the dollar....

The energy crisis thus develops the energy of crisis. *Deregulation* is promoted in the West as a principle of government. The monetary and tariff fluctuation, principle of uncertainty raised to the status of a means of economic pressure, is succeeded by a *destabilization of détente* where, as with the monetary standard, it seems the 'nuclear standard' is abandoned in a sort of political fluctuation where 'terror is the realization of the law of movement' (Hannah Arendt), outside all effective localization, outside any ideological distinction, and where, as long ago, military anarchy belongs less to long-term history than to the *time of instantaneous exposition,* outside any sanction, since speed is a violence which is not politically sanctioned. We begin to catch sight of the double effect of what is incorrectly named 'the crisis'. If the energy crisis tends to justify the importance of *geostrategic proximity,* with the pursuit of logistical support,[48] the revival of activities of support destined to preserve the flow of supply, the energy of the crisis tends conversely to challenge the very notion of *geopolitical proximity.*[49] We are witness to the beginnings of a remarkable event: *the decline of territorial politics.* As an official of the Israeli parliament claimed in Jerusalem: *'Israel is too small to make peace'.* From now on, the whole world is too limited to carry on with geopolitics, i.e., with *relative peace,* this innovation of a bygone epoch where the expanse of territories was not even known....

The experience of the concentration camp is, therefore, no longer that of camps or gulags, these were still only 'small-scale models' of the progressive restriction of political territory, whence *this disintegration on the way to generalization* which begins with the illusion of decolonization, continues with economic and monetary deregulation,[50] and extends, with the demand for regional autonomy, to the deurbanization glimpsed here and there,[51] to which the American continent is testimony, to end tomorrow in 'transpolitical' anarchy, *the inertia of a relative war*, exemplified by the negative utopia of Cambodia. The hate and extreme horror of what is close, familiar, are merely the indirect and politically unperceived consequences of the logistical capacities that reach the extremities of the world without delay. *No more delay, no more relief,* the neighbourhood becomes insipid, leading to the introversion of communities, this inertial confinement of *societies infinitely too small to make civil peace.*

'*Immediacy is a deception*', wrote the theologian Dietrich Bonhoeffer. The perverse effects of this deception are measured by observing that what is *common* is today disqualified by the immediacy of what is not. When a user of *CB radio* explains, for example, that his transmitter allows him to speak 'preferably with people he doesn't know', to enter into communication '*outside of his circle of geographic affinities*', this implies that what is not *here* prevails by far over what is present.... Finally, audiovisual pressure represents the *decline of the unity of vicinity,* and through it, the expression of the next stage in the decline of territorial politics. From this arises the insidious discrediting of geopolitical extensivity, for more than twenty years, to the benefit of an unsuspected transpolitical intensivity, the decline of the state of law and the accelerated deregulation of different governmental systems which lead, even at this very moment, despite the illusion of the international market, to a reversal of the aggregative federative principal,[52] an auspicious dissociation, the figure of an *illusory decentralization which is only the extension of liberal decolonization.* Thus follows an infinite series of 'divorces', carried out in the name of liberties, between the sexes, the generations, the ethnic and social groups, and up to the vast national social entities, and thus the advancement of an administration, or rather an *empire of time itself,* whose nature may already be evaluated, thanks to the evolution of industrial production, through the precariousness of the status of *temporary* personnel tied to both cyclical unemployment and *intensive schedules*, with no connection to any other physiological cycle, any cultural rhythm, so as to realize *the management of a continuous time that would be to transpolitical intensity what colonial and federal extension was once to geopolitics.*

Industrial restructuring [*redéploiement*] thus illustrates perfectly this phenomenon of panicked dispersal, where the increased concentration of power implies conversely the geographic and transnational deconcentration of companies, the greatest possible economic and social anarchy.

Thus we better understand the subtle diversion in the procedures of liberation that today drives entire populations to become not merely *migrant workers* forced into an industrial deportation, *temporary proletarians*, the unemployed of a lockout planned in advance, but equally, more and more frequently, refugees, exiles in their own country, enemies, or, more exactly, an internal threat to a power without any exteriority at all, *where those absent are inevitably right.…*

In fact, this obscurantism more or less renews the dichotomy of body and mind, whence the conflict, the unprecedented competition that develops between 'priest' and 'warrior' for a supremacy of which the *transpolitical beyond* [*au-delà*] is the stake, after the extinction of the covetousness and constraints of the geopolitical here below. Henceforth, asceticism extends into unsuspected domains. With the propensity of 'advanced technologies' to annul the space and time of long durations, *less is more;*[53] the ecological inversion becomes the criterion of a global logistics (ecologistics) where *'in order to reinforce the State, to do less is better'*.[54] All this is because teleprocessing opens certain inquisitorial perspectives with no similarity whatsoever to any other capacity of control, whence this decline of real coexistence and cohabitation[55] to the dubious mutual advantage of a 'post-political' detachment [*distanciation*] where the old containment becomes a pure and simple renunciation, a great 'abandoning of all', in the name of liberation from supervision: lies and the deception of an immediacy which will enslave supernumerary populations soon to be deprived of their 'civil rights'. We need, finally, to stop deceiving ourselves, stop taking a will to *autonomy* as a desire for emancipation, which is only in fact the desperate search for an *inertia* which already extends beyond geopolitical limits attaining every delimitation. *The imperceptible disqualification of the proximate environment by the acceleration of transports and transmissions now affects the fundamental nature of politics.* The invention, the original survey of the inscription of laws, of the rights and responsibilities of every individual, not only on clay tablets but in the precise configuration of a town or land registry, has so thoroughly marked the history of nations and the memory of peoples that none seem to notice its progressive disappearance, as well as the imminence of a management of time, of an *emergency chronopolitics*, excluding all other representation.

'Democratic Kampuchea' serves here to analyse the end of territorial politics. More than 30 years after Auschwitz, Kampuchea effectively constitutes the life-size model of a *suicidal state* capable of exterminating more than half of its population in three years, and this outside any sanction, since certain leaders of the Angkor still dared to intervene at the UN with the assent of the West....

The decisive importance of the socialist ideology in the Cambodian experience unfortunately allows lessons of a general nature to be drawn which apply to a number of contemporary situations. As early as the first days of Khmer Rouge power, one witnesses, not, as has been claimed, a situation comparable (given the small size of the country) to the circumstances associated with the creation of extermination camps within Nazi Germany, but rather a radically inverse movement of *deconcentration* attaining simultaneously total conglomeration. Exodus, now a total logistic reality, has become the absolute weapon of a revolution where *deurbanization* must assure no longer the justice of the classes, but 'the vengeance of the classes'[56] by separating the wheat from the chaff, in other words, the old people of the countryside from the new people of the cities. The 'liberation' of Cambodia sees, therefore, the end of the city–country opposition and the most radical *decentralization* possible. With the forced evacuation of the political capital, *the revolution becomes an efficient religion, and the country, a purgatory* where justice is now nothing more than expeditious for a people corrupted by consumption, money, and a life-style of an urban proximity perceived as reactionary.

'Let us consider the difference between revolution and religion', say the Khmer Rouge, 'In Buddhism, the sinner was condemned long after having committed his sin: the punishment was deferred until later, to an alleged other life, this was a deferment that could drag on indefinitely.

This encouraged people to commit other sins, because they never knew at what moment they were to be punished. *But then the revolution did away with this delay, the person guilty of a serious transgression is immediately punished, he does not wait, that is real justice: revolution purifies more quickly than religion.'*[57]

The absence of incarceration being the consequence of this postulate, deregulation must soon reach not only the urban morphology, the territorial infrastructure inherited from an abhorred past, but all institutional constraints, leading to the disappearance, simultaneously with that of the prisons, of parts of the civil state, of birth certificates....

The utopia of Khmer military socialism reveals itself, therefore, as first of all the atopia[58] *of an eschatological power determined to hasten the Last Judgement.*

Instantaneity is, therefore, to the 'warrior' what eternity is to the 'priest'. No more duration, no more topography! The raising up of the 'people on the bottom' requires the inertia of an absolute *self*-sufficiency in isolated villages where no freedom of movement is allowed, nor any free time tolerated, and where the most important of the communal tasks are the giant irrigation projects, in a watertight country where communications are banned, trips prohibited ... *the dictatorship of the liberation movement leads thus to a fixation*, a pathological fixation which affects the mentalities and activity at the heart of a *society without class,* but also without expanse and without depth, where all is immediate, from whence the practical uselessness of any delimitations of the land, of any hierarchic or social distinctions, since all this, including taxation, will disappear.

The geographic exiguity of Cambodia and its weak demography facilitates the 'reduction', the real country becomes its representation, *a representation deprived of dimensions, where each agricultural camp is identified with the 'democratic' Kampuchea.* The fatal omnipresence of the Angkor in each of them thus attains a 'stereopolitical' confinement where *self-punishment* is the emergency imperative of a population which has become the raw material of an endless purge ... outcome of a necessary popular resistance, the Khmer peasants only pushed to the extreme, that is to say to the absurd, a tendency apparent *each time that popular struggles organize to endure.* Rebelling against an unjust order, the 'militants' thus reconstitute the formation of 'military' castes.

Progressively, the political character of their opposition movement is supplanted by a military, indeed radically militaristic, system; what can now be verified in Ireland with the IRA, or in Spain with the separatist Basque movement of the ETA, *is being reproduced everywhere today due to the excessively long duration of antagonisms* resulting indirectly from nuclear deterrence. Because of a capacity to produce or acquire deterrent weapons, the armed movements of political opposition must absolutely continue the combat. *For each of them, whatever their initial ideological motivations, the victory is identified with the infinite prolongation of the war game,* a permanent war, another name for an 'armed revolution' that thus becomes a vicious circle where each protagonist wants to conserve at all costs, with the security of the employment of his ultimate 'profession', his weapons and a power acquired throughout the years of the fratricidal struggles.[59] The incessant harassment of the 'military-militants' thus faithfully reproduces the permanent effect of tribal war in the societies analysed by Pierre Clastres.[60]

Contrary to the extensive 'great wars' which historically installed the unifying political state, the intensive 'little war', i.e., guerrilla war, opposes the state, that is to say, opposes the constitution of a durable political pacification, a consequence which geopolitics takes into account by marking the limits of respective influence, above all by managing with the state-city a strategic theatre of operations (the fortified wall) founded on the primacy of the centre over the periphery, and then, with the frontiers, a national territory where the city dominates the countryside, the capital itself becoming an over-determined political pole.

The end of the extensivity of conflicts recreates today the conditions of an intense local enslavement; *wars of liberation are no longer anything but a liberation of war* which affirms the supporters of political non-violence.

Based on the return of the 'tactical' primacy and autonomy of numerically limited 'grassroots groups', unlike the large battalions or 'groups of armies' which depend strategically upon a great power, open war requires that the disciplinary power necessary for action be divided up into networks of *military self-defence* where mastery is assured by an infinite number of delegates, small 'warlords' of a neo-feudal system of which the current separatist or fractional demands are the obvious symptom. The recent generalization of terrorism can, moreover, be explained by this new-found tactical autonomy, this *local inertia* of 'grassroots militants' escaping democratic control, where the balance of terror signals henceforth the *global inertia* of a strategy of deterrence which is itself escaping, more and more, the political control of different governments[61] with the constant development of 'theatre' *tactical nuclear weapons*, the medium-range missile, the computer-guided cruise missile, and, especially, the 'enhanced-radiation weapons' said to be capable of restoring the defensive by allowing a *limited nuclear war*. In other words, these tactics constitute the logistical complement of domestic terrorism where the national state would soon become the target of a double assault, hostage of a double game: in the name of the *ideologies of liberation* on the one hand, and, on the other, in the name of the apparent deterrent necessities of a *defence of the free world* which transcends the ideological options of states subject to the blackmail of the 'capital nations', another designation of the great militarily over-determined powers, in both the East and the West.

Thus, deterrence progressively expands to all the geostrategic levels of nuclear or conventional armaments and to all geopolitical degrees, from traditional diplomatic means to individual actions and other 'state attacks'.[62]

As the American General Bennie Davis, chief-of-staff of the Strategic Command of Intercontinental Missiles declared publicly, in the summer of 1981: '*We are going to delegate more and more authority to the leaders on the ground*'. The fact that thereafter both the commanders on the spot,[63] and pilots[64] were given this latitude, confirms, if it is still necessary, *the escalation of a now chance interventionism, the notion of an accidental or preventive act of war*, the return to a 'tactical' activism favoured by the prolonged duration of tensions (national and international), the endemism of a *relative war*, which gives up, by virtue of being excessively random, every other strategy save that of the 'accident-test' or attack, and whose increased likelihood has been indicated by a number of recent incidents.

Can one envisage the extension of deterrence without understanding, if a little belatedly, that what is called 'deterrence' is nothing other than *the strategy of a war which would appear less in its execution than in its preparation? a logistical preparation which would be, in fact, its perpetuation beyond [au-delà] all limits* (economic, political)? the fatal drive of industrialization toward the non-development of a *zero growth* where the ecological demands of the Club of Rome would be suddenly reinforced by the 'ecologistical' imperatives of the army, the imperious necessities of a generalized deterrence?

By the beginning of the 1960s, the abandonment of the doctrine of *massive retaliation* to the advantage of that of *flexible response* had given the signal for the rise in power no longer of the armaments whose destructive capacity were going to be constantly limited, but of a scientific and industrial 'war machine' supposedly capable of deterring the adversary-partner through a game of war become military-economic that General Eisenhower, a specialist in logistics, had himself denounced on his departure from the White House.[65]

From this perspective, the current manipulation of opinion would indicate, above all, a solicitation for a new leap forwards, the announcement of a new 'military-industrial revolution', advent of the third nuclear age[66] and this one, during a full recession, in a period of worldwide economic crisis....

The ever volatile threat of a possible vitrification of European ground: wouldn't this be some form of psychological incentive for the organization of a new Yalta?... 'Yalta', certainly a bit specific, but of which the *bilateral* accords of Moscow in 1972 offered a glimpse, along with the multilateral accords of Helsinki, not to mention the closed doors meetings in Geneva between Russians and Americans, or again to the practical uselessness of the conference on European security in Madrid.... A 'Yalta' that this time is less interested in the delimitation of spheres of geopolitical influence than in the limitations on the sovereignty of nations subject to the system of blocs.... A *'Yalta' where the level of development of the mode of destruction would suddenly take precedence over that of the mode of production,* a *New Deal* of a military consumption, of an economy of pure war, between partners–adversaries who have reached the epitome of political emptiness, causing in their train the collapse of their 'allies' and the bankruptcy of their 'satellites', unable to pursue any longer 'an arms race with no finish line' (General Buis).

For that matter, let it be noted that if atomic deterrence prevented total war, none were deterred from arming themselves, since it contributed instead to the exponential development of the technologies of war. In less than ten years, strategic arms limitation agreements led essentially *to the multiplication of miniaturized nuclear warheads and, correlatively, to the perfecting of the guidance of delivery systems with the most extreme precision,* with the disastrous consequences which this supposes for the practical efficaciousness of 'first strike' and, therefore, for the very credibility of strategic deterrence....

Contrary to the affirmations of certain authors, victims of disinformation,[67] the problem is no longer that of a *quantitative strategy* but, for a long time already, that of a *qualitative strategy*[68] which continually destabilizes nuclear deterrence and contributes to the advent of a war economy. This economy is insupportable for states of average power engaged in an escalation to the extremes of an absolute economic war, where there are no friends or enemies, but only *threats,* and above all the *threat of armaments become the real enemies of the sovereignty of societies*; no longer so much a threat to those for whom these weapons are destined in the eventuality of an aggression, but paradoxically to the societies that produce them or thoughtlessly contribute to producing them *for their defence.*

The notion of *threat* that today characterizes the strategic ambiguity of the doctrine of security, clearly contrary to the politics of national defence, has not allowed this 'transpolitical' dimension of global logistics to be taken into consideration. *This strategy of the perpetuation of war in the escalation in the power of a military-economic programming will contribute sooner or later to the non-development of states engaged in the research and development of a mode of destruction which is supposedly a deterrent to the potential adversary,* but which is in fact first and above all a deterrent to the development and progress of the society that one intends to safeguard.

Just as in Yalta in 1945, where agreements between 'allies' subjugated entire nations under the virtuous pretext of assuring the geopolitical balance between the Eastern and Western blocs, so also in 1972, in the name of a necessary balance of the American-Soviet strategic forces, the Moscow Accords contributed to the accentuation of the 'technologistical' risks. *The increase in the threat of the means of deterrence, along with the sophistication of the weaponry, furthers the capacities of pure war,* war on the political autonomy of countries approaching total disqualification due to their imminent powerlessness to further engage their resources in a military-industrial wager which constitutes in itself a major risk to the economic and political survival of the states in question, European states which henceforth find themselves much closer than they would like to those of the Third World.

The SALT Accords and the bilateral negotiations of Geneva aiming at the preparation of the future START Accords,[69] much less than the dawn of universal disarmament, constitute, in fact, *the announcement of the third revolution in the mode of destruction.*

If the first *military-industrial* revolution of 1870 had facilitated the rise of European colonial imperialism by means of the development of naval force and the railway system and had seen the rapid economic collapse of this continent leading to the war economy, just after the first global conflict, the second *military-industrial and scientific* revolution of post-World War II led, at the same time as decolonization, to the economic and cultural subjugation of these same European nations in the sectors of influence of the zones of total peaceful coexistence, and this thanks to the terrorist innovation of atomic weapons and of stratospheric missiles.

In accordance with this tendency, the third revolution should mark the entire and definitive supremacy of the mode of destruction over different modes of production, declaration of pure war on the entire world where, beyond bygone ideological enemies, the politically incalculable threat of destructive technologies rises to the fore.

Deterrence on all levels would thus consist in extending the regime of pure war on the totality of productive activities to the eschatological and 'post-industrial' perspective of the non-development (economic and social) of productive forces – a contamination of political thought but also, and above all, of a scientific discourse definitively engaged with negativity, whose extreme perversity is already indicated by certain practices of military control of intellectual resources.[70]

In fact it is this agonistic situation that necessitates in the short term *a last Yalta* between the 'great powers' threatened with political powerlessness in their spheres of influence. A 'Yalta' that no longer, as in the past, consists in negotiating between 'allies–future enemies' but between 'enemies–future allies', faced with the non-calculated risk of a fundamentally enigmatic internal adversity: *science*, the improbable sudden appearance of knowledge. In effect, the real redeployment of the 'mode of destruction', the generalization of deterrence on all levels of weaponry, *not at all deterring, however, the invention of new weapons*, never deters the fortuitous discovery of definitive means, available to all, at any time, anywhere (the logic of a logistical terrorism become in turn absolute). The issue in these future negotiations would involve *an attempt, before it's too late, at agreeing upon the sharing of responsibilities in the control of knowledge*; faced with the last of the 'declared enemies', the war machine at work in a scientific production about to be engaged by military intelligence. The desperate attempt to impose, not the *zero option* of non-deployment of weapons, but the *degree zero* of the development of knowledge, the definitive crisis of a 'civil scientific community reduced to acquisitions'. This crisis is already symptomatized by the failure of university research, an obvious sign of the degradation of political intelligence, the decline of a 'providence state', advent of a 'destiny state' destined with the progress of knowledge to abolish civil consumption and social assistance, while fostering extreme military consumption.

The current debate on the risks of the *transfers of technology* to the Third World, and to countries of the East as well, in which Caspar Weinberger, the American Secretary of Defence,[71] took part, clearly indicates the tendency: a division of the world established on *ideological* givens is replaced, bit by bit, by a division founded on *technological* considerations. As Raymond Aron explains, if it is *technological* excesses that yesterday replaced war objectives with ideologies,[72] it is *scientific* excess that tomorrow will install the technologistical idolatry (the Gnostic belief in a transcendence of science) in place of political economy. Improperly named 'deterrence' by the apologists of nuclear conflagration, *pure war* is, therefore, only the emergence of a cult, the institution of a *military-scientific messianism* founded on the logistical capacities of vectors of extermination escaping the control of a political intelligence corrupted by materialism, a materialism which progressively turned away from the contemplation of death (individual and collective), contemplation that all the same maintained tight relations with the origin of politics. Powerless, we witness thus today a catastrophic hybridization, a fusion/confusion comes about between mystical apocalypse and the apocalyptic mystification of a *cult of the arsenal*, analogous in many respects to the 'cargo-cult' of Papua New Guinea.[73]

The participation, the enlistment of everyone, no longer amounts to a conscription for the defence of the nation, but rather to the conversion of masses forced to take up *the nuclear faith* [*foi*], the hope for salvation through the virtues of an absolute armament[74] where the incessant reinforcement of destructive achievements assumes the role of a common centre, a *cratos*[75] of a transpolitical city, deprived of both [*à la foi*] territory and corporeality, a city built beyond the regime of law, an *auto-da-fé* that prohibits all political reasoning in order to generate a regime of panic superstition, founded under the sign of the *immediate survival of the body* and no longer, as in the past, of the *postmortem survival of the soul*.

In this parody of the religious state – which plays out in this 'ecological' return to regimes of simple subsistence and non-development – lies the beyond, the hereafter [*l'au-delà*], of progressive perspectives, the end of hope for any 'paradise on earth', for any economic and social success, the obscure advent of a *universal purgatory* for supernumerary populations deprived of civil rights, in deferment, in permanent suspension, subject to the decay of the quotidian and the many recent excesses that betray the scandal. *It is hard to imagine a society that would deny the body just as we had progressively denied the soul. This, however, is where we are heading.*

Notes

TRANSLATOR'S INTRODUCTION

1   p. 28.
2   p. 30.
3   p. 26.
4   p. 30.
5   p. 30.
6   p. 32.
7   'The Idea of Natural History', in *Telos* #60, 1984, p. 115.
8   Ibid., p. 120.
9   In 'Anaximander's Apeiron: Fault Lines at the Foundations of Thought', to appear in an anthology of essays in response to Bucher's *L'Imagination de l'origine* entitled *Death, Language, and Thought: Gérard Bucher's Imagination of Origins.*
10 I have altered the translation here to avoid confusion between *das Seienden* and *Sein.* Hullot-Kentor's rendering 'the existing' is another alternative.
11 'The Anaximander fragment', in *Early Greek Thinking*, p. 20. Translation altered.
12 *The Specters of Marx*, New York, 1994, p. 28.
13 *Op. cit.*, p. 118.
14 p. 47.
15 p. 42.
16 *The Archaeology of Knowledge*, New York, 1972, p. 90.
17 Ibid., p. 12.
18 'Nietzsche, Genealogy, History' in *Language, Counter-Memory, Practice*, Cornell, 1977, p. 154.
19 Ibid., p. 154.
20 In *The Origin of German Tragic Drama*, London, 1977.
21 Referring here, of course, to Nietzsche's *The Birth of Tragedy.*
22 *The History of Sexuality*, Vol. 1, New York, 1978, p. 93.
23 p. 99.

24 *Homo sacer: Il poetere sourano e la nuda vita*, 1995, translated as *Homo Sacer: Sovereign Power and Bare Life*, Stanford, 1998.

25 Ibid., p. 6.

26 Ibid., p. 3.

27 Ibid.

28 *Op. cit.*, p. 8.

29 Ibid., p. 27.

30 See 'The Caesura of the Symbolon in Aeschylus' *Agamemnon*', *Arethusa*, vol. 34, 2001: 61–95.

31 *Op. cit.*, p. 111.

32 p. 57.

33 A more complete treatment of these odes will be presented in a forthcoming article to be entitled, 'Slipping through the hands: the parallax of antiphor in Aeschylus' *Agamemnon*'.

34 An explanation of the active dynamics of Empedoclean optics and the role of these optics in the suspension of the mythico-symbolic order is detailed in my article in *Arethusa, op. cit.*

35 This moment plays a key role in Agamben's discussion of the King's two bodies when he turns to Vernant's study in *Myth and Thought among the Ancient Greeks* of the mimetic figure of the colossus (*Homo Sacer*, pp. 91–103), which take the form here of the statues of Helen stationed at the city limits of Argos. Vernant's account does not, however, uncover the full significance of this passage as *the* key moment underlying all that Agamben is pursuing in the *homo sacer*.

36 p. 48.

37 p. 114

38 *Op. cit.*, p. 170.

39 'Innocent detainee found unlikely ally', *The New York Times*, 30 June 2004.

40 'Blair says illicit weapons may never be found, but "we know" Hussein had them', *The New York Times*, 7 July 2004.

41 p. 59.

42 p. 44.

43 p. 200.

44 In 'Regarding the torture of others', in the *New York Times Magazine*, 23 May 2004.

45   ED: Hilare was the first mobile robot designed by LAAS (Laboratory for Analysis and Architecture of Systems) at the Centre National de la Recherche Scientifique in 1977. The name means something akin to 'hilarious'.

FOREWORD

1   ED: Art critic Michel Tapié coined this term to describe the European counterpart to American abstract expressionism and specifically action painting.
2   TN: The French *entre-deux*, used to indicate the space between, means literally 'between two'.
3   TN: Virilio is expanding upon the art term '*fond*', 'ground', as in figure/ground to include the other connotations of the word such as bottom, depth, core and background.
4   TN: '*Voyant*' has essentially the same connotations as 'seer', namely those of the visionary or even clairvoyant.

FIRST PART

1   TN: There is, unfortunately, no way of rendering the double entendre of this term, '*passager*', which is at once the noun 'passenger', and also a substantive adjective meaning 'the fleeting'. Both senses are in play throughout the chapter.
2   TN: Here we have the first instance of the simple French term '*voyage*' which will prove surprisingly difficult to translate throughout the course of the text. The somewhat antiquarian or adventurist tone of the English 'voyage' will prove poorly suited to many of the contexts in which the French term will figure later in the text. In this instance it seems reasonably appropriate to employ the cognate; however, it will be necessary to resort at times to 'trip' or 'travel'. The reader should be aware that these terms are all linked together in an important chain of references. The importance of the term itself will be seen again below when Virilio speaks of the '*voyager/voyeur*,' where again I will opt to retain the cognates.

3   TN: '*Femme-de-charge*' as opposed to '*bête-de-charge*', 'beast of burden'.

4   TN: '*Femme-de-bât*' as opposed to '*cheval-de-bât*', 'packhorse'.

5   Aragon.

6   TN: The verb *monter*, 'to mount', is commonly used for mechanical vehicles as well as horses.

7   TN: Virilio employs the term *déplacée* here to establish in the next sentence the charge of 'displacement' for the term '*déplacement*' which it will carry throughout the text. See note 14 below for an explanation of this term.

8   TN: Here Virilio establishes the emphasized charge of 'displacement' on '*déplacement*'. See note 14 below.

9   F. Benoit, *L'héroïsation équestre*, Ophrys, 1954.

10 Consider the political and economic functions of the dovecote in the Middle Ages.

11 'I looked and there was a pale green horse! Its rider's name Death, and Hades followed with him...' Revelation 6:8.

12 TN: Virilio's play on various connotations of the word '*enlever*' is not translatable.

13 TN: See next note.

14 TN: Having established the literal charge of 'displacement' for this term as discussed above in notes 7 and 8, Virilio enhances the distinction between '*mouvement*' and '*déplacement*'. '*Mouvement*' signifies the action of being in movement, whereas '*déplacement*' signifies moving from one place to another as well as the literal sense of 'displacement'. Thus, the terms are very close in meaning to their English cognates; however, the meaning of 'displacement' is more restricted and technical than '*déplacement*', which is used more broadly in French. At times it will make sense to retain the more limited connotations of the English 'displacement', i.e. the sense of being moved away from a (rightful) place; in other instances, however, it will be necessary to resort to the broader range expressed in 'movement'. This is unfortunate, for in the latter cases we lose something of what is conveyed in the technical sense of 'displacement' that remains in the background of the French. I seek to suggest what is at stake in this distinction with the half quotes on 'displacement' which actually means something closer to 'movement' here.

15   TN: Here is an exemplary instance, as discussed above in note 2, in which it is unfortunately not possible to rely on the cognate of the original '*voyages*'. Again the reader is advised to be aware of this shortcoming in what follows as it would be too cumbersome to point out each instance.

16   It is enough to point out all the various constraints and controls of the highway system to verify this point.

17   G. Dumézil, *Le problème des centaures*, Guenther, 1929.

18   TN: Here is an exemplary instance in which '*déplacement*' is not well translated by its cognate. See note 14 above.

19   TN: Although 'skedasos' appears in Virilio's text, it must be assumed he is referring here to 'skedasis' the Greek term for scattering, or dispersing, particularly in battle.

20   TN: Perhaps a bit forced, this phrase seeks to reproduce Virilio's double entendre on *étalon*, 'stallion' and 'standard', as in gold standard.

21   Nicolet, 'A propos de l'ordre équestre' in *Problèmes de la gurre de Rome*, Mouton, 1969.

22   TN: Virilio is playing here on *appareiller*: in the nautical sphere, 'casting off'; in the medical, 'fitting with a prosthesis'.

23   TN: Virilio's word play is untranslatable: '... *nous sommes moins des gars, des graces, que des gares*'.

24   TN: Virilio's word play on *election/ejection* is nearly as strained in French. He is addressing the devaluing of territory as a chosen [*élection*] place to dwell by the displacement of travel [*éjection*].

25   TN: This technical term, '*rupture de charge*', indicating a trans-shipment, is reversed just below. See note 27.

26   TN: The term is Greek for 'scattering'.

27   TN: The phrase '*charge de rupture*' reverses the term indicated above at note 25. Virilio plays on the shipping term '*rupture de charge*', 'break of load', that refers to the break-up of a shipment at transshipping points. His reversal of the term here, '*charge de rupture*', conveys the notion of the break-up or rupture of a charge on defences.

28   TN: The term derives from the Greek *poliorketikos*, 'siege of a city'.

29   TN: Virilio is using the term here in its original theological sense of a 'procession'.

30   TN: See note 27.

31   TN: Virilio is referring to the two senses of *appareillage*: first, matching up or coupling, even in the sense of sexual reproduction; second, the sense of fitting out in preparation for departure on a voyage, especially of ships.

32   TN: The term refers simultaneously to a dance partner and a rider.

33   TN: These are simultaneously equestrian terms and the names of nineteenth-century dances.

34   TN: The term '*défiler*' that Virilio introduces here will resurface repeatedly in different configurations throughout the text to follow figuring similar links between dynamics of moving bodies or forces and the cinematic sequencing of images. At times it will be translated as it is here, at other times it will be translated with some form of the notion of 'sequencing'.

35   TN: Virilio is playing on *mobilier*, 'furnishings', just above, which derives from *mobile*.

36   TN: Here, and in the instances of *déplacement* to follow in this chapter, the restricted sense of 'displacement' comes to the fore. See note 14 above.

37   M.-R. Davie, *La guerre dans les sociétés primitives*, Payot.

38   TN: The Greek term for the public auditors of outgoing magistrates was used in Latin as the title of an imperial official who supervised the spending of municipalities.

39   Gilles Deleuze, *La logique de sens*, Éditions de Minuit, 1969 (*The Logic of Sense*, Columbia University Press, 1990).

40   ED: The *chevaucheurs royaux* were royal messengers of the mediaeval era of a status not always indissociable from that of an ambassador and who were equipped with a network of horses.

41   The officer responsible for the review of armies and materiel under the Ancien Régime.

42   ED: The intendant was an officer in charge of supplies for the army in a capacity comparable to that of a quartermaster general.

43   A. H. De Jomini, *Précis de l'art de la guerre*, Champ Libre, 1862.

44   P. Rousseau, *Histoire des transports*, Fayard.

45   P. Rousseau, ibid.

46   P. Rousseau, ibid.
47   *Signal*, November, 1941.

SECOND PART

1   ED: Virilio is playing here on the similarity between the verb for applying facial make-up that refers as well to broader implications of dissimulation, '*maquiller*', and the name for the scrubland vegetation from which the French Resistance took its name, '*le Maquis*'.
2   ED: The Camisards were members of a Calvinist insurgency in the southern mountainous region of France known as the Cévennes who derived their name from their distinctive shirt, or 'camiso', which is Occitan for 'shirt'.
3   ED: The term, which also derives from Occitan, meaning 'butterfly', was pejorative.
4   If very early on the camera took its place just above the cannon of the machine gun of aerial dogfights to facilitate the acquisition of the target, the recording of enemy planes brought down, it was because the function of the weapon and that of the eye were from their very origin fused in aiming, the eyepiece of the gun with a telescopic sight, the telescopic sights of long-range artillery. The invention by Nadar of 'aerostatic photography', the systematic industrialization of the image of aerial reconnaissance through the course of the First World War, had elsewhere perfectly illustrated this cinematic dimension of a mode of destruction operating on the level of entire regions, an incessant upheaval of a countryside that it was necessary to reconstruct as quickly as possible with the aid of successive photographs, a cinematic tracking of an uncertain territory, geographic decomposition and recomposition where film succeeds the map of the major state. Total war would only accelerate this play of the changing scene of battle. (See P. Virilio, *War and Cinema: The Logistics of Perception*, London and New York, 1989.)
5   *Is it necessary to raze the suburbs?* In the hour when the suburbanites claim their specificity, the great complexes of the sixties are living

through a sort of revolution. In la Courneuve, preparations have been made to destroy 1,500 public housing units, in Gagny, 500 apartments, etc. Everywhere around the large cities the problem is posed. An economic study undertaken by the Association for the Development of Communication, came to following conclusions: 'The demolition of 300,000 apartments in five years would cost 10 billion francs each year, but it would allow the creation of more than 100,000 jobs. Even better, at the end of the five years, the fiscal income arising from the demolition/reconstruction operation would be 6 to 10 billion francs greater than the public investment. So, why not?' A. Silber, *Le Nouvel Observateur*, 1982.

6   We understand better in this way the destitution of certain large American cities, in particular to the east of the Mississippi where, from Chicago to Washington, from Saint-Louis to Boston, urban centres are being depopulated in record speed, a menacing economic equilibrium of urban zones on the Atlantic coast and in the Midwest. *In ten years Saint Louis lost 27 per cent of its inhabitants, Cleveland 23 per cent, and Detroit more than 20 per cent....* Certain of these cities' neighbourhoods already seem like the ghost towns immortalized in American films. It is the same thing in Europe, with the crisis of industrial cities: Liverpool and Sheffield in Great Britain, Dortmund in West Germany, without even mentioning the situation in the urban zone of Lyon in France, whose deterioration has reached such a point that the building minister Roger Quilliot has recently undertaken a study of a *demolition programme of a million public housing apartments* judged not to be in conformity with the new 'way of life', unhealthy conditions being no longer officially the sole criteria, the sole pretext for the destruction of buildings.... *Is the demolition of the large industrial cities in the process of replacing the politics of great public works, typical of a period of economic crisis?*

7   'A true decentralization must be accompanied by a large deconcentration, notably as regards urbanism and housing'. A. Mauroy, *Le Matin*, 21 April 1982.

8   'On both sides, guided missiles are targeted to destroy the enemy's launch capacity. In order to successfully strike their targets, they

must be fired before the enemy's missiles even leave the silos. *The reaction time has become so short that, in the course of a crisis, peace and war are decided by computer.'* R. Barnet, *Le Monde diplomatique*, April 1982.

THIRD PART

1   TN: This technical painting term describes an error in the application of varnish wherein the varnish soaks through the canvas in a particular spot causing a dullness or matt appearance.

2   TN: Virilio returns to the art term he employed in his discussion of perception in the foreword.

3   TN: As awkward as this translation may seem in English, there is good reason to render it in this fashion. The notion of 'mounting' goes back to the references in the first section to the horse and runs as a motif through the entire work.

4   TN: It is necessary to retain the French term here, which means 'collision', to follow Virilio's line of thought.

5   'As confirmation let us look at a complex object. A ball 10 cm in diameter, made of thread of 1 mm in diameter, possesses, in a certain latent way, several distinct physical dimensions. At a degree of resolution of 10 m, it appears as a point, therefore as a zero-dimensional figure; at a resolution of 10 cm, it is a ball and therefore a tridimensional figure; at a resolution of 10 mm, it is a collection of threads and therefore a unidimensional figure; at resolution of 0.1 mm, each thread comments a sort of column, and it all becomes again a tridimensional figure; at 0.01 mm, each column is resolved into spindly fibres, and it all becomes again a unidimensional figure and so on continuously, the value of the dimension continuously alternating.' (B. Mandelbrot, *Les object fractals*, p. 13, introduction, Flammarion, N.B.S., 1975.)

6   See *L'insécurité du territoire*, Stock, 1976, chapter entitled 'Véhiculaire'.

7   To return to Europe from San Francisco, aeroplanes pass above the glaciers of Greenland. At certain times of the year, one is witness to a surprising phenomenon: there is no night. Behind, the red

glow of twilight and, at the same time, in front, the green glow of dawn.

8 'Cinema, in whatever way, is a vision', René Clair.

9 D. H. Lawrence, *Apocalypse*, preface by Fanny and Gilles Deleuze, Éditions Balland, 1978.

10 If tools extend the body and if weapons extend it much further still through projectiles, *must we not consider the rectilinear line as a geometric weapon? The Euclidean postulate as a sublimation of speed?*

11 B. Mandelbrot, *Les objects fractals, forme, hasard ed dimension,* Flammarion, N.B.S., 1975,

12 'The French and German research institute of Saint-Louis has just perfected a device for *flash cineradiography* that is capable of capturing *40 million images per second.* This instrument used primarily in connection with ballistics and explosives, provides for a more dynamic view of the inner state of matter.' F. Jamet, *La Recherche*, May 1982.

FOURTH PART

1 The reasoning behind automobile aerodynamics considers the route to be a mirror. The car and its image are reunited by the purchase of the tyres. The performance of the car depends, therefore, on the forces of contact internal to the 'car-image' system.

2 According to a law of physics the maximum speed varies proportionately to the square root of the weight.

3 ED: Aéropostale was the first French airmail service between Europe and South America.

4 'Sliding home', an expression invented by the record breakers. Paul Clifton, *The Fastest Men on Earth*, 1967.

5 P. Clifton, ibid.

6 P. Clifton, ibid.

7 Shakespeare.

8 Shakespeare.

9 The scientific definition of a surface.

10   Since the invention of the laser, the measure of one of the most
      fundamental constants in physics – the speed of light – has
      enjoyed a spectacular improvement. Certain modifications in the
      international system of units of measure will ensue from this. See
      in *La Recherche*, n. 91, 1978, an article by Patrick Bouchareine:
      'Le mètre, la seconde et la vitesse de la lumière' ['The metre, the
      second, and the speed of light'].

11   ED: Virilio uses the term *gnosie* here, which derives from the Greek
      gnosis and carries with it some sense of the conceptual experience
      or cognition that arises from perception.

12   TN: Virilio is playing on the multiple senses of *asservis à* which
      indicates 'enslavement', but is also used to indicate the remote
      control of electronic or motorized devices.

13   It is sufficient to consider the historical influence of the arsenal on
      the development of the sciences and the increased importance of
      military financing in contemporary scientific research, as well as
      the very notion of the civil and technological repercussions of war.

14   TN: The French '*mode*' also carries with it, beyond the connota-
      tions of its English cognate, the notion of fashion or style.

15   ED: With this phrase, Virilio is playing on the name of the French
      equivalent of the FBI, namely, *les Renseignements généraux*, or the
      RG, for short.

16   TN: The association between the elements in the list to follow
      arises in a more obvious fashion in the French usage of '*communi-
      cation*'. For the semantic range of this term includes everything
      that is expressed in its English cognate but adds as well the sense of
      'transmission', as appears in the more limited usage of the English
      phrase 'communication of forces'. It is often preferable, therefore,
      to translate the term instead as 'transmission' as has been the case
      in other instances. In this case, however, it is important to see that
      such media as radio and television are listed together with trains
      and automobiles as means not only of the communication of
      information, but simultaneously also of *force*.

17   TN: Virilio is playing on the homonym *sens*. The first term '*sens*'
      is directly cognate with 'sense' and derives from a Latin root; the
      second term '*sens*' derives from an unrelated Germanic root and
      means 'direction'.

18 TN: Virilio is playing here on the term 'corps' in its sense of a military corps, that is, an expeditionary corps or task force, and of 'body', that is, the body of the cameraman sent forth in an 'expeditionary' capacity for the sedentary voyeur in the cinema.

19 TN: See note 12 above.

20 The Stealth owes it unique characteristic, it seems, both to its design to avoid angles – notably those of the jets that grab radar rays – with a shield that dissimulates the infrared rays of the escaping gases, as well as to a special coating, the SIRMPF that covers the plane and absorbs the radar.

21 By means of spy satellites and other means of teledetection.

FIFTH PART

1 N. Loraux, 'L'autochthonie athénienne, le mythe dans l'espace civique', *Annales*, January–February 1979.

2 TN: Virilio is playing on 'foule', 'crowd', and 'folles', 'the mad' or 'the crazed', as in the folly of May.

3 For Clausewitz, the political State is 'a non-conductive medium that blocks the complete discharge ...'. See *On War*.

4 TN: Virilio follows this term in his text with [*sic*] presumably to retain the implication of the 'stadium'.

5 *On 1 August 1793, the Convention voted for the complete extermination of the Vendée*. 'Let us burn the villages, this harsh measure will be an act of justice since the innocents that are in the middle of the revolt are cowards that we are not obliged to save'. And Carrier (of those drowning in Nantes) exclaimed: 'We will rather make a cemetery of France than fail to see it regenerated in our way!'

6 In particular in Brazil. In Argentina, since February 1978, the government has demanded the registration of all non-Christian associations in order to better control them.

7 See on this subject 'La révolte des Indiens du Brésil' *Monde diplomatique*, December 1980.

8 See *Birth of the Clinic* and M. Foucault's other works.

9 See Roland Pressat's text: 'Situation démographique de l'URSS à

la veille de son cinquième recensement' in *Population*, 1979 [4/5], p. 863.

10 T. B. Granotier, *La planète des bidonvilles*, Éditions du Seuil, 1980.

11 See 'L'escadron de la mort', 'la Main Blanche', et 'ORDEN', an organization created by General Medrano.

12 We can also observe an *industrialization of the living* with *organ banks* for transplants, with *sperm banks* for artificial insemination, the recent use of *human fetuses* for the treatment of diabetes, as well as that of *fresh cadavers* as 'crash test dummies' for automobile safety research.

13 A. Rouquié, 'Argentine, anarchie militaire ou État terroriste?', in *Études*, October 1977 and *Argentine: dossier d'un genocide*, Flammarion, 1978. Also the article dedicated to the North/South industrial redeployment in the November–December 1980 issue of the revue *Économie et Humanisme*.

14 On 31 January and 1 February 1981, there was a senate, in Paris, at an international colloquium entitled *La politique de disparition forcée des personnes* [*The politics of forced disappearances*], organized by several associations of legal experts.

15 N. Loraux, *Annales*, January–February 1979.

16 N. Loraux, op. cit.

17 TN: 'The European Social Space'.

18 Dietrich Bonhoeffer.

19 TN: The Oxford English Dictionary defines this specialized use of this word from the Greek θεωρία as, 'A body of theors sent by a state to perform some religious rite or duty'. It is important to note for Virilio's use here that these theors would partake in a procession to a sanctuary.

20 Paul Klee.

21 ED: Loraux's phrase '*prose laïque*' recalls the Greek etymology of the term from λαός which refers to the class of commoners who formed the essentially anonymous ranks of foot soldiers.

22 N. Loraux, op. cit.

23 Philostratus, *De Gymnastica*.

24 In this 'civilization of competition' where democracy is nothing but a name concealing 'the government of the elite with approbation

of the masses ...' (Plato): 'Marathon is like the indispensable prologue to the history of Athens, therefore to the history of the Athenian empire, this empire actually initiated in Salamis and that the democratic party dreams of reconstituting. Thus the first historical act just barely goes beyond the boundaries of myth; it is something of an analogy to the first exploits of the noble, or to the labour that the hero must face in order to affirm himself as such, a certain initiation: *the speed with which the victory was immediately won and announced, does this not evoke a race [course], a rite of passage and integration in martial society?*' N. Loraux, 'Marathon ou le l'histoire idéologique', in *Revue des études anciennes*, 1973, p. 29.

25   Victor Hugo.

26   P. Virilio, *Esthétic de la disparition*, Balland, 1980. (*The Aesthetics of Disappearance*, translated by Philip Beitchman, Semiotext(e), NY, 1991.)

27   J.-P. Vernant, *Mythes et pensées chez les Grecs*, Maspero, 1966. (Translated as *Myth and Thought*, Routledge and Kegan, 1983).

28   In Paris and in other capitals, the same ceremony would take place before the embassies every Thursday at noon, and this, despite the abduction and torture of several of the 'mad of May', like Noemi Esther Gianotti de Molfino, who disappeared in Lima on 12 June 1980 and was found dead in Madrid on 21 July, executed, according to her son, by Argentine agents with the assistance of members of the Peruvian secret service.

29   For example, the driving of the population of Phnom-Penh out of the city during the reign of the Cambodian *Angkar*.

30   With the conflict of the Falkland Islands between Argentina and Great Britain, the situation of the 'mad of the Plaza de Mayo' would become more and more critical. During the fifth anniversary of their protest, in May 1982, there were about 600 women in front of the government palace (nearly double the usual number) despite the general disapproval of the passers-by who accused them of undermining national unity. On one of their banners we read: '*We, mothers of the Plaza de Mayo, give our total support to the soldiers defending our fatherland. But as the mothers of the disappeared, we fight ourselves also as*

soldiers, for the living appearance of our children. Long live the fatherland!.'

31 ED: *Groupe d'intervention de la gendarmerie nationale,* special tactical force of the French police.

32 TN: The term here, '*au-delà*,' echoes the title, '*La stratégie de l'au-delà*' where it signifies in its substantive form both 'the beyond' and 'the hereafter'.

33 13 May 1981, a more or less manipulated Turkish terrorist, Ali Mehmet Agca took a shot at the Pope … a year later, on the same day, in Fatima, a fundamentalist priest, Jean Fernadez Krohn, attempted to stab Jean Paul II.

34 The 'Lodge of the Liberators of America' in Argentina, or also the 'P2 Lodge' in Italy.

35 P. Virilio, *Défense populaire et luttes écologiques,* Galilée, p. 77.

36 Let us recall here the sacrifice of Bobby Sands and his comrades interned during the summer of 1981.

37 The bombardment was preceded by the attack on the shipyards at La Seyne-sur-mer, near Toulon, that caused the equally *pre-emptive* destruction of components of the reactor core 'Ozirak' destined for the processing facility of Tamuz.

38 The conflict of the Malvinas here provides a startling confirmation: *confronted with a major economic collapse, Argentina occupied the Falkland Islands on 2 April 1982.…* Faced with the unforeseen and inordinate character of the British counterattack, the South American continent manifests a cohesion as perfect as it is paradoxical since we see Nicaragua and Cuba on the side of the Argentinean military junta.

39 'For twenty years, the Soviet Union experimented with a mode of nonviolent struggle against religion while creating a new atheist religion from scratch', B. Karlinsky, *Le Monde diplomatique, 3 January 1982.* Concerning this matter, it is interesting to read the work of Leonid Pliouchtch dedicated to Soviet 'Philopaganism'.

40 As explained by the Chilean National Commission on the Rights of Man, military power is disposed to the creation of '*A feeling of collective terror before bringing about submission and the voluntary relinquishing of the exercise of the rights of man*'.

41 TN: Both the terms '*dégénération*' and '*dégénérescence*' have as their

primary meaning the privation of the qualities which determine a genus. The latter term, however, includes as well the familiar sense of 'degeneration' which is not the case in the former, uncommon in French usage.

42   TN: Virilio's use of the French for 'blockage', '*blocage*', incorporates the term '*bloc*' as in the Western or Eastern blocs.

43   It is enough to consider the state of the economic decline of Eastern countries, but also of England.

44   We must analyse here, not only the military operations in the 'foreign theatres of operations' in Africa or elsewhere, but above all, the threats of Head of State to Head of State (Khadafi-Reagan for example) not to mention *state attacks* like the pirating of the Falklands by the Argentines preceded, let us not forget, by a similar attempt of occupation of the Seychelles (Islands) in the Indian Ocean fomented by South Africa, in November 1981.

45   TN: Virilio employs a double entendre on 'parée': 'adorned' and 'protected'.

46   'Cruise missiles', neutron bombs, chemical weapons recently reintroduced, as well as most of the 'tactical' nuclear weapons, *without omitting missiles like the 'Exocet', capable of sinking the 'Sheffield' destroyer....*

47   The statements of President Reagan on the probabilities of a 'limited nuclear war' in Europe, illustrate the escalation: *throughout the 1960s we posed the question regarding the threshold of nuclearization of a conflict engaged with conventional weapons; from the beginning of the 1980s, the question posed was that of the limitation of a war begun with tactical nuclear weapons.*

48   In particular, in the Indian Ocean with the growing importance of the islands, Diego Garcia, the Seychelles, etc., but as well in the Southern Atlantic Ocean, with Ascension Island, the Malvinas, and as far as Antarctica, junction of three oceans. See Paul Virilio's article, 'Le pôle Sud, toit stratégique de la citadelle planétaire', in *Libération*, 11 May 1982.

49   Thus the Yalta Accords are called into question, as are the first results of an American–Soviet discussion concerning the settlement of disputes affecting their spheres of influence. We cite here the example of the United States 'ready to engage in

the dialogue with the Soviet Union, *in order to defuse the crisis in Central America* (Washington, 15 March 1982).

50   See: 'L'omission monétaire', report of the International Monetary Fund on world economic perspectives, an article by Paul Fabra in *Le Monde*, 21 July 1981.

51   With regard to this, the urban riots of the summer of 1981 in Liverpool, Sheffield, and Brixton in the suburbs of London indicates clearly the 'post-industrial' tendency.

52   '*Federate to separate*', curious slogan of the Belgian separatists in the 1970s; see also the plan of Marie-France Garaud to transform France into a '*federal republic*' (June, 1984).

53   Mies van der Rohe.

54   Gaston Defferre, Minister of the Interior and of Decentralization of the Mauroy Government.

55   From which follows a crisis in the *management of territory* involving uncertainty regarding the future of the great urban conglomerations sprung from the industrial era of which the *civil defence plans* (American or Soviet) are a symptom; as if the real objective of these measures of anti-nuclear protection were never anything other than the progressive conditioning of populations for the evacuation of cities, evacuation necessitated by an imminent 'post-industrial' restructuring [*redéploiement*].

56   Pin Yathay, *L'utopie meurtrière*, story of a survivor of the Cambodian genocide, Robert Laffont, 1980.

57   'L'utopie meurtrière des Khmers rouges', an article by the same author, published by *La quinzaine littéraire*, special edition of 1 August 1981: 'La cité idéale'.

58   TN: The term is a Greek adjective, *atopos*, that is the negation of the term *topos* 'place'. The Greek adjective means literally 'no place' and was used to describe the extraordinary or bizarre.

59   To verify these assertions, it is enough to consider the fate of the Lebanese today, who describe themselves as *incapable of getting out of their civil war*.

60   This concerns the last two texts published by the author before his accidental death: *Archéologie de la violence* and *La guerre contre l'État*, in the journal *Libre*, 1977.

61   The development of 'terrorism' could appear until now to be the

acts of extremist minorities, as it was nothing but the reflection
of an *escalation to extremes attaining a balance of force and power
between the military and the political.*

62   For example, the taking of hostages in the embassy of Tehran as
the aborted intervention of the Americans in Iran (see P. Virilio
'Tabas, la stratégie de l'accident' in *Libération*, 7 May 1980). Also
the act of pirating the Argentinean dictatorship on the Falkland
Islands, which took place three days after the mass demonstration
in Buenos Aires, the slogan of which was 'Bread, Peace and
Work'.... Beyond these, a precise list of different *state attacks*
would be quite long. For a dozen years, we have been witness to
a disturbing *proliferation of acts of war without war,* destruction,
taking of wages, hostages, etc. At first limited to the Near East,
these practices are now spreading to Europe and the entire world.

63   The affair of the Soviet submarine *Whisky 17,* run aground in
front of Karlskrona in Sweden, with nuclear mines on board,
evoked this disillusioned thought of General Gallois: '*This incident
is the perfect demonstration that it is impossible to control nuclear
weapons*'.

64   For example, the aerial skirmish of the 'Black Aces' squadron
of the American aircraft carrier *Nimitz,* shooting down in the
Syrian Gulf Libyan aircraft, without *President Reagan having been
informed of the situation.*

65   'We must never let the weight of this combination endanger our
liberties or democratic processes. We should take nothing for
granted. Only an alert and knowledgeable citizenry can compel
the proper meshing of the huge industrial and military machinery
in defence with our peaceful methods and goals, so that security
and liberty may prosper together.' Farewell address of President
Eisenhower, 17 January 1961.

66   See the book by C. Delmas, *Le second âge nucléaire*, PUF, 1974.
The third age, in other words the senescence of this weapons
system, referred to above as characterized by the *armaments of
enhanced radiation,* neutron weapons, particle, laser, and other
doomsday machines.... Concerning this matter, the Pentagon
claimed early on to be in a position to carry out instantaneous
nuclear attacks.

One better understands, therefore, the developments of the debates on nuclear first strike, the calls of MacNamara, Georges Bundy, Kennan, and Smith (who was a negotiator of the SALT I Accords), exhorting President Reagan to renounce as quickly as possible *the doctrine of first strike*, explaining that 'the refusal, traditional until now, of western powers to be the first to resort to atomic weapons implies *unacceptable risks to the life of the nation*', and that a change of attitude on this point is today 'the best means for maintaining the unity and the effectiveness of NATO'.

In fact, it is not a question for these *warmongers* (one owes to Mr MacNamara and Mr Bundy the count of strategic carriers in the thousands and no longer in the hundreds, and to Mr Nixon and Mr Smith, the qualitative escalation this time of high-precision nuclear delivery systems as well as the number of warheads) *advocating peace*, but *making it seem as if they are acting politically* with the moral, electoral, and other benefits that this implies, so that today, each of the partners/adversaries is constrained by the violence of the speed of nuclear delivery, *be it in definitively renouncing the qualitative escalation*, otherwise known as the sophistication of the surprise first strike, *or definitively renouncing political power of decision-making*, from which follows this reference to the unacceptable risks to the life of the nation.... It is not a question here of the risk of Soviet missiles, nor of the financial one of the arms race or of the corresponding civil defence (the seven-year plan of President Reagan), it is above all a question of *transpolitical apocalypse*, the end of all delay of reflection concerning the triggering of hostilities, the end of the initiative of the head of state concerning attack as with nuclear counterattack, to the exclusive benefit of the instantaneity of the *machine of the last judgement*, where the old 'war machine' becomes suddenly the 'declaration-of-war machine' ... (regarding this subject, see the last chapter of *Vitesse et Politique* by Paul Virilio, Éditions Galilée, 1977, translated as, *Speed and Politics, an Essay on Dromology*, Columbia University Press, 1986).

67   In particular, C. Castoriadis, in his book *Devant la guerre, les réalités*, Fayard, 1981.

68   The delays of the manufacturing of submersible nuclear launching

devices are extremely revealing: '13 months had separated the "*Terrible*" and the "*Redoutable*" ['Formidable'] (first French nuclear submarines), 17 months the "*Foudroyant*" ['Lightning'] from the "*Terrible*", 31 months the "*Indomptable*" ['Invincible'] from the "*Foudroyant*", 42 months the "*Tonnant*" ['Thundering'] from the "*Terrible*", and around 60 months (5 years) the "*Inflexible*" from the "*Tonnant*", and nearly 9 years will separate the new submarine from the "*Inflexible*" that will not be ready until 1985', Jacques Isnard, 'La défense nucléaire', an article in *Le Monde*, 6 December 1981.

69 START, acronym for the negotiations on the *reduction* of strategic weapons, the SALT Accords was only concerned with their *limitation*.

70 The ultimate objective of military research: 'To centralize all scientific information and to assure a full-scale watch, in the manner of an arms-system under the remote control of radar that sweeps the horizon'. J.-E. Dubois (Director of military research), cited in G. Menahem's book *La science et le militaire*, Éditions du Seuil, 1976.

71 In Munich February 1982, during his participation in the 'Wehrkunde Gesellschaft,' private association specializing in strategic problems.

72 R. Aron, *Les guerres en chaîne*, Gallimard.

73 The 'cargo cult' is a religious, pagan, and then syncretistic phenomenon that recurs in 1871 and extends through many periods strangely marked by significant global conflicts. *At the origin, it corresponds to a sort of adoration of sea-going vessels, hence its name, and then with the installation of aerial bases in the Pacific, to a cult of aerial vehicles.* To get more details on the 'cargo' movement, see the book of P. Lawrence, *Le culte du cargo*, Fayard, 1974.

74 During the summer of 1981, Monsignor Hunthausen, Archbishop of Seattle, declared: '*The actual crisis goes much deeper than the political.* I have heard a lot of enlightened political analyses concerning the nuclear situation, but their common element is despair. The nuclear arms race could add in a few moments the violence of tens of thousands of years elevated to a power of

nearly infinity. *But politics itself is without power to vanquish the evil in its heart*, it needs another dimension.' Denouncing with the TRIDENT project, the tragic aberration of the first strike doctrine, he concluded '*We must refuse to make offerings (and in our times the offering is tax dollars) to our nuclear idol*'.

Several months later, in the spring of 1982, despite the indignation of American churches, the Pentagon decided to baptize the most recent nuclear submarine: *Corpus Christi*.

75   TN: '*Cratos*' is Greek for 'power'.

Index